Praise for **THE O**

"A spellbinding story . . . [Benjamin Gilmer's] writing is lucid and compassionate."   —Minneapolis *Star Tribune*

"Fans of both true-crime podcasts and medical mysteries are in for a treat. . . . The search for answers sends [Benjamin Gilmer] on a years-long crusade through the legal and prison systems, where medical compassion can be hard to come by."
                    —*The Washington Post,* "10 Noteworthy Books for March"

"A remarkable true-crime account . . . The story makes a fascinating real-life mystery, but *The Other Dr. Gilmer* is more than that. Benjamin Gilmer argues that, as asylums have closed and mental health centers have seen budgets slashed, the criminal justice system has become a holding pen for many of the nation's mentally ill. . . . [He] calls for humane reforms to ease the system and perhaps to prevent crimes in the first place."
                    —Wilmington *Star-News*

"A haunting, insightful story of justice and humanity . . . In this engrossing, powerful memoir, Gilmer recounts a story of medical mystery and criminal justice. . . . Gilmer's narrative is gripping, and he writes deftly and with compassion."
                    —*Library Journal* (starred review)

"Family physician Gilmer's gripping debut starts out as a murder tale, morphs into a medical mystery, and lands as a heartbreaking account of how poorly the American prison system treats the mentally ill. . . . The author does a fine job humanizing everyone involved. This painful look at a terrible social injustice deserves a wide audience."   —*Publishers Weekly*

"Antitheses abound—mercy versus punishment, intuition versus preconceptions, coincidence versus destiny—in this unsettling combination of murder mystery, medical detective tale, and plea for criminal-justice reform."   —*Booklist*

"A remarkable, true-life medical detective story–cum-memoir, grippingly told . . . I was drawn in by every part of it—the bizarre murder, the mystery of what really happened, Dr. Benjamin Gilmer's gumshoe work to get to the bottom of that mystery, and all that followed when he did."

—ATUL GAWANDE, #1 *New York Times* bestselling author
of *Being Mortal: Medicine and What Matters in the End*

"A knockout debut that gripped me from the very first line . . . Benjamin Gilmer masterfully peels away the layers of a long-closed murder and drops us into an unbelievable true story of medical mystery, mental illness, and the terrifying injustices of our justice system. Meet *The Other Dr. Gilmer,* a man you won't soon forget."

—MAUREEN CALLAHAN, *New York Times* bestselling author
of *American Predator: The Hunt for the Most
Meticulous Serial Killer of the 21st Century*

"There are too many in prison who should be in hospitals or mental health facilities. *The Other Dr. Gilmer* is one man's story, but it represents the stories of so many. We all know that there is more broken than not within our system of mass incarceration, but this book does more than point at a broken system; it humanizes the people trapped within it. They have names. They are suffering. And they need a physician like Dr. Gilmer to lead the way to healing."

—ANTHONY RAY HINTON, *New York Times* bestselling author of
The Sun Does Shine: How I Found Life and Freedom on Death Row

"While this book is many things—a grisly story of true crime, a medical mystery, a deep-dive into the inequalities of rural health-care, and the story of a good man walking in the footsteps of a killer—it is, most important, very, very good. Benjamin Gilmer has written nonfiction that flows like a novel and a piece of investigative journalism full of heart and grace."

—WILEY CASH, *New York Times* bestselling author of
When Ghosts Come Home and *A Land More Kind Than Home*

"A complex, unlikely medical mystery and true crime story along with one man's relentless quest for justice."

—CHARLES FRAZIER, *New York Times* bestselling author of
Cold Mountain, winner of the National Book Award

"*The Other Dr. Gilmer* is an extraordinary true story by a physician of how an inheritable brain disorder destroyed two lives: a father and a son. More important, it gives a view into a criminal justice system that has destroyed many more.... Powerful, profound, and compelling."

—JAMES R. DOTY, M.D., *New York Times* bestselling author of
*Into the Magic Shop: A Neurosurgeon's Quest to Discover
the Mysteries of the Brain and the Secrets of the Heart,*
founder and director of the Stanford University Center
for Compassion and Altruism Research and Education

THE OTHER DR. GILMER

THE OTHER DR. GILMER

TWO MEN, A MURDER, AND AN UNLIKELY FIGHT FOR JUSTICE

BENJAMIN GILMER

BALLANTINE BOOKS

NEW YORK

Ballantine Books Trade Paperback Edition

Published in the United States by Ballantine Books,
an imprint of Random House, a division of
Penguin Random House LLC, New York.

Originally published in hardcover in slightly different form
in the United States by Ballantine Books, an imprint of Random House,
a division of Penguin Random House LLC, in 2022.

Library of Congress Cataloging-in-Publication Data
Names: Gilmer, Benjamin, author.
Title: The other Dr. Gilmer: two men, a murder,
and an unlikely fight for justice / Benjamin Gilmer.
Description: First edition. | New York: Ballantine Group, [2023] |
Includes bibliographical references.
Identifiers: LCCN 2021032935 (print) | LCCN 2021032936 (ebook) |
ISBN 9780593355183 (paperback) | ISBN 9780593355176 (ebook)
Subjects: LCSH: Mentally ill offenders—North Carolina. | Clemency— North Carolina.
Classification: LCC HV9305.N8 G56 2022 (print) | LCC HV9305.N8 (ebook) |
DDC 364.3/809756—dc23
LC record available at https://lccn.loc.gov/2021032935
LC ebook record available at https://lccn.loc.gov/2021032936

Printed in the United States of America on acid-free paper

randomhousebooks.com

Book design by Elizabeth A. D. Eno

*I dedicate this book to Dr. Vince Gilmer and all
those suffering from mental illness behind bars.
May they all be healed.*

The degree of civilization in a society can be judged by entering its prisons.

—Fyodor Dostoevsky

CONTENTS

THE OTHER DR. GILMER

1.

GOOD HOPE ROAD

On June 28, 2004, in rural Appalachia, a man with my name and my profession strangled his father in the passenger seat of his Toyota Tacoma.

The other Dr. Gilmer was a family medicine physician in North Carolina, at a small clinic he'd founded with his wife near the tiny town of Fletcher. He was recently divorced, living alone in a house on the hill above his office. In the weeks and months before that night, he'd been drinking more than usual, going out to bars during the week. He'd also been making some impulsive decisions—like buying the brand-new truck he was driving, even though he was massively in debt.

After a full morning of seeing patients, Dr. Vince Gilmer left his practice on the afternoon of June 28 to drive to Broughton Hospital, a psychiatric facility in Morganton, North Carolina, where his father had lived for the previous two years. Vince's father, Dalton, was sixty years old, a diagnosed schizophrenic, and had landed at Broughton after a time of delusional behavior, drug abuse, and intermittent homelessness. Now, though, he was being released. His son was getting him out.

Dr. Vince Gilmer wasn't particularly close to his father, but he had arranged for Dalton to be cared for at a facility called Flesher's

Fairview Health and Retirement Center, a five-minute drive from his house, so he could keep a closer eye on his care. Vince told his co-workers that he was going to take his father into the outdoors before taking him to his new home, that the two of them were going canoeing on Watauga Lake in Tennessee. It was a place Vince knew well. He had often escaped there to relax during his residency after medical school.

If anyone thought it was strange for Vince to drive two hours in the wrong direction so that he could take his schizophrenic father on a quick evening boat outing, they didn't mention it. This was the sort of thing he did often. Vince's nurses and co-workers would not have been surprised that he thought a trip to the lake might be therapeutic. Dr. Vince Gilmer was well known for his unconventional, friendly, and personal approach to life and medicine. He was a big believer in the power of the outdoors, the sort of doctor who had been known to take depressive patients on walks to help them clear their minds rather than just give them medicine. Patients and nurses called him "Bear" because of his hulking presence and warm hugs.

None of Vince's co-workers knew how much his father had deteriorated while at Broughton. If any of them had, they would have realized how difficult canoeing would have been for him. Dalton Gilmer was a frail man, heavily medicated, barely able to stand on his own. He would have needed to be lifted into the boat and certainly could not swim.

Still, along with the usual lawn care tools—garden shears, gloves, clippers—that Vince used to maintain the landscaping at his clinic, there was a poorly tied-down canoe rattling in the bed of the truck that afternoon, throughout the hour-long drive from Cane Creek Family Health Center to Broughton.

Vince made good time. At five-thirty P.M. an orderly wheeled Dalton out in a wheelchair and loaded his meager possessions into the rear cab. He lifted Dalton into the front passenger seat after

Vince moved aside a dog leash, suspending it from the headrest. Then father and son headed north, toward the North Carolina–Tennessee border.

What happened next has never been fully explained. Sometime that night, they stopped at an Arby's for dinner, Dalton's first meal out in over a year. Sometime that night, Dalton turned to Vince and began to hum the song "Baa Baa Black Sheep." Sometime that night, Vince wrapped the dog leash around Dalton's neck.

Just before midnight, Thomas Browning, coming home from a late movie in Abingdon, Virginia, an hour north of Watauga Lake, saw what he thought was a drunk man sleeping in a ditch on Good Hope Road. He and his wife pulled over and called the cops. When the police arrived, they found Dalton Gilmer's body, still warm, with contusions and a bruised ring around his neck. He had soiled himself.

He was missing all of his fingers.

By the time a report was filed with the Washington County Sheriff Department, Dr. Vince Gilmer was already back in North Carolina, over a hundred miles away. He'd driven south in the predawn, on the winding two-lane country roads and slightly straighter highways that penetrate the heart of Appalachia. He'd passed through the moonlit shadows of the Blue Ridge Mountains, through fog-filled hollers and sleeping mountain communities, crossing the North Carolina state line through the Cherokee National Forest.

Ask Vince how he got home that night, and he probably wouldn't be able to tell you. The precise route is lost to time, lost to the shadows, lost to darkness. The night only comes back into focus again at three-thirty A.M., this time bathed in fluorescent, twenty-four-hour light. That's when a receipt from a Walmart outside of Asheville shows a ten-dollar purchase of hydrogen peroxide, paper towels, and a pair of gloves.

Vince used the hydrogen peroxide on his hands, and to wash the blood from the bed of his truck. Back at his house on Ivy Lane, he took an Ambien but couldn't sleep. The next morning, he showed up on time to clinic at Cane Creek, ready to greet his patients. The day after killing his father, Dr. Vince Gilmer worked a full day, eight in the morning to six in the evening, and no one—not his nurse, not his receptionist, not a single one of the fifteen or so patients he saw that day—noticed anything different about him.

I now work in that same clinic. I know some of the previous staff. I see Dr. Vince Gilmer's patients. I use his exam rooms.

I am Dr. Benjamin Gilmer. Though we are not related, for the last thirteen years, I've lived in the other Dr. Gilmer's shadow. I know his story better than anyone except Vince himself.

It's a complex, twisting, and often frightening tale. To many people, it doesn't make much sense.

But there are a few facts about the night of June 28, 2004, that everyone—detectives, a judge, a jury, and Dr. Vince Gilmer himself—can agree on:

Dalton Gilmer was strangled with a dog leash. His son, Vince Gilmer, was holding it. Using a pair of garden shears, Vince Gilmer amputated all of the fingers from his father's hands, then laid the body on the side of Good Hope Road and drove home.

The detectives had lots of questions—the most critical one was *Why?*

Why did Vince Gilmer kill his own father?

Why did he leave the body in an easily discoverable place, on the side of a busy road, when there were so many other secluded spots—including Watauga Lake—only five minutes away?

Why did he want to take his frail, mentally impaired father canoeing at night, two hours north of the facility where his new caretakers were anxiously awaiting his arrival?

Why did he wait almost two days to file a missing-person report?

Why did he tell everyone that his father had wandered off, an easily disprovable lie?

Why didn't he run?

Why did he cut off his father's fingers, and what did he do with them?

Why did a caring doctor become a brutal murderer?

A few weeks after Vince killed his father, mine officiated at my wedding on a North Carolina mountaintop a short drive from Watauga Lake, where the murder occurred. I was looking forward to starting a family and my professional life as Dr. Gilmer.

Back then, I had no idea there was another Dr. Gilmer.

I had no idea what the other Dr. Gilmer had done.

And I had no idea that it would change both of our lives forever.

2.

HOME

In April 2009, after years of effort—rejections from medical schools, eight grueling semesters once I finally got in, a master's degree, and three years as a family medicine resident at MAHEC, the Mountain Area Health Education Center, in Asheville—I finally interviewed for my first job as a doctor.

Sitting in the air-conditioned conference room that day, facing down a room full of experienced doctors and administrators, I was nervous. Unlike many of my fellow residents, I wasn't in my twenties. I was thirty-nine, married, with gray in my hair. I had a two-year-old son, a daughter in utero, and a thirty-year mortgage.

I was a bit of a late bloomer.

The job was at a tiny six-room clinic in rural North Carolina. Shuttered for three years, it had recently reopened and was in high demand. It desperately needed another doctor to help address the needs of a historically underserved population.

Family medicine was my chosen path. Rural practice was my calling. And the job involved teaching medical students, which the former high school teacher in me couldn't wait to do.

But also? I desperately needed work. Medical school was not cheap. The loans I'd taken out were only growing. I had mouths to feed and a baby on the way.

You can't say that in a job interview, of course. So when the head of the hiring committee asked me to tell the assembled room full of MAHEC leadership about myself, I reached for something deeper. "Where to begin?" I said.

For the next twenty minutes, I gave the MAHEC leadership a CliffsNotes version of my life. I told them about my father, an Episcopal priest who became a hospital chaplain, then a Jungian psychotherapist; my mother, an elementary school teacher; and my stepmother, a nursing professor. I talked about my stepfather, a Presbyterian minister who during the week ran a mental health clinic in the rural Tennessee town where I grew up, and on weekends spread the good news at tiny rural churches as a traveling preacher.

I told them about the moment I first knew I wanted to be a doctor, tagging along with my dad in the hospital at age eight, watching the white-coated docs walk briskly across the polished linoleum.

I painted a picture of Martin, Tennessee, the small town where I grew up angling for catfish in small ponds with my stepfather, playing in the woods with my brother Nate, and shaking our neighbor's pecan trees to gather nuts for pecan pie.

I described my bifurcated childhood, taking the Greyhound to visit my father and my stepmother, Jo—first in Chicago, then Charlotte—and how it felt to transition from cornfields to gated communities, where split-levels became three-stories and Fords became BMWs.

I explained how I always felt like I was somewhere between two worlds: northern and southern, urban and rural, sophisticated and country. How I learned to move between houses—and what I learned from each parent. From my schoolteacher mother: a voracious intellectual curiosity and a dogged, pragmatic persistence. She always knew what she wanted and wasn't afraid to get her hands dirty to get it—or to have her mind changed when new facts presented themselves. From my chaplain father: a moral framework for medicine. He believed that healing was a matter not only of the body but also of the spirit, and that we had a moral duty to help heal each other.

I told them about Davidson College, where I majored in neurobiology, with a minor in religion and French, because I didn't want to be boxed into a premed track. I recounted my years in Paris, teaching in a high school so I could study medicine at the Sorbonne, and how my fascination with the human brain led me to a master's degree in neurotoxicology.

I told them about applying to medical school and not getting in. Twice.

I told them what it felt like to get rejected from *everywhere* in the state—UNC, Duke, Wake Forest. How retaking the MCAT and rewriting my essays dozens of times only made me want to be a doctor more. How there's a kind of person who takes rejection as a sign—the sort of person who, after two failed attempts, regroups and recalibrates. And then there are others like me, or my mom—tell them *no*, and they'll just keep coming back until you say *yes*.

I told them dogged persistence was what got me through med school at Eastern Carolina, the oldest male student in my class, cramming for exams and memorizing pages of facts like all the branches of the cranial nerves or Ranson's criteria for staging acute pancreatitis.

I shared how incurable optimism kept me afloat as a Schweitzer fellow in Gabon, West Africa, where every mosquito carried malaria, and most children experienced hunger. I told them how inspired I'd been by my fellowship's namesake, Albert Schweitzer, the doctor, humanitarian, and theologian who had viewed it as his sacred duty to bring healing and medicine to thousands in French Equatorial Africa—at first in a chicken hut, then in a hospital he built himself in Lambaréné.

I described my own experience treating a young man my age

there, who was rapidly deteriorating from a neurologic disease called Guillain-Barré syndrome. His lungs were paralyzed, and he needed a ventilator to survive. But there was only a bag-mask, which meant that someone had to breathe for him. I breathed for him for hours. After my shift, I lay down to sleep on the hospital grounds. When I awoke he was dead, because no one else had breathed for him.

I told them that we need to breathe for each other. That this was a young man who would not have died in America. That in Gabon, life and death were determined by simple means: available food, access to medical resources, and sheer luck. This man had lacked all three.

I explained how that moment provoked a total sea change in how I envisioned myself and my career in medicine. How setting broken bones, prescribing antimalarial pills, delivering babies, treating depression, and addressing food scarcity revealed to me the vital importance of the basics: primary care at its most elemental level. How even though that young man wouldn't have died in America, he made me realize that we had our own issues with treating patients across racial and socioeconomic divides—especially in rural areas.

I compared rural North Carolina to rural Gabon, which shared the same basic needs: education, a functional economy, and access to healthcare. I told them how rural medicine was everything I loved about being a doctor. How it required me to be a part of the community, a valuable member of it—how it made me realize that you have to know the *place* to know the *people.*

And once you know them, you become a part of the fabric of their lives.

I told them that practicing rural family medicine in Africa enabled me to see patients as my minister father saw them: whole, complete spiritual beings. It required my mother's persistence and curiosity. It meant approaching care like my stepfather approached preaching in those tiny country churches: as a necessary, humbling act of grace and healing.

This, I told them, is what I want to bring to rural North Carolina, to Cane Creek. This is the work I've been put on earth to do.

Roughly thirty minutes later, I leaned back in my chair, exhausted. I thought I'd done pretty well.

But the room was hard to read. Drs. Heck and Hulkower—friends and mentors of mine—seemed on board, but a few of the other faces revealed concern. I started to wonder if I'd said something wrong, or just too much. There's a fine line between passionate and overconfident: Had I crossed it?

"Do you know why this clinic was closed?" a broad-shouldered man in his sixties asked after a few seconds. Built like a linebacker and wearing a sweater reminiscent of Mister Rogers, he was Dr. Teck Penland, the CEO of MAHEC.

"Broadly, yes. But I don't really know the details."

This wasn't quite true. Everyone in the area knew about what had happened at Cane Creek: The beloved town doctor who went crazy and killed his own father, then showed up to work the next day like nothing ever happened. The arrest, the trial. The missing fingers.

"Do you know that you and the previous doctor there have the same last name?"

I nodded, and there was a pause—a long one. It was clear from every face in the room that I was supposed to fill it. That this was actually the biggest question they had for me.

"Listen," I said. "I get it. We're both named Gilmer. That might be odd for patients at first. But the truth is, it's just a coincidence. That community has little access to care. They need another medical home, another doctor. I don't think my name will affect the way they treat me—or if it does, it won't for very long. And I know one thing: The other Dr. Gilmer will have no effect on the way that I treat them. I'm ready to take the risk."

Dr. Penland still looked unconvinced. But the other doctors seemed relieved that we had addressed the elephant in the room and could move on.

"Well, I think we've heard what we need to hear," he said. "We'll let you know in a few days."

It was actually a few minutes. Before I was even halfway across the parking lot, keys in hand, Dr. Heck ran out to catch me.

"Congratulations," he said. "You got it."

On the way home, I swung by the grocery store for some fancy cheese and wine, splurging on a ten-dollar bottle. No two-buck Chuck for us tonight.

"Look at the doctorcito," my wife, Deirdre, teased when I got home. She always called me that—we appended the Spanish suffix "-cito" to nearly everything, an affectionate reminder of our previous life in Ecuador, where we worked in an Amazonian hospital.

Deirdre and I met in the early 2000s at the Governor's School, a summer camp for gifted high school students in North Carolina. I was teaching neurobiology, and she was teaching modern dance. We fell in love over discussions of epistemology, how neurons enabled bodies to dance, and where we would travel together. I couldn't resist her curiosity, her vivacity, her sarcastic sense of humor. For a couple of years during medical school, I traversed the Eastern Seaboard every few weeks to see her in Queens, New York, piloting my beat-up Honda Civic wagon up I-95 and across the Verrazzano-Narrows Bridge, nervously dodging cabs and buses all the way to Twenty-ninth Street, next to the Neptune Diner.

But we really became partners when I convinced her to move in with me one summer at North Carolina's most notorious mental institution. I was doing my first clinical rotation in medical school at Broughton Hospital, working with severely traumatized teenage girls. And when Deirdre agreed to pack up all her things, drive down to Morganton in her beat-up Chevy Cavalier, Bella, and teach my patients yoga—just to be with me—I knew that she was the woman I wanted to marry. It's not every woman who can see the potential for romance at a mental hospital.

Wine in hand, Deirdre and I sat on our back porch after we put our son to bed. It took a while. Kai was two at the time, and sleep was not his forte. And I think he could sense how excited his parents were—the smiles extra-large, the hugs extra-long.

"Remember when we bought this place?" Deirdre asked, her legs stretched out in front of her chair. She was six months pregnant with our daughter, so the glass of wine was ceremonial for her. She took one glorious sip before handing it to me. "Thought we'd never clear this damn yard. Remember the jungle we inherited?"

"I thought we'd never pay for the place," I said.

"We still might not. You're going to have to work harder," Deirdre said with a smirk.

We were both quiet for a moment, watching the June fireflies. For years, we had scrimped and saved, living the unsettled life of a late-to-the-game med student and a professional artist. But that night, everything seemed to be coming together. Sitting on the back porch of the home we owned together, our son softly snoring in his bedroom, I thought: *You know what? I think we're finally going to make it.*

"This is what we always wanted," I said to Deirdre. "Finally a job that will pay the bills, a home together."

"A new child," she said, resting her hands on top of her belly.

"A new life," I said. "I think the hard years are behind us."

"You better be right," she answered.

But I wasn't right.

I was so, so wrong.

3.

CANE CREEK

On the first day of my new job, I woke up early. I slipped out of bed without waking Deirdre, stumbled into the closet to grab my most conservative button-down, poked my head into Kai's room, and silently made my way to the kitchen for coffee. I showered and dressed before sunrise and was in the car by six A.M., just as the first beams of light filtered through the pines in the valley below our house. As the business-lined streets and tidy subdivisions of Asheville gave way to forested hills, I thought about the day ahead of me.

What would my first hours as a full-fledged doctor bring? How would it feel to be greeted by the staff and patients with whom I might spend a career?

Driving east past the Blue Ridge Parkway, up Burney Mountain, I was struck by the beauty of the landscape: the ancient green of the forest, the shimmer of morning dew in the clearings, the meandering creeks alongside the narrow two-lane country road. This was rural Appalachia, a world away from the big city, as most mountain folk referred to Asheville. These mountains were old—the oldest in the world, in fact. The hollers around them had been worn by millions of years of settling earth, the valleys filled with families that had been there for generations.

Poverty was common in the country. But money was pouring in. You could see it from the road: dilapidated trailers next door to new construction, overgrown lots abutting staked-out developments. Like much of the rural South, the community was changing, an influx of new money bringing wealth to the area—without the correlating infrastructure.

That's what the Mountain Area Health Education Center was trying to address with its first rural outpost. Named for the creek running behind its parking lot and the valley surrounding it, the Cane Creek Family Health Center is sandwiched between a gas station, a Baptist church, and the valley's only veterinarian. The building itself is unassuming, a small house whose twelve hundred square feet had been only slightly remodeled for its new medical purpose.

In fact, on my first day of work, I drove right past it.

But by the time I'd turned around, found a parking space, and locked my car, a woman about my age with thick glasses and pink scrubs was already walking toward me, a gigantic smile on her face.

"You must be Dr. Gilmer," she said, in a musical southern drawl. "Welcome, welcome, welcome."

I recognized her voice: This was Terri Ippolito, the office manager. Effusive and accommodating, she'd helped me fill out some necessary paperwork and had reviewed the daily schedule with me. And now she was ushering me through the office's front door into the waiting room, where a group of my future patients sat on mismatched chairs reading *The Fairview Town Crier.* It was early—ten minutes before the clinic officially opened—but the room was already brimming with activity.

"This is Laura, our receptionist," Terri said, motioning to a friendly-looking woman behind the counter. Laura raised one hand, taking note of my presence, and simultaneously answered the phone with the other. I heard then, for the first time, the cheerful question I'd hear hundreds of times a day for the next year: "Cane Creek, this is Laura. How can I help you?"

Terri buzzed me through a locked door and into the hallway, which was narrow and crowded with nurses and lab equipment.

"Those four exam rooms down there used to be the garage," Terri said brightly, pointing to her left like a real estate agent showing off a newly renovated house. "This central room was the kitchen."

We walked down the hall, almost colliding with a nurse wheeling a portable EKG. I had to press myself against the wall to let her pass.

"And here," Terri said, "was the dining room. This is your side."

If it had been a dining room, the table couldn't have seated more than four. Every square inch was taken up with equipment: a refrigerator for vaccines, a scale for weighing patients, shelves of neatly stacked folders and lab supplies. Terri and I took up most of the available space. I didn't see how anyone else could fit—that is, until a woman in her late fifties with a well-coiffed bun walked in.

"That's Robin," Laura said. "She'll be your nurse."

"Honey, let me help you get started, it's going to be busy today," Robin said. Within seconds she'd made sure I could access the charts on our electronic health record.

I liked Robin the moment I met her. Warm and maternal, she'd lived in the area for decades, and the impression she gave off was of a longtime local, a native to Cane Creek. She wore a big gold cross around her neck, and though she was originally from New Jersey, she had an accent that rivaled any of my patients'. I could tell that she had a gift for connecting with people. She was like one of the elders in my father's church—someone who brought people together, who welcomed them and made them feel at ease. I trusted her almost immediately, and I knew she'd help bridge the slight gap between me and the community.

I was worried about being perceived as an outsider. Unlike the previous Dr. Gilmer, who'd transformed the clinic with his bare hands and lived a couple of blocks away from it, I was commuting every day from "over the mountain." Progressive West Asheville, where I lived, was anathema to much of the conservative, rural patient population I'd be serving. It was a place they viewed with distrust, a place where liberals and hippies lived.

Having grown up in the country, I found myself with a foot in both worlds, but Cane Creek didn't know that yet. I knew I'd have to make a concerted effort to connect.

The other doctor at Cane Creek, who'd been seeing patients there for the past year, was someone I'd known since residency. Mike Coladonato, a tall, laconic man with black curly hair and a dry sense of humor, was spiritually grounded by nature and a committed patient advocate. But he was no country boy, and most Cane Creekers knew *he wasn't from 'round these parts*—though they realized he was approachable and committed to serving them with care.

Like me, he was a commuter, driving the thirty or so minutes from Asheville every day in his old-school Honda Civic. But unlike me, he didn't feel conflicted about it. When I'd asked him, soon after getting the job, if he'd ever thought about moving out to Fletcher, the small town closest to the clinic, he laughed.

"Nope," he said. "Just because I work in the country doesn't mean I have to live there."

Now, in the cramped back office, he looked up from his computer and high-fived me.

"Welcome aboard, bro," he said. "Your desk's over there."

Mike pointed to the corner. He'd taken the spot near the window, and had hung his diplomas—UVA, MAHEC—on the wall, alongside pictures of his smiling wife and his child, who was Kai's age. They brightened the room, which was otherwise dark and dank and smelled slightly of mildew. The carpet was gray and pitted, my desk chair rusty. It resembled a relic from my grandfather's small-town Georgia insurance agency.

I set my bag down, then peeked into the shared kitchen: a scuffed table that had clearly been imported from someone's basement was covered with random snacks, all of them past their prime. On the kitchen counter was a microwave dotted with grease. But through the back window, there was a glorious view of Little Pisgah Mountain, ablaze in the early morning sunlight.

Next to the mountain, the clinic was tiny and shabby, insignificant. And standing in the cramped kitchen that morning, I felt—in addition to nerves, excitement, and an eagerness to get started—something akin to disappointment. For a second, in my mind's eye, I saw the excitement of the bustling ER where, once upon a time, I'd thought I would end up after med school. I looked at the overgrown lot behind the clinic and thought: *All that effort—med school, residency, and fellowship—for this? Diagnosing diabetes in a room that used to be a garage?*

But then I remembered Gabon and the framed photos of my patients there that I'd brought with me to hang in my exam rooms. I remembered the looks in people's eyes when I treated them *en brousse*, in the jungle. We practiced medicine simply, using basic medications and creative means to solve complex problems. It wasn't the building that made the doctor. It was the doctor's duty to fill whatever space he was in, whether it be the hallway of an abandoned school, the entry of an old church, or a two-bedroom house at the foot of the Appalachian Trail.

"It's no Taj Mahal," Dr. Coladonato said from the doorway of the kitchen, taking a last swig of coffee before his first patient of the day. "But it's home."

My first patient that day was a Cane Creek regular.

"This'll be a perfect introduction to the kind of patients we see here," Robin said, handing over her computer chart for a sixty-five-year-old man with a history of high blood pressure. "Don't call him William."

"What should I call him?"

"His family calls him 'Mule Man,'" Robin said, smiling. "He's the only guy on the mountain who still plows his land by hand. Uses a couple of old mules."

The first thing I noticed when I opened the door to room six was the smell. It wasn't that Mule Man smelled bad, exactly. It's that he didn't smell like anyone I'd ever met. He smelled like a house on fire, or a burning brush pile, or ten thousand pipes—smoke, mixed with aged wood and rich tobacco. I'd later learn that he heated his house with a perpetually burning woodstove, in front of which his ailing wife, Evelyn, spent much time, warming her aching joints. He also burned his own trash and cleared brush with fire.

Mule Man was lean, with skin the color of walnuts. Though it was August and pushing ninety-five degrees outside, he was wearing a pair of seasoned Carhartt overalls over a faded flannel shirt, the sleeves rolled up to reveal scarred, thickly calloused hands.

"How d'you do," he said when I walked in, rising with a slightly courtly flourish and a smile that was warm, but also skeptical. I could tell right away that the doctor's office was not a comfortable habitat for him.

"What seems to be the trouble?"

"Got a cough," he said. "So you just stick me with some penicillin and I'll be on my way."

I laughed.

"That's a little old-fashioned," I said. "Let me examine you first."

"It's what the vet gave me when I was a boy," he said gruffly. "If it was good enough for them horses it was good enough for me."

"Why were you getting shots of penicillin at the vet?"

"Son, 'cause I grew up in Yancey County," he said. "Weren't no doctors there."

I listened to his heartbeat and lungs. He seemed remarkably healthy for his age, and I told him so.

"My blood might be a little high today," he said. "Fell off the plow."

I checked his chart.

"It looks like we already have you on hydrochlorothiazide," I said.

"I know it," Mule Man said, eyeing me suspiciously. "Don't work."

Mule Man, however, did. Quite a bit. Over the course of our twenty-minute consult, he told me about his boyhood growing up in the Yancey hollers before coming to Buncombe County, his decades of farming tobacco for cash and a variety of vegetables for sustenance, his pride at having bought, in the late seventies, the plot of land he and his brother still farmed today. He had left western North Carolina only twice in his life and did not plan on doing so again.

"Did you ride your mule here today?" I asked, trying to strike a jovial tone.

His face darkened somewhat.

"Son, you don't ride mules," he said, drawing out the last word into an endless, elongated syllable. "Them animals are for working. Don't you know nothing?"

I blushed. Mule Man was right: I knew nothing. Nothing about him, nothing about his life growing up in the country, and certainly nothing about mules.

I apologized for the insinuation, prescribed a different antihypertensive, and invited him to come back in a month for a checkup. He reluctantly agreed and shook my hand, and before I left shyly reached into a paper bag at his feet.

"For your troubles," he said, and handed me a sealed mason jar.

"What is this?"

"Chowchow," he said. "The other Dr. Gilmer liked it."

I grew up in the country. I'd had chowchow before. But this looked nothing like the yellow pickled relish my grandmother used to make. This was a dusty jar filled with a grayish wispy substance, vaguely reminiscent of cured brains.

I thanked him, conjuring up what was left of my West Tennessee accent, and left the jar on the table with the museum of other aging snacks.

Although I was tempted many times out of respect for his gracious gift, I could never bring myself to open that jar. It sat there for a very long time.

My second patient was Mule Man's opposite: a woman in her early forties wearing a pantsuit, with an expensive-looking haircut and an enormous diamond wedding ring. I'd taken an extra five minutes with Mule Man, and she was a bit peeved about how long she'd had to wait in the exam room.

"I need a referral to an orthopedist," she said. "My elbow is killing me. I can't even play tennis anymore."

She was new to the area, she explained. Her husband had recently retired, and the two of them had moved into their dream house, a four-bedroom place on a former horse farm, about ten miles from the clinic.

"Big enough for the kids," she said as I examined her elbow. "Not that they ever come back."

Although I had pride in my sports medicine and ultrasound skills, it was clear that the only thing she wanted was a specialist. Never mind that I could do the exact same steroid injection at a fraction of the price right now—she wanted to see someone who only treated elbows. I referred her to a sports medicine doctor in Asheville, and she was out of the office in short order. It seemed like she couldn't wait to leave, a phenomenon I would see again from some of the wealthier patients at the clinic, who were uncomfortable having to sit in the waiting room with some of the area's poorer citizens, who were mostly Medicaid patients or entirely uninsured.

Patients like the twenty-one-year-old boy I saw after lunch, a recovering opioid addict who hadn't eaten in two days. He'd been clean for almost six months, he told me, but he was struggling to make enough money to feed himself.

"Dollar General had Campbell's soup for a dollar thirty-three," he said. "But last week it went up to two dollars. And I just can't afford that."

Everything in me wanted to reach into my wallet, take out a twenty, and hand it to him. He was rail thin, his heart beating like a terrified bird's when I lifted his shirt to press my stethoscope to his chest. He sat there, pliant as a child. Which is exactly what he was.

The stories I heard that day were like a farmer's almanac of rural twenty-first-century life: drug addiction and successful journeys to sobriety, struggles with too much food and not enough, shimmering economic success and utter poverty. There was the wealthy lawyer with a heart condition who'd represented several local farmers in a lawsuit against a chemical fertilizer company. There was the preacher drinking a sixty-four-ounce Mountain Dew, happily reporting his sugars and getting a refill on his diabetes medication. There was the taciturn police officer admitting that he'd been having worsening anxiety and occasional suicidal thoughts, but wouldn't dream of scheduling an appointment with a "shrink."

And there was my last patient of the day, a woman in her sixties, wearing a long dress and black leather slippers. She'd come into the clinic because of recurrent back pain, and after Robin described her symptoms, I was prepared to prescribe a muscle relaxant to help with her spasms.

It seemed like it would be a routine visit.

But when I opened the door to exam room five, I was faced with a person in total panic, gulping air as if she were drowning. She was hyperventilating, terrified of something.

It took me a moment, but then I realized: She was terrified of *me*.

I closed the door, sat down next to her.

"Focus on your breathing," I said, in my softest, most reassuring voice. "It's all right. Just look at the picture on the wall, try to count all the people in it."

During my lunch break, I'd decorated this exam room with photos of my family and of my time in Gabon at the Albert Schweitzer Hospital. I wanted my patients to get to know *me,* not my diplomas, as they knew the personal side of the previous Dr. Gilmer. I wanted them to feel safe and secure with me.

Evidently, it wasn't working.

"I just didn't know what to expect today," she said after she calmed down, her breathing back to normal. "I know it's been five years, but I saw 'Dr. Gilmer' on my appointment reminder and didn't know who was going to walk through that door."

"Would you like to talk about the other Dr. Gilmer?" I asked, as her breathing returned to normal.

"Oh, I *loved* him," she said. "He was so nice to me. Used to drive out to my house when I couldn't get a ride out here. But that was before..."

I waited for her to finish.

"Well," she said. "That was before everything happened."

All through that first day—and the days and weeks and months that followed—I met people who had been cared for by Dr. Vince Gilmer. I didn't provoke any more panic attacks by my mere presence, thank God. That wasn't the therapeutic relationship I was going for.

But my patients didn't shy away from mentioning my predecessor. I sensed they needed to talk about him. Not because they were scared of him, or because they thought he was an evil man. In fact, it was just the opposite.

Vince Gilmer's old patients *loved* him.

And starting on that very first day, they told me stories about his unconventional approach to caring for them. A woman who had suffered from depression told me that Vince had led her out of the exam room and on a thirty-minute walk to look for four-leaf clovers in the backyard.

"He really listened to me," she said. "I didn't expect that from a doctor. I expected he would just start me on an antidepressant like most doctors do. But then I was crawling around in the grass, looking for the luck of the Irish, and you know what? I did feel better. I thought it was a little crazy, but it helped."

A construction worker told me that Vince had changed the clinic's hours—opening at seven in the morning and closing at eight in the evening—so that working people like him could actually go to the doctor. "Never made much sense to me that doctor's offices were only open right when you were supposed to be at work," he said.

A farmer told me that Vince had once accepted a bag of tomatoes and twelve ears of corn in exchange for taking care of him during a time when he was flat broke. And several former patients told me that Vince had sometimes refused payment altogether.

Vince, it seemed, had taken pains to integrate into the community. He'd bought a giant left-field advertisement from the baseball team at the middle school down the street, and often could be found in the stands, eating peanuts and watching the eighth-grade squad. The principal told me he would come down and do free sports physicals for the children. Vince and his wife, Kathy, had befriended several local couples and frequently went square-dancing on Thursday nights. Vince and Kathy's front porch, which overlooked the school from the top of the hill, was often full of friends and neighbors, drinking beer and playing music.

Patients described the other Dr. Gilmer as one of them—a hulking, back-slapping country boy, quick with a smile and generous to a fault. One woman said she'd been surprised, on her first visit, when Vince had asked if she wanted a hug.

"People call me 'Bear,'" he'd told her, before wrapping her up in a huge embrace.

I couldn't imagine hugging a patient on the first encounter. Medical school and residency teach you to keep your professional distance. But I was a new doctor, and hearing patients describe how much they liked Vince's friendliness and openness—his willingness to collapse the distance between doctor and patient—made me think that maybe his approach was what patients wanted. Vince hadn't just commuted in to serve Cane Creek—he'd moved there, made friends, become a part of the daily fabric of life in the community.

I envied that, my first months on the job. I grew to love my patients—the farmers and the schoolteachers, the single moms and young men struggling with opioids—but at first, I felt like an outsider among them. In my mind, I never quite matched the folksy appeal that the other Dr. Gilmer brought to the exam room.

In Appalachia, everything was defined by the mountain. You were going up the mountain, you were going down the mountain; you were from this side of the mountain or the other side. I was definitely from the other side of the mountain. And I felt guilty, sometimes, at the end of the day, throwing my computer into the back seat of my old Subaru and retreating to my suburban security in Asheville.

But I didn't have much energy to spare second-guessing my choices. My life was changing in huge ways. My daughter, Luya, was born on Thanksgiving, and Deirdre and I were in the process of remodeling our eight-hundred-square-foot house to make room for her. Every day, when I got home from work, I took off my white coat and put on a ratty pair of old jeans and a T-shirt, doing demo, replacing floors, mowing grass, and simultaneously entertaining Kai. I had the best job of my life, but with two kids, mounting debt, and remodeling our house, Deirdre and I were flat broke.

I was also teaching again—students from the inaugural class at Asheville's first medical school, a branch of the University of North Carolina.

It was a unique campus, designed to shatter the antiquated paradigm of traditional medical education, which exposed students to disciplines one by one and required hundreds of hours of passive observation. Our mission, by contrast, was to expose students to all the disciplines at the same time, and to integrate them into clinics as student providers, actually responsible for patients.

It was a curriculum built on *doing*. Students needed to be active to learn.

Laura Cone was my first student at Cane Creek. I realized right away that she was going to be a huge asset to me: wicked smart, unflappable, always professional, and ready to learn.

That was a good thing, because all of us at Cane Creek were learning how to navigate a medical landscape that was changing radically. Soon after taking office, President Obama had signaled that healthcare would be his number one legislative priority, setting off months of contentious debate. His proposed Affordable Care Act would allow tens of thousands of people to get medical insurance for the first time, a major victory for public health.

But before it became the law of the land, we were in a different world. Laura grappled with the fact that medical care was different for each patient, depending on their insurance status or lack thereof. Our treatment was the same for everyone, but each patient's access to services or medications was distinctly based on their socioeconomic status—whether or not they had insurance. We worked in a system that was inherently designed to serve the most fortunate, rather than the most vulnerable.

How do you explain that to a student without crushing their idealism?

"This is just not right," Laura insisted one afternoon, after watching me teach an uninsured patient how to mitigate her excruciating knee pain. Although she'd been dreaming of a knee replacement for years, she wasn't poor enough for Medicaid, and with her preexisting conditions, no remotely affordable insurance plan would touch her. Her leg made it difficult for her to work, and all I could offer her was a Band-Aid: ice, ibuprofen, and a steroid shot.

At Cane Creek, the healthcare debate stared us right in our faces. Every day, I treated Medicaid patients, patients who had robust private insurance plans, and patients who had never paid a premium in their lives. There were patients who had been waiting for decades for something like the Affordable Care Act, as well as patients who opposed it with every fiber of their political being.

And oddly, some of the law's most vocal opponents were those who would benefit the most from it.

"What do you think about all this socialized medicine crap?" a patient asked me that fall, when the debates had reached their feverish peak. Wayne Watson was a fifty-five-year-old diabetic, a mid-career roofer who had always been an independent contractor and needed insulin to survive. The expansion of Medicaid would be incredibly beneficial to him as an uninsured, self-employed laborer.

I was always very careful to answer this question respectfully but honestly, leaving space for my patients to talk about their own views. But mine were pretty unequivocal, and I wasn't shy about expressing them. Laura was with me that day, so I felt compelled to be an example for her. I didn't want to be a clinical robot. Vince Gilmer certainly wasn't. I wanted my patients to see me as a person, as a physician who could be real. And that meant sharing my opinion and being vulnerable, too, just like them.

"Well, I think healthcare is a basic human right, like schools and roads," I said. "I believe that everyone deserves access to it, and my job—my moral *duty*—is to make sure that happens in our community. And I think that for many, Obamacare will be helpful—they'll get more care, and their taxes won't even go up."

That's about all I would say. I learned pretty quickly at Cane Creek that even the mildest of progressive views would get me labeled a socialist or a crazy liberal from Asheville.

Which is what I was, at least in part.

But I also learned pretty quickly that if I approached my patients with respect, if I really listened to them, they didn't really care what my political opinions were. As fiercely independent as they were, my patients respected a multitude of viewpoints. They knew that despite my dream to drive an electric car rather than a Ford F-150, at heart I was a country boy from Tennessee who had one real mission: to advocate for their health. They knew that my primary concern was helping them get well. I knew they were just teasing me when they called me a socialist—and that they'd roar with laughter if I asked them when the next Tea Party meeting was.

Just before Christmas, as the mountains were blanketed by snow, Wayne returned. He was wearing his customary NRA hat, Carhartts, and a big smile.

"You're in a good mood," I said.

"Christmas spirit, doc," he said, then thrust a copy of the Asheville *Citizen Times* at me. There on the front page was a picture of Kai, Luya, and me posing next to a beautiful Christmas tree with Pat McCrory, then the Republican governor of North Carolina.

"Gotcha, I knew you were a Republican!" Wayne said, eyes gleaming.

I simply smiled and said thanks—to him and the dozens of other patients who ribbed me as they dropped off Christmas goodies at the office. I didn't tell anybody the truth, which was that my kids and I had snuck into the governor's Christmas party, or that I'd spent most of my time after the photograph giving him a piece of my mind about Medicaid reform.

They still didn't know who I really was. But it didn't matter. Because over the course of my first year at Cane Creek, I realized something crucial: My patients just wanted someone who took their health seriously. Someone who listened. Their community had been abandoned so many times, by so many people and institutions, that they didn't trust mere good intentions. What they valued was action: a prescription refilled, an ultrasound probe touched to their chest, or an extra fifteen minutes of my undivided attention. They wanted care and a kind word from a doctor they could trust, even think of as a friend.

That was why they'd loved the other Dr. Gilmer: He was one of them. He made house calls. He remembered your grandmother's birthday. He worked the sideline at the high school football game as the team doctor, no questions asked (and no fee charged).

Which made the fact that he was currently sitting in prison for murder all the more perplexing.

Throughout that first year, I noticed something peculiar: It was as though the man who had killed his father was someone else. My patients seemed unwilling to believe that their doctor had done all the things of which he'd been accused—or, if not unwilling, unable to accept it. When I occasionally asked patients about it, they usually clammed up.

"I just can't see it," one old-timer told me. "He just wasn't the type."

"I try not to think about it too much," another patient said. "I just remember the man I knew, who helped me so much. I come to my appointments and still halfway expect to see him."

That first April, when all the flowers began to bloom, we had a mouse problem. Since Cane Creek was surrounded by forest and bordered by an enormous open field, the clinic was a magnet for small vermin—not exactly the kind of guests a sterile medical environment needs.

We tried everything: hired exterminators, set traps, had the clinic's doors and walls repaired. But every morning, we'd find evidence of mice in the kitchen. Once, Laura even saw one in the waiting room.

At wits' end, I mentioned the problem to a patient one day. Not just any patient—I didn't want our mouse problem to go public. But Terri Worley could be trusted. A friendly, warmhearted woman, she'd been Vince Gilmer's previous office manager, and dear friend. I thought that maybe if I let her in on a secret, she'd tell me about my predecessor.

"Oh, we had the same issue," she said as I tapped her knee with a mallet to test her reflexes. "Nasty little things."

"What did you do about it? How did you kill them?"

"We didn't," she said. "Vince couldn't bear to kill little animals like that."

"You're kidding," I said.

"No, I'm not," she replied. "He wouldn't let us poison them. He bought a bunch of no-kill traps, caught 'em, then carried them back out to the field."

It was an image I couldn't get out of my head, as that first year came to a close: a murderer currently serving a life sentence, gently holding a mouse in his hands, then releasing it out into a grassy field.

I had to know more.

4.

PARANOIA

There wasn't one moment that tipped my curiosity into fear, my fear into paranoia. Instead, it was an accumulation of things, any one of them easily absorbed into the relentless momentum of my busy new practice. But taken together, they amassed into something larger, a dark black cloud on the periphery of my vision.

There was the day, a little over a year into my new job, when I found out what the fenced-in patch of weeds behind the parking lot was.

During my lunch break I had the habit of stepping out the back door for a breath of fresh air. After hours in the refrigerated, fluorescently lit exam rooms of the clinic, the searing heat and wet-towel humidity of a North Carolina summer was oddly refreshing. Usually, I'd walk out to the edge of the field that lay behind the clinic, past a fenced-in area that I assumed had once been a garden. I'd breathe deeply and stretch. With Deirdre's help, I'd even developed a meditation exercise: For five minutes or so I'd train my eyes on the mountain in the distance and try to empty my mind of all the morning's patients—their illnesses, their pain, their anxiety. Then I'd go back to work.

My attempts at mindfulness didn't always go so well. I often struggled to be in the moment, distracted by what Deirdre called my "monkey brain." Always focused on the next patient, distracted by the multitude of unfinished morning tasks, I'd struggle to attain any moment of zen. But the mountains always made me feel more peaceful and grounded.

Turning back to the clinic one afternoon, after a particularly lackluster lunch session, I realized I wasn't alone. A woman in scrubs was standing at the fenced-in area, her fingers through the chain-link, a cigarette between her lips. She was noticeably embarrassed that I had busted her smoking.

I recognized her from MAHEC's main campus; she was filling in for one of our nurses that afternoon. Cane Creek was such a small clinic that when a nurse took the day off, we had to import substitutes from Asheville. This nurse was an old-timer, a MAHEC lifer. Her name was Colleen, and she lived in the valley, so it wasn't hard for her to come to the clinic that day. Some of the patients knew her already.

"I'm trying to quit," she said, motioning at the cigarette.

"It's okay," I told her. "No lectures from me."

It's sometimes surprising to people how many doctors and nurses smoke. You would think that constant exposure to the ravages of lung disease would turn even the most hardened two-pack-a-day type against tobacco. But medicine is a high-stress job, and many who practice it take relief in any form. For me it was the mountain, for her it was nicotine.

Colleen took another drag and stared through the fence. I stretched and stared beyond the field at the mountain. Both of us just needed a brief escape.

"I never quite understood what this area was for," I said, motioning to the rectangle of overgrown land, where weeds, cattails, and thistle had overcome a marshy area. "A garden?"

"It was a pond," Colleen said. "The other Dr. Gilmer used to stock it with big koi."

I noticed, for the first time, a cracked concrete bench at the edge of the pit, near the clinic's septic tank.

"Was it supposed to be for patients? It's weird that he would put it all the way back here."

She took a final drag. "Maybe Dr. Gilmer just thought it would be cool. He was kind of an odd bird."

We both paused and stared at the overgrown pit for a moment.

"I heard the cops fenced it in," she said. "After the murder and everything?"

"Why?"

"Because that's where he dumped the fingers," she said.

Then she stubbed out her cigarette and walked back inside.

A few months later, I walked into exam room number seven to find a seventy-three-year-old gentleman staring at me, sizing me up. We had never met each other. Most of the time, he saw Dr. Coladonato.

"Hello, Mr. Burris," I said. "Everything okay?"

"Yes, sir," he said. But he kept looking at me with an eerie smile.

I'm accustomed to patients' personality quirks. Some want to tell you their life story. Others remain intensely private, reluctant to even tell you their symptoms. Still others try to defuse the tension of the exam room by cracking jokes—as though it is you, the doctor, who is uncomfortable.

That's what I thought Mr. Burris was going to do. He was a weathered man with wispy gray hair, wearing a beat-up pair of jeans and a faded black T-shirt. His chart told me that he'd been suffering from knee pain associated with his work as a hobby farmer. Part of me expected a dirty joke, or a tale about his sweet potatoes. I would have been fine with that, if it made him feel better.

But before I'd even gotten around to asking him about the osteoarthritis in his knees, he flashed a toothy grin and said something that stopped me in my tracks.

"The other Dr. Gilmer knows about you," he said.

"Excuse me?"

"The other Dr. Gilmer," he said again. "You know. Vince Gilmer? The one in prison?"

I nodded.

"You look like him, you know," he said.

"I do?"

"Oh, sure," Mr. Burris said. "And he knows who you are, too. I bet he's not real happy about you taking over his life."

At that moment, something happened that I hadn't experienced in an exam room since Gabon, when an eleven-year-old boy came into the clinic one day with an ax sticking out of his head: I briefly went into shock. My body went cold and stiff, my vision narrowed, and for about five seconds, I couldn't hear anything but the blood rushing through my head. Then the world returned to Mr. Burris, his cracked smile, and the absolute confidence he had in sharing this news.

Mr. Burris could see that I had lost my color, and he seemed to be enjoying it. His smile just got bigger. He chuckled, pleased with himself.

"How do you know?" I asked after regaining my composure.

Mr. Burris didn't answer me. He just scratched his head pensively and leaned back on the exam table.

"He's getting out," he said. "And when he does, he's gonna want to take back what's his."

Was this true? I realized, standing there in the exam room, that I didn't actually know. I had always assumed the other Dr. Gilmer was serving a life sentence for first-degree murder, but I had never confirmed it. And if he was getting out, of course he would come here and find me.

Clumsily holding my stethoscope to his back, I asked him, "How do you know he's getting out?"

It took me far too long to hear his heartbeat.

"I heard it from someone last week," he said.

He sounded so convincing that I didn't doubt him.

At that point, Robin knocked on the door. She needed to draw some blood. But when she saw my face, she motioned me out into the hallway.

"What's wrong?" she asked. "You look like you've seen a ghost."

When I told her what had happened, she looked concerned, an expression I hadn't seen before on her face.

"It's time to look this up," she told me. "But let me take over for a little while."

So I took a few minutes to compose myself in the hall, staring at Mr. Burris's chart blankly while Robin drew his blood. I took deep breaths, visualized the mountain, tried to use the centering techniques Deirdre had been teaching me.

When I'd slowed my heart rate, I checked in with the patient in room six, who was there for a routine diabetes follow-up. I went on total autopilot—*Sugars well controlled. Continue metformin. Repeat hemoglobin A1c in six months. Daily exercise. Avoid eating anything white*—until she was on her way out the door.

Then I was in the cramped hallway again, staring at the door to room number seven. I'd managed to calm myself down, but I was surprised at how frightened I was. Medical school and residency tend to beat the fear out of you. It isn't the blood and guts that most doctors are afraid of—it's the possibility of failing a patient. Harming a patient, or making a mistake that leads to suffering or death, is what keeps doctors up at night.

But what I was feeling outside the exam room now was a different kind of fear, one that I'd never felt as a doctor. It was fear for my own safety.

The door opened, and Robin walked out.

"All done," she said.

She looked calm—normal, even.

"I think he's moved on to other topics," she added in a low voice. "I just heard a lot about Obamacare."

And it was true: By the time I stepped back inside to talk about a knee injection, Mr. Burris seemed to have forgotten all about our earlier conversation. He was staring intently at the bandage wrapped around his forearm, and nodded when I described the potential risks of a steroid injection and pain medication.

"Now remember, don't take this while you drive, or mow the grass," I said, as he slowly got to his feet. "Just at night. Don't want any wrecks."

"Appreciate the concern," he said at the door. "I won't."

He paused in the doorway, then flashed another haunting smile.

"And, Doc?"

I looked up and saw him testing the door handle with his calloused hand.

"I'd think about changing the locks, if I were you."

He grinned again and was gone.

That night, when I told Deirdre what had happened, she was unconcerned.

"Oh, come on," she said, feeding Luya tiny bits of banana while I shoveled rice and beans into Kai's mouth. "Maybe he's a little demented and trying to freak you out?"

"Well, it worked."

Trying to keep my voice calm in front of the kids, I explained why: I was an easy target. I was the person who had benefited from Dr. Gilmer's incarceration. I was the man who had continued the life he had worked so hard to build for himself. I knew he couldn't practice medicine again, but it seemed obvious he would want to return to his community.

"I'm screwed," I said to her.

"I think you're being a little dramatic," Deirdre replied. "This isn't *Cape Fear,* honey."

My brother Barrett was considerably less sanguine about the situation when I called him that evening. In fact, he amplified all my fears.

Barrett and I couldn't be more different. I'm a country doctor; he's a finance guy. I wear a faded Obama T-shirt when I play doubles at the public tennis courts; he wears tennis whites on his club's grass courts and describes himself as a "fiscal conservative." To him, I am an idealistic socialist whose worldview is not fully rooted in reality. Despite my many attempts, he has never bought my arguments that America is *not* a meritocracy or that healthcare should be a human right.

But we're brothers, and we love each other. And that night I didn't give a damn about talking politics. I wanted to know what he thought of my situation. Barrett is calm, composed, and honest to a fault. I could always count on him telling me exactly what he thought.

Also? Part of his job is buying multimillion-dollar companies. He is really good at assessing risk.

After dinner, while Deirdre bathed the kids, I stepped out in the yard so I could freely pace, my default for intense phone conversations.

Barrett's response to the situation was not what I wanted to hear.

"Are you fucking kidding me?" he asked after I told him about Mr. Burris. "That's insane."

"I know," I said softly, keeping my voice down so Deirdre wouldn't overhear through the open window. "What do you think I should do?"

"Isn't it obvious?" Barrett answered. "Get out of there. Move to Charlotte or Nashville."

I laughed.

"I can't quit my job," I said. "I've only had it a year."

"You're a doctor. You can get a job anywhere. The one you have right now puts you one step away from a cold-blooded murderer. What happens if he gets out?"

A movement at the edge of the yard caught my eye, and my breath paused, stuck in my throat for a moment. But it was just a groundhog, making its evening rounds through our Leyland cypresses.

"He's not getting out," I said after a pause. "I looked it up. Life sentence, no parole."

I sounded unconvinced, even to myself.

"Don't be naïve, Benj. He tried to plead insanity, right? One of those Innocence Project freaks will get him released. Think about your future. Think about your family. You need to put some serious distance between yourself and him—*now*."

That night, after we put the kids to bed and Deirdre fell asleep reading, I checked all the locks twice. I stared out the window, certain that every movement in the darkness—a waving tree branch, a passing car, a deer placidly chewing grass at the edge of the lawn— was my ghostly predecessor, out of prison and ready to take back his life.

Unable to sleep, I thought about my family dozing peacefully in the rooms surrounding me, and tried to imagine what would happen if Vince Gilmer tried to break in. It was strange—when I imagined the other Dr. Gilmer out there in the darkness, I had a hard time imagining what he looked like. He was just a shadowy figure, as obscure and wild as one of the black bears that occasionally stumbled into our backyard.

As a rule, I don't drink much hard liquor. But that night, deep in the bowels of our kitchen cabinet, behind the olive oil and the cooking sherry, I found an old bottle of scotch I had bought on a trip to the Isle of Skye. After the first peaty sip, I moved a rusty kitchen knife to a space behind the bookshelf near the front door—just in case. After the second, I unearthed one of Kai's wooden baseball bats from the basement and stashed it in the laundry room, within reach of the back door.

By two in the morning, I was researching home surveillance cameras on the internet. Near three o'clock, I tiptoed into the bedroom, avoiding the creaky spots on the floor, and grabbed my wallet off the dresser. I entered my credit card number and hit BUY before I had time to change my mind.

When I arrived at Cane Creek the next morning, exhausted and on edge, I found a stack of papers on my desk. A note on the top indicated that they were from Laura at the front desk.

Robin told me about yesterday, so I did some research. Hope this helps ease your mind.

Attached to the note were pages of printouts: stories from the *Bristol Herald Courier*, dating from June 2004 to 2008. Headlines like FUGITIVE DOCTOR ARRESTED and MAN WANTED IN SLAUGHTER OF FATHER blared at the top of every page.

I thought about them all day as I saw patients. But it wasn't until five-thirty, after I'd seen my last patient for the day, that I had time to read them thoroughly. Neglecting my charts and reports, I flipped through the stack of papers from Laura, looking for something—I wasn't quite sure what. But over the course of an hour, I learned a lot.

For one thing, Vince Gilmer was still behind bars at Wallens Ridge State Prison, a maximum-security facility in southwest Virginia. He'd been there for seven years and was serving a life sentence, without the possibility of parole.

That was certainly a relief. But the gruesome particulars of his case did not ease my mind.

One, Vince Gilmer had been my age when he killed his father.

Two, his arrest site was a place I knew well: the parking lot of the Lowe's in Asheville where, for the past three months, I'd been buying lumber to build our new deck.

And three, after the killing, Vince had waited two days to report his father missing. In the meantime, he'd told an easily disprovable lie: After picking his father up from a psychiatric hospital, Vince was planning to take him canoeing. Dalton, he said, had wandered off sometime that evening. He was a wanderer, Vince had told people, and this was not his first time getting lost.

I couldn't get that lie out of my head. *Taking him canoeing after getting him released from a mental hospital, then he just wandered off.* It was so amateurish and nonsensical. How far could a severely disabled sexagenarian have gone? Why were the two of them canoeing at night, when they were supposed to be a hundred miles in the opposite direction? Why had no one at Cane Creek asked these questions for two days?

And if you'd murdered your father, why report him missing at all? Why not run?

With this new information, I couldn't stop thinking about the other Dr. Gilmer's co-workers. What had it been like for them, in this very office, that week he was back at Cane Creek? Had they suspected anything? Had anyone observed any behavior changes?

Terri Worley, his office manager, had always spoken well of Vince Gilmer. She'd told me stories about his good humor, his love for square dancing, and his deep commitment to his patients. She'd mentioned his eccentric side, too—how once, when a staff member advised Vince that communication was not going so well, he impulsively drove to Walmart on his lunch break and returned with six walkie-talkies for the staff to use.

It was a ridiculous idea, of course. One could whisper from one side of the building and be heard at its farthest corner.

"But that was his sense of humor," she'd said.

What else was his sense of humor? Or, more pressingly, what was his sense of right and wrong? Of vengeance? What kind of person was Vince Gilmer, really?

Sitting at my desk that evening, a mountain of reports and paperwork still ahead of me, I resolved to ask Terri more pointed questions about life at Cane Creek before and after the murder the next time she came in as a patient.

I needed a more complete picture of him before and after the killing. Just before I got up to leave that night, I caught a slight glimpse of the after. One of the last pages in the stack was a grainy, pixelated image of Vince Gilmer from *The Charlotte Observer*. It showed a sad-eyed man with a shaved head, wearing an orange jumpsuit and gripping the iron bars of a jail cell.

Mr. Burris had told me that I resembled Vince Gilmer. But I couldn't really see it. Sure, his skin, like mine, was pale—it was not hard to imagine that, hundreds of years ago, we shared an ancestor in the Gilmore clan of northern Scotland. But our similarities ended there. Vince was a big, burly, football-player type, while I was tall and wiry, a tennis player. He was completely bald on top; I had most of my hair, even if it was graying. He was forty-two when the photo was taken, and I was forty when I first looked at it, but I was astonished by how much older than me he looked. Prison had aged him beyond his years.

Still, despite his war-torn, shackled appearance, his eyes were surprisingly bright. Despite everything, he looked gentle, empathetic, and curious.

So why was I so afraid of him?

The mind abhors a vacuum. And with relatively little information to go on, mine invented all sorts of implausible scenarios. For most of my second spring at Cane Creek, every crunching twig outside my bedroom window was Vince Gilmer, crouching in my yard. He was at the wheel of a silver pickup tailing me on Cane Creek Road. He was in the hospital, disguised as a pediatrician with a shaved head.

None of this fear made any logical sense, of course. I knew that the other Dr. Gilmer was serving a life sentence in Virginia, and that he wasn't even eligible for parole. Mr. Burris's rumored information seemed to be just that: a rumor. I wondered if his mild dementia was getting the best of him. I knew that practically speaking, I was in next to no danger.

But the only way I can describe that spring was as a period of existential anxiety. After the busy rush of my first year and a half at Cane Creek, a part of me was finally coming to terms with the fact that I'd inherited a killer's practice, and that my name was inextricably linked with his. And the more I learned about the other Dr. Gilmer, the more real his actions seemed to me, the closer they came to my own life.

It was as though I'd been trying not to drown. Inundated with a steep learning curve—new patients, new co-workers, new responsibilities as a teacher, a doctor, a parent, and a spouse—I'd been just trying to keep my head above water. Now the waves had calmed, and I could finally see the horizon—and realize just how far from land I really was.

It gave me a chill to see the other Dr. Gilmer's patients in the very rooms he had furnished. It made me both anxious and curious to talk to people who had known him. I was always afraid someone else was going to say something about how my predecessor was being released, how he'd be coming back for his old life—and me.

During this period, I was exhausted and distractible.

"You on call last night?" Robin would ask, her eyebrows arched. "'Cause you sure seem like you didn't get any sleep."

"Life with two sleepless children," I lied.

At home, things were growing tense, too. In addition to life and work stressors, my preoccupation with Vince's story was starting to take a toll. The other Dr. Gilmer creeped into our marriage.

"You're like a different person," Deirdre yelled at me one night, when we were struggling to get the kids bathed and into bed. She was on her knees in front of the bathtub, kids' shampoo spattered across her shirt, a sobbing Luya standing in the warm water. Kai was holding on to my leg as I dried his hair with a towel.

"How?" I asked. "How am I different?"

"You're not here," she said, pointing to her forehead. "You aren't present. You're not the person I married right now."

"I'm the same," I said, picking Kai up.

"The man I married doesn't bookmark gun websites," she replied. "What the hell are you thinking, Benjamin?"

I felt myself turning red. In the depths of the night earlier that week, unable to sleep, I'd done some research on Deirdre's laptop. First I'd googled Vince Gilmer's name, and read again the stories that by then were a kind of lullaby: AREA DOCTOR MURDERS FATHER; FLETCHER PHYSICIAN SENTENCED TO LIFE IN PRISON. Then I'd started browsing the Remington and Smith & Wesson websites, looking for a gun I could keep at the house, the whole time hearing my Episcopal priest father's voice in my head: *Guns aren't the solution. They're the problem.*

"I don't know," I said softly. "You're right. I don't know."

"You need to do something about this," said Deirdre as I led Kai to his room. "You cannot live like this. *We* cannot live like this."

What I did about it: I watched our home security footage religiously. I assured Deirdre I wouldn't buy a gun—but I asked my brother in Nashville if I could borrow his .22 rifle. I told her I would stop obsessing about the other Dr. Gilmer, now that I knew he was safely behind bars—but I drafted questions to ask Terri the next time she came in for a visit.

One Saturday, at the Mast General Store, buying a new tent, I came across some bear spray.

"How well does this work?" I asked the guy at the register.

"Pisses bears off," he said, ringing me up. "And it could blind a person if you aimed good."

"I'll take two," I said.

In the car, I shoved one into the back of my glove box. The other I kept in my backpack, just in case.

Bear spray for the bear. A morbid joke that didn't even make me smile in the rearview mirror.

None of these measures made me feel better. In fact, they made me feel worse.

It was like boarding your house up before a hurricane. You know that doing so will make you safer indoors, but once you put hammer to nail, you're consumed by waiting for the first drop of rain.

I knew that the only thing that would bring me peace was to learn more about the other Dr. Gilmer. And I knew that working at Cane Creek, I was in a unique position. The problem was, most of the people who knew Vince—my patients—didn't understand what had happened, either. People like Mule Man and Terri didn't remember a man who was capable of killing anyone. They couldn't answer the question that radiated through my brain: *How could this caring doctor become a cold-blooded killer?*

I felt like I was staring at a paradox. I felt terrified, lost, and I didn't know where to turn.

And then I met Tommy Ledbetter.

5.

SEROTONIN

One Saturday in April, after a long night of being on call, I found myself at the edge of the Asheville farmers market, a restless Kai buckled into the stroller in front of me. Deirdre and Luya were about a hundred feet away, wending their way through the crowd to retrieve kale and squash so that I wouldn't have to push the stroller into the fray. I could just see Deirdre's blond hair, pausing in front of the Farm and Sparrow stand where a line was building for their fresh artisan bread. I thought about calling out to her, asking her to buy us a pain au chocolat, Kai's favorite. But the crowd was too thick, and we'd spent the morning squabbling, so I let her go.

The Asheville farmers market is a local institution, and it more than lives up to the city's crunchy reputation: stand after stand of organic produce, clothing, and farm-fresh eggs, all sheltered beneath a rainbow of colorful umbrellas and rusty trucks. Deirdre and I tried to buy most of our groceries there on the weekends. But more than any produce, over our first few years in the area, we'd grown to love the experience of going to the market. It was reminiscent of my previous life in France and an easy way to discover Asheville's mountain community. We loved meeting our neighbors, staying plugged in with the city, and supporting local farming. Coffee in hand, we'd wander past funky hemp sandals and tables stacked with perfect heirloom tomatoes, through a cross section of twenty-first-century western North Carolina: aging Black Mountain hippies, musicians playing guitars and harmonicas, and young professionals like us. The people-watching was good—and the dog-watching even better.

That Saturday, the chatter of the crowd felt more overwhelming. I hadn't been sleeping well for weeks, my mind constantly filled with thoughts of Vince. And the night before, I hadn't gotten any sleep at all. My night on call had been a tragic one: I had lost a patient, a well-known local artist, to a spontaneous head bleed. Before dinner, he had been telling me about his mobile steel dinosaur sculptures. But when I returned from a quick trip home to grab a bite and tuck everyone in, he had died. I didn't even have a chance to say goodbye. He had no idea his platelets had been almost non-existent before coming in, let alone why. His brain quickly became overwhelmed by uncontrollable bleeding.

The market was a portal back to life and family. I was happy to just be standing in the sun. But Kai started to get restless. To kill time—and keep him entertained—I started sampling the wares of the farm stands closest to us: first the cheese stand, then a jam producer.

"Your raspberry is delicious," I told the man behind the table, a forty-something guy with long hair. He was wearing the Asheville back-to-the-land uniform: faded jeans, muddy boots, a frayed straw cowboy hat.

"Thanks," he said. "Try the mixed berry. That's my favorite."

After I tasted it I saw why. I bought four jars. And while I waited for Deirdre to come back, I started asking the man, Tommy, about the history of his business. How did a guy in his midforties end up making jelly for a living?

"I used to be a medical assistant," he said. "It kept me indoors all the time, which I didn't like."

To get outside after work—and make use of the wild blackberry and blueberry bushes on his property—Tommy started making jam. Sometimes he'd take jars into the clinic, and one of the doctors liked it so much he gave Tommy a loan to start a business.

"Nice guy," I said. "Where'd you work?"

"Out in the country," he said. "Small family medicine clinic off of Cane Creek."

"You're kidding," I said, feeling, even as I said it, some of my ambient dread return. "That's where I work!"

Tommy squinted, studying me like I was playing a prank on him.

Just to break the silence, I asked him who the doctor was who loaned him the money. But I already knew the answer.

I didn't have to tell Tommy my last name, either. Still dressed in scrubs from the night before and embarrassingly still wearing my hospital badge attached to my hip, I could see that Tommy had zeroed in on my name.

When he saw it, he went white as a sheet.

"I was wondering when I would run into you," he said.

A few weeks later, I met Tommy at Sunny Point Café, my favorite breakfast spot. I wanted to know more about his friendship with Vince Gilmer—specifically, what Vince had been like in the weeks leading up to the killing.

Also, I was ecstatic to eat their huevos rancheros without having to wrangle pancakes into a three-year-old's mouth.

Sunny Point was one of Tommy's biggest wholesale customers. They carried his Berry Blast, a mix of blackberry, raspberry, and blueberry. I saw the flicker of pride on Tommy's face when his biscuit arrived with its telltale purple slather.

"So, what was Vince like?" I asked. "As a doctor, I mean."

I'd already filled Tommy in about the clinic and how I'd come to work there. He'd been interested to hear about the reopening, and surprised that MAHEC had taken over the clinic, after everything that had happened.

"Vince was just a good guy," he said. "Real friendly, salt of the earth. Great doctor. We'd hang out after work sometimes, grab a beer or two. On weekends, we spent a lot of time together on friends' porches, playing music, enjoying the outdoors. When I told him about the jam I was making and how I was thinking about trying to make a business of it, he just straight up offered to give me starter money. I didn't even have to ask. It hadn't even entered my mind."

Tommy paused and mindfully took a bite of his biscuit.

"I mean, I know now that he didn't really have the money to give me. By then he was in a lot of debt."

"How do you know?"

"Well," Tommy said, "he didn't pay himself for the first two years. It wasn't until the third year in practice that he and Kathy made their first profit."

Kathy was Vince's wife. I'd known she'd helped him start the practice, but I didn't know where she was now, and no one had been able to tell me much about her.

"So why do you think he offered?" I asked, making a mental note to research Kathy's whereabouts more fully.

"That was just him," Tommy answered. He looked like he was about to say something else, but then he stopped.

"What?"

"Well," Tommy said, "that spring, there was also something just kind of . . . off about him."

I cocked my head, willing him to go on. But he didn't. He just sliced a piece of sausage in half, then into quarters and eighths, progressively smaller pieces that he pushed into a pile at the edge of his plate.

"What do you mean?" I finally asked.

"He was . . . I don't know, he was more impulsive than usual."

Tommy tore open a sugar packet, emptied it into his coffee, then folded the brown paper into a tiny square.

He was struggling to articulate himself, and I couldn't help but think he was intentionally holding back. He didn't know me, but certainly he could appreciate that I must be having a truly unusual experience in the clinic as the second coming of Dr. Gilmer.

I pressed, very gently.

"Nothing really crazy," he said. "It's just, after he and Kathy split up in December, he started drinking a lot. Would go to Jack of the Wood on weeknights even. Stuff that wasn't really him, like buying a new truck and womanizing. But, hey, everyone has a midlife crisis when you hit forty. His just seemed a little more severe."

We were quiet for a moment then. I ordered another cup of coffee and asked for the check. When it came, Tommy pulled out his wallet, but I waved him off.

"When's the last time you saw him?"

He wouldn't meet my eye, and beneath his thick head of curly hair I saw his face grow red.

"The last time I laid eyes on him was the trial," he said.

I did the math. About six years.

I wanted to know more, but by the time I started to ask my next question—*What was Vince like, the days before and after the killing?*—the waitress had come back with my receipt. I took my eyes off him for a second, just long enough to sign and tip. And when I looked up again, Tommy was standing by the table, ready to leave. He graciously thanked me, but he seemed a little rattled. I asked if we could meet again sometime.

"Yes, I'd like that," he replied.

But from the expression on his face, I couldn't be sure if he was telling the truth.

So, I went back to the internet. From newspaper articles, I learned that Vince Gilmer had used a rope to strangle his father and a pair of pruning shears to cut off his fingers. I learned that he came back to practice in the clinic for several days until he was placed under house arrest. I also learned that the facility where Dalton was being treated—where Vince had picked him up, the night of the killing—was one I knew well. It was Broughton, the mental hospital where I'd moved with Deirdre for my first clinical rotation.

Broughton Hospital was infamous. Built in 1875 at the urging of pioneering mental health advocate Dorothea Dix, it was originally one of the country's most enlightened facilities for treating mental illness. When it was built, the facility was like a gorgeous château, five stories of Victorian and Greek Revival buildings sitting on three hundred acres in the foothills of the Smoky Mountains. During the early twentieth century, the hospital was nearly self-sufficient, with patients raising vegetables, building roads, and working at an onsite dairy. Conditions were—for the time—largely patient- and community-centric.

Originally named the Western North Carolina Insane Asylum, over the next hundred years it slowly became one of the most dreaded facilities in the state. After World War II, the patient population exploded, and the standard of care slipped. The greenhouses went to ruin, the dairies were abandoned. After the war, Broughton became the terminus for severe mental illness, a place many patients feared they would never leave.

By the time I arrived there in 2003, as a third-year medical student, it had come to rest somewhere in between its ambitious beginnings and its fragile nadir—a place with a fascinating history that was running on managed care fumes and a limited state budget. I had fantasized that my inaugural clinical rotation would be in the emergency room. Instead, I had landed in a mental hospital. Deirdre and I were ensconced in Broughton staff housing, a second-story flat on the grounds that looked like a time capsule from 1972: dirty linoleum under our feet, cracked Formica countertops, a window unit that blew musty air and dripped water all over the carpet in the bedroom. But it was ours, our first home together.

Every morning Deirdre accompanied me to work along a beautiful tree-covered walk to the locked west wing of the adolescent ward, where my patients—thirteen disturbed, highly emotional adolescent girls—waited for me. In their short time on earth, these young women had already experienced more hardships and racked up more diagnoses than I could imagine. They were, in my fledgling psychiatric terms, "messed up."

And me? I was fresh bait to them. I bought all of their stories, hook, line, and sinker.

Those stories still remain vivid in my mind. The young woman—a girl, really—who had been in an L.A. gang for almost half of her life and had, she confided in me one day, killed a man. The girl from Chicago who had been abused by three separate sets of foster parents. The girl from Charlotte who looked like an eighth-grade honors student—hair in a neat ponytail, a stuffed Winnie-the-Pooh in one arm, and a book in the other—who had threatened to kill her mother.

They were sweet but also volatile. Bipolar disorder and either physical or emotional trauma were the norm for these children, and almost daily, one of them had to be restrained due to extreme outbursts. There was a sense of learned helplessness in them that was wholly unfamiliar to me, as a privileged middle-class kid who had been nurtured for his entire childhood. At the age that I was collecting baseball cards, they were receiving their first psych diagnoses. Unlike mine, their childhoods had been fragile and dangerous, and they imagined their futures to be no different. They knew Broughton was their last refuge before going to "juvie," and in their minds, they had already lost the game of life. Their stories wounded me.

During the day, I led rudimentary counseling sessions. Seroquel, Zyprexa, Abilify, Haldol, and Ativan were my first medical tools. But as time went on, and the girls began to trust me, I started to understand how listening was more powerful than prescribing. Most of my patients had never had a doctor so eager to hear their stories. Of course, I wasn't a full-fledged doctor, but I found that if I allowed myself to be vulnerable with them, to be real with them, they saw me as an ally in their healing—not just an authority figure to distrust. And watching Deirdre with them, as she skillfully led the group through yoga poses, taught me something else—there was more than one approach to mental illness. As a neurobiologist, I knew that a good deal of my patients' problems were due to brain chemistry. But as a budding physician, I was learning that healing was about far more than neurotransmitters and hormones.

My patients felt ground down by life, and instead of hurling pills at them, what I really wanted was to help them lift off from their circumstances. They didn't need me or medications; they needed parents and a stable home. They needed to remember how to dream.

My dream at their age was to fly. Maybe that's why, during my last week at Broughton, I told the whole floor of girls to look out the south-facing windows of their dorm at two-thirty P.M. A field trip to nearby Burke Mountain would have been the best way for the girls to experience the excitement of flight, but there was absolutely no way anyone at Broughton was going to let me drive a bus of teenage girls with suicidal tendencies to the precipice of a mountain. So, I decided, I would fly to them, soaring from the mountain with my bright yellow paraglider.

The plan: run off a cliff near the peak, catch a thermal, and then soar out above the grounds of Broughton, landing in a field adjacent to the hospital. It was a broadly symbolic action, and I knew it sounded crazy, like the sort of thing that might get me committed to Broughton myself. So I didn't tell my supervising doctor about it. I just drove to the top of the mountain with the glider.

I had a grand vision of what would happen next: I'd soar above the verdant valley, descending in majestic swoops, the yellow wing of the glider illuminated by the sun. And my patients would see that even their straitlaced student doctor had a little crazy in him, a willingness to risk himself to inspire a brief smile on their faces.

In the end, it didn't happen that way. Like so many other things in those girls' lives, the storybook ending did not arrive. Towering cumulonimbus clouds were developing as I unfolded the glider to inspect it, and the wind started blowing from the backside of the mountain. It was impossible and too dangerous to launch. Two-thirty came and went, and I was stuck under a tree at the top of the mountain, gazing down into the valley, imagining my students' faces peering up through the rain-streaked window. It was just another disappointment to add to their long list.

Nearly ten years later, it seemed appropriate that my life was intersecting, in yet another way, with Vince's. Because not only had Dalton been confined to Broughton just before his death—he'd actually been there when I was doing my clinical rotation.

Sitting in my darkened office after hours, newspaper articles spread out before me, I couldn't help but ask myself: Had we ever met? I could remember almost every square inch of Broughton's geriatric ward, and in my time there I had spoken with nearly all of the dementia patients. But I didn't recognize the face staring at me from the newspaper articles covering Dalton's death.

I'd learned from Terri that Dalton had been admitted to Broughton in 2002, as Vince could no longer take care of him at home. Dalton suffered from hallucinations, which were likely exacerbated by self-medicating with drugs. His behavior was often impulsive and unpredictable. The doctors at Broughton had believed that he had a form of schizophrenia, layered with a progressive dementia. I wondered, again, why Vince had thought it was a good idea to go canoeing with him instead of delivering him immediately to the medical care he so obviously needed.

At around six-thirty, just as I was wrapping up charting and emails, there was a hesitant knock on my office door.

"Come in," I said without looking up.

"You're still here," Laura said shyly, her purse on her arm. She had another stack of paper-clipped pages in her hand. "I found something else. Something you should see."

On the pages she handed me was a list of names, cities, and countries, along with brief, often gruesome capsule summaries: *killed wife, killed sister, killed father.*

At the top of the first page was a picture of a young boy and his grandfather, each holding a large fish—a bass, I think—and smiling exuberantly. The text below was sobering:

> Christopher Pittman, aged 12 (Paxil then Zoloft).
> Known amongst family as "Pop-Pop's shadow," he had
> always been very close to his grandfather. Shortly after
> being prescribed Zoloft he shot both his grandparents
> dead and burned the house down. Imprisoned, he
> waited 3 years for trial, and was then tried as an adult—
> a practice acceptable in the USA. Defense pleaded in-
> voluntary intoxication. Preparing for the expected
> homicidality-Zoloft link, Pfizer lawyers involved them-
> selves early into the case with prosecution. Jury opted
> for murder verdict. Ongoing appeal against the sentence
> lodged.

"What is this?" I asked, flipping through the rest of the pages.

"It's a list of people who have committed violent acts," she said, "after starting or stopping an SSRI. That's what the other Dr. Gilmer said was the reason he killed his father."

I frowned. "I don't remember the class on murderous medications in medical school."

I continued to scour the packet, which had been compiled by a woman in Great Britain and posited a link between SSRI discontinuation syndrome and violence. Page after page, homicide after suicide, the list trudged on. People of all ages, from twelve to seventy-five. Many different types of SSRIs—selective serotonin reuptake inhibitors, the most common antidepressants on the market. Some violent acts by those who had just started taking the drugs, others following cessation. Mothers who killed their babies; young adults who indiscriminately attacked strangers; violent acts by adults who had never acted that way before.

I wondered whether these stories could be verified, if there was any validity to the list. A few cases had links to other sources, but most did not have any supporting evidence.

Then I read page four:

> Vince Gilmer, 42 (antidepressant withdrawal), of
> Fletcher, N.C., strangled his father and mutilated the
> corpse. Withdrawal from an antidepressant medication
> left him unable to resist the impulse to kill.

I kept flipping, and another name caught my eye: the father of a close friend. I'd heard pieces of the story for years: My friend's father, a successful doctor, was convicted for shooting his wife. I knew that she'd survived—in fact, I'd met her. But what I didn't know was that my friend's father had actually gone to prison, then pleaded temporary insanity, due to SSRI discontinuation syndrome—and that it had worked, reducing his sentence to only two years.

Seeing two names I knew on the list erased some of my skepticism. Maybe it was true—maybe SSRI withdrawal could explain some of Vince's violent behavior.

Laura cleared her throat.

"Listen, Dr. Gilmer," she said. "I know this is true. My mom, she had a bad accident when I was a kid in Texas. She got hit by a train in her car. She lived, thank God, but had a brain injury and they had to put her on medication to control her crazy mood changes. One of the pills she was taking was an SSRI. I spent my whole childhood making sure she took her meds. And any time she ran out of them, it's like..."

She paused and I saw tears come into her eyes.

"It's like she became a different person," Laura said.

That night at the clinic, long after Laura had gone home, I read through the stack of grisly SSRI-withdrawal incident reports again. Then I flipped back to one of the news stories from the *Bristol Herald Courier*. One line popped out at me:

"I have serotonin brain," Vince said. "It's like jellyfish electric stings in my head."

From the night of his arrest on, he had told police officers that his mind wasn't working, and that coming off the medication Lexapro was the reason. He also claimed to be experiencing bizarre physical symptoms, which showed up sometimes on the jail's cameras: facial tics, stooped posture, and an awkward, shuffling gait. And, judging from the tone of the articles I'd read, no one had believed him at the time. Not in the county jail, not during his trial, and apparently not after that, in federal prison.

But as a neurobiologist, I knew that SSRIs like Lexapro, by design, altered a person's brain chemistry. And as a physician, I knew that coming off them could be tricky. I had seen this many times before in my own patients.

Maintaining a functioning brain requires a marvelous physiological balancing act. Ultimately, our ability to function, our consciousness, our moods—all are dependent on simple amino acids that orchestrate a complex dance between our billions of nerve cells. They're called neurotransmitters: chemical substances that sit at the end of a nerve cell which, when they receive an upstream signal, transfer the message across synapses to downstream neurons. Neurotransmitters are the nervous system's messengers, allowing the brain and the body to communicate. Some neurotransmitters are designed to excite nerve cell conduction, while others are designed to stop it. Like computer circuits turning on and off, our neurons dance between these opposing states of excitation and inhibition. It's a simple binary code, but the most complex act of nature.

Serotonin is one of the most famous—and misunderstood—neurotransmitters. It helps to regulate vital functions such as sleep, vision, and pain, but its association with well-being and happiness is what has made it the subject of decades of pharmaceutical research. Since the late 1970s, psychotropic medications have been designed to combat depression by selectively bolstering serotonin in the brain. The first of these selective serotonin reuptake inhibitors, or SSRIs, was Prozac, released in 1986. Currently, one in six Americans take an SSRI daily, and the overwhelming majority of them experience few ill effects.

Serotonin normally breaks down after it has accomplished its primary job of stimulating its neighboring neuron. SSRIs work by preventing that breakdown, causing a surplus of natural serotonin and, voilà, an improved mental state.

Seems straightforward, but it's not that simple.

The truth is, altering synaptic neurotransmitter concentrations can be a double-edged sword. Nerve cells are *designed* to turn on and off very quickly so they don't burn themselves out. That's why stimulants such as cocaine and amphetamines are so dangerous—they can overwhelm cells' ability to self-regulate, ultimately damaging or even destroying them, by producing excessive amounts of another excitatory neurotransmitter, dopamine. When neurons are stimulated too much, feelings of love and well-being can turn into feelings of aggression and agitation.

The abnormal release of neurotransmitters can be detrimental.

At the same time, low serotonin and dopamine release—as happens in Parkinson's disease and certain forms of dementia—is not ideal, either. Neurochemistry is an elegant balance. Manipulating this balance with drugs is an imperfect science, and despite amazing advances in neurobiology, we remain like cavemen using very simple tools.

Still, we have seen how drugs like LSD can create meaningful, mind-expanding experiences. Medicine and psychology have noted how MDMA—also known as ecstasy or "molly"—can inspire empathy. And it is clear that SSRIs can reduce anxiety and combat depression. In my own practice, I have seen a full spectrum of clinical responses to psychotropic agents. I've seen SSRIs like citalopram save people from profound depressions. But I have also seen them make anxiety, sleep disturbance, agitation, manic episodes, and even suicidal thoughts worse.

Stopping these medications introduces other problems. SSRIs were not originally designed for long-term use; in clinical trials, it was assumed that patients would use them for a period of three to six months. Nowadays, patients routinely take them for years or even decades at a time, terrified of what awaits them when they stop.

Altering the mind is an unpredictable science, because every brain is so unique. Everyone has their own threshold for becoming reactive, arriving at depression, or having a panic attack. One size does not fit all when thinking about the most complex biologic structure to ever exist. Our wildly different brains are what make us so brilliant, so human, but also so fallible.

Was there a medical reason to explain the other Dr. Gilmer's crime? Vince appeared to think so. A Google search showed me that soon after his arrest, a local TV station captured video of Vince saying, "My mind is not working right. I need help!" From another article about his trial, I learned that he had accumulated medical papers and other publications on serotonin discontinuation for use during his trial.

But something was odd about his phrasing. In the articles describing the trial, Vince Gilmer never used medical terminology. He didn't say he was suffering from serotonin discontinuation syndrome. He'd just say "serotonin brain" like everyone would understand what he was talking about. He didn't say that cessation of his daily Lexapro had induced psychosis, the way a doctor would. Instead, he'd described a "man-of-war" in his skull.

From what I could tell, he didn't call an expert witness to the stand at his trial, a psychiatrist or a medical doctor to lend credence to his theory. In fact, I learned later that he hadn't even used a lawyer—he'd fired his counsel and attempted to defend himself.

Why?

The more I stared at that photo of the other Dr. Gilmer behind bars, the more questions I had. Was he telling the truth about his brain? Could stopping Lexapro really turn someone violent? Or was SSRI withdrawal just a convenient scapegoat, a way to minimize responsibility for his actions?

If Lexapro wasn't to blame, what was? What could drive a universally beloved, gentle man to brutal murder?

Below all of these questions, like an anxious heartbeat, was the question I hadn't stopped asking since the day I met Mr. Burris in exam room number seven:

Am I safe?

That night, after hours of reading studies about SSRIs and accounts of violent acts attached to them, I had a dream I was shepherding a group of children on a long road trip. We were driving across the desert in a pickup truck, an old Chevy. All of us knew that Vince Gilmer was out there in the darkness somewhere with a gun. It was my job to keep us all safe.

He was out, just like Mr. Burris had warned me. But he wasn't a free man. He was being hunted by the authorities.

And he was also hunting us.

It was night, and I was keeping watch over the children sleeping in the bed of the truck. I heard a shuffling noise, then the click of a safety being switched off. Then I saw him: the other Dr. Gilmer materializing out of the darkness, an AR-15 in his hands.

I was terrified, the hair standing up on the back of my neck. My fight-or-flight response was telling me: run, run, run.

But I didn't. I stepped in front of the sleeping children.

Vince and I were face-to-face. He was larger than I'd imagined.

"This has to end," I told him. "It's time to go."

"I know," he said.

Then he raised the gun.

The cries of the children filled the truck while my alarm went off. It was six o'clock.

6.

THE LETTER

When Sarah Koenig first called me in the spring of 2011, asking to interview me for the nationally broadcast radio show *This American Life,* I told her no thanks.

She'd heard about my story from my cousin Jonathan Milner, she said, an old friend of hers from Winston-Salem. She thought my situation would be perfect for a fifteen-minute segment on co-incidences: a short, offbeat tale with a gothic twist.

When she called, I was in the middle of a faculty meeting and didn't recognize the Pennsylvania area code. After the nightmare about Vince, my paranoia had shifted into overdrive. I was double-checking locks, looking in on my sleeping kids several times a night. I was on edge, anxious, and finding it hard to concentrate at work. So the last thing I wanted was to bring an investigative reporter into my life to produce a story—a story that would be heard by millions of listeners. That would tie me, now and forever, to the murderous doctor bearing my name.

I politely declined.

Then I tried to put the whole thing out of my mind. I thought that maybe, if enough time went by without incident—if the bear spray went unused—my fear would fade, and I would come to terms with the ghost of my predecessor.

I wanted to believe that Cane Creek was big enough for two Dr. Gilmers, one of them safely in the past—and locked up, hundreds of miles away. I wanted to believe that I could take the good that he'd done here and use it to become a better doctor, leaving the violence and the bizarre nature of his case behind me.

I wanted to believe that I could get over the other Dr. Gilmer, and go on with my life.

But I couldn't.

Days, weeks, months went by, and I couldn't forget the look on Tommy Ledbetter's face when he talked about his friend. Couldn't forget the list of grisly murders, Vince Gilmer's name in the middle of them. Couldn't forget the Tacoma, the gardening shears, the image of a man my age behind bars, staring out.

So one day, in the spring of 2012, I called Sarah back.

"I think I'm ready to do this," I said. "It's become pretty clear to me that the ghost of Vince Gilmer isn't leaving Cane Creek, and if I'm ever going to find peace, I need to know as much as I can about him. I need your help."

"Hello to you, too," said Sarah.

Sarah arrived in Asheville a few months later, on the busiest night of the year at the Gilmer household: the evening of our annual music festival fundraiser. It was a benefit to raise money for Shoulder to Shoulder, an NGO that supports medicine and community development projects in one of the most impoverished parts of rural Honduras. Every year, several other doctors from MAHEC and I took our UNC students and MAHEC family medicine residents there to provide care and support the local schools.

To our seven-acre backyard we had invited hundreds of people, all of them donating money to our cause. In return, they got free barbecue, Twin Leaf beer, a bouncy castle for the kids, a silent auction filled with work from local artists, and live music. That year was special because Sarah Lee Guthrie, Woody Guthrie's granddaughter, and her husband, Johnny Irion, were coming. I was a big fan and starstruck to have Woody Guthrie's legacy play in our backyard.

It was a hectic scene, and at first I worried that Sarah Koenig would feel overwhelmed. But from the second she pulled up in her rental car, spraying dust from our gravel driveway, I knew she would have no trouble.

"Hi, I'm Sarah," she announced, springing out of the car, a microphone already strapped to her like some supra-evolutionary appendage. I knew nothing about Sarah besides what she sounded like on the radio, but she looked like her voice: loose-fitting clothes, glasses reminiscent of my high school English teacher, a mess of black curls framing an alert, inquisitive face.

Flashing a smile, she offered me a confident handshake and exclaimed, "Nice party!"

I was busy for most of the night—hauling a spent keg with Dr. Coladonato, introducing Johnny and Sarah Lee to the crowd, welcoming guests, serving them drinks, and delivering my annual ask: *"For a hundred dollars, you can provide ten people with their chronic disease-controlling medications for a year, or send a child to school who would otherwise be turned out to the fields at the age of twelve."*

I had no time to check on Sarah. But every time I looked up, she was mingling comfortably, projecting her fuzzy microphone to a healthy cross section of Asheville. She'd already started working.

When Johnny and Sarah Lee started playing their first song, "Probably Gone," I sat down to reflect for a moment. We'd just come back from seeing a thousand patients in Honduras, I was about to delve deep into the story of a violent killer, there were two hundred people in my backyard—and one of them was a Peabody Award-winning journalist.

But for the first time in months, I felt something approaching peace. All that commotion silenced the voices in my head, and watching Sarah circulate among my friends and family calmed me. A weight I'd been carrying all by myself was about to be shared.

I wasn't going to just worry about Vince Gilmer anymore. I was going to do something about him.

The following night I joined Sarah in her hotel room to prepare for our week of research. I was nervous and unsure of what to expect, but I had compiled a list of names and addresses of all the people I thought we should interview: Terri Worley, Tommy Ledbetter, Detective Michael Martin, whose name I'd found in the *Bristol Herald Courier*. Some part of me thought it would be like a scene from *Law & Order*: a bulletin board full of names, all of them linked by pushpins and red string to spell out their connection to Vince Gilmer.

But when I got to her room, Sarah glanced at my list, then pushed it aside.

"We'll get to them soon enough. Right now, though," she said, "I just want to hear the story from you."

She was fiddling with a pair of black wires attached to an electronic recorder. I realized the taping was about to begin.

"Ready?" she asked, finger poised over the RECORD button.

I nodded, somewhat tentatively.

"Okay, why don't you start from the beginning?"

I didn't know where the beginning was: My summer at Broughton with Dalton? Getting married down the road from where Vince dumped his body? My first day at the clinic? There was no time to think it over, and I had never read the playbook on how to sound good when being interviewed for national radio.

Sarah could tell I was nervous. She was smiling, urging me to get started. But there was a slight edge to her voice that let me know she was in control.

"Just tell me your story," Sarah said in her calming radio voice.

So I did. It was awkward and halting at first, but eventually, after some encouragement—and my first lesson in interviewing: *Be specific*—I got into enough of a rhythm that I had to stand up and pace. For the next two hours, I recounted everything: the first days at the clinic, the encounter with Mr. Burris, the nights staring out my window. I told Sarah about the SSRI withdrawal, the mounting collage of patient stories that he was a good guy—all of it.

I was surprised how emotional I was. Tears came to my eyes as I told her that something was not right, that something wasn't adding up. My voice shook.

Then I was done, sweating slightly in the hotel chair. For the first time, I noticed how cold it was in the room, and how loud the buzzing air-conditioning unit was.

"How did that feel?" Sarah asked.

"Cathartic," I said. "I've never told anyone the whole story from the beginning."

"Well, now we need to see where it ends," Sarah said.

But as we'd find out over the next week, we weren't even close to the middle.

From our very first encounter, I realized that Sarah would not hesitate to call bullshit if she sensed it. She had a way of tilting her head, grimacing and smiling at the same time, which I soon came to associate with disbelief. The first time I saw it was that night in the hotel, when I speculated that the pure coincidence of two Dr. Gilmers might be the result of some kind of divine intervention.

It came out again the next day, on our drive to Cane Creek, when I told her that the French Broad River was the third oldest in the world.

"Really," she said, tilting her head and squinting. I could see her making a mental note to Wikipedia it later, when I wasn't looking.

We were very different. I'm southern and a people pleaser, she's clipped and East Coast. By nature, I'm somewhat accommodating, and my years treating patients have taught me how to put nervous people at ease. Sarah is more direct and to the point, and although she's very friendly, she is not shy about asking difficult questions. She is perpetually unruffled.

Our first full day together was at Cane Creek. She wanted to see the clinic Vince had built and meet the community he'd cared for, she told me. But as the day went on, I realized she was really watching me. As we diagnosed thyroid conditions, treated diabetes, and looked at undifferentiated masses with ultrasound, Sarah—who my patients assumed was a local journalist writing a story about rural health—got a pretty good idea of what I was like on my home turf.

This would be useful, I knew, in two ways: It would give her some insight into how to bounce off me in our later interviews with Cane Creek residents who had known Vince, and it would help her figure out who I was as a person. Sarah had already told me that she didn't just want to get to the bottom of what had happened to Vince—she wanted to show listeners my pursuit to discover the other Dr. Gilmer. The story was about our two random paths colliding, about both Dr. Gilmers, not just the one in prison.

Under her watchful eye at the clinic, I felt myself becoming a character. And at the end of the day, as I was walking her past the filled-in koi pond, I asked her what she'd learned.

She confessed that she'd had no idea what primary care really was until that day—that rural medicine could be so different from the urban medicine to which she had grown accustomed. She said it seemed like we really cared about the long-term relationship with our patients, and she was surprised we could treat so many different illnesses well.

"That's nice to hear," I said.

"I'm also realizing how little I take advantage of my doctor," Sarah said, laughing. "I'm the kind of person who just sees whomever—I don't have a relationship with my physician. But these people, they know you. You know their kids' names. You have private jokes."

"That's what Vince had," I told her. "To an even greater degree, too."

I tried to explain that in a weird way, despite everything, Vince had become a kind of mentor to me, that I admired the way he'd treated his patients. But it didn't come out the way I wanted.

"He seemed like a really good guy," I said, finally.

Sarah didn't say anything at first. But she cocked her head and grimaced.

"We'll see," she said.

Our first interview together was with Terri Worley, Dr. Gilmer's office manager. I'd arranged for us to meet in a small office near the clinic, a neutral space, and had already told her that Sarah was a professional journalist who was making a story for the radio. I didn't say it would air on NPR—to Terri or anyone else. In rural North Carolina, NPR stood for "liberal," and we needed everyone to trust us.

Sarah tapped on the microphone.

"Benjamin is gonna conduct the interview, more or less," she told Terri. "I'll probably get bossy and interject sometimes."

I had been adamant with Sarah that I wanted to be a part of her story—to partner with her in creating it. I wasn't a journalist, but I wanted to learn from her. Also, I wanted some input about how my story would be told. Sarah understood this and let me take the lead in many of our interviews. This was strategic for her, too, of course. At the clinic, she'd seen that people would open up to me quicker than they would to her, an outsider.

"Sarah will probably ask you clarifying questions about the South," I said to Terri. "I had to explain to her what a biscuit was this morning."

Terri laughed, but I could tell she was nervous, shifting in her seat behind the black microphone. So I threw her a softball.

"What was Vince Gilmer like as a doctor?"

Recalling her friend and old boss, she smiled. She recounted a story I'd heard before about a man who showed up with dangerously high blood pressure. He didn't have much money, and when he realized how much the visit would cost, he was ready to leave without being seen. Vince wouldn't allow it and took care of him for free. Later in the afternoon, the patient returned with a bushel of beans, fresh corn, and squash from his home garden.

"That's how Vince and Kathy built their practice. They weren't into making a lot of money," said Terri.

At ease now, Terri told us about Vince's generosity, sponsoring her kids' basketball teams and attending games after work. He loved kids, she said, but had never wanted any of his own. Apparently, that was a point of contention between Vince and Kathy.

This was the first time I'd heard much about Vince's marriage. According to Terri, Vince and Kathy had met in medical school, in Mobile, and after marrying, they moved to Bristol, Tennessee, for their residency training. On a vacation to the Blue Ridge Mountains one year, they found a small house for sale in Cane Creek. They bought it, imagining it could be converted to a clinic, which they'd run after finishing their residency. A young woman about their age, Dr. Leigh Ann Hamon, was doing the same thing next door, creating a veterinary office.

Vince didn't talk much about his family back in Alabama. They were closer to Kathy's people, Terri said. But one day Vince got a call that his uncle had put his father on a bus to Asheville. At the time, Dalton was struggling: drinking, wandering, acting out. It had become too hard for the family to take care of him, so they'd shipped him off to North Carolina, where Vince could be responsible for him.

"I didn't have much contact with him," Terri said. "But Vince and Kathy, they'd have to go home at lunch to check on him, make sure he was okay. And one day, he wasn't there. He'd just disappeared. They had to drive around for hours looking for him, and then they found him out on Highway 25. He said he was going back home to Alabama. That's when we had the little incident."

"What incident?" I asked.

"Well, they brought him back to the office and they asked me to give him his medicine," Terri said. "When I tried, he slung the pills across the table at me and said I was trying to kill him. He was yelling that I was from the Mafia."

I asked what the pills were for.

"I don't really know," Terri said. "Vince said he was schizophrenic. It seemed like he had dementia or something, but he wasn't that old, just in his midsixties."

Vince was struggling to maintain his busy practice while taking care of his father, so he moved Dalton to Broughton Hospital after that. And then, in the fall of 2003, Kathy and Vince split up without much warning.

"It was like a light switch," Terri said. "Nobody anticipated it. By the time he told Kathy, he'd already found a place to live. It was like he just decided and that was it."

"Did he have a reason?" Sarah asked.

"I don't know," Terri said. "Kathy said he never gave her one."

After that, Vince started going out a lot. His friends thought he was having a midlife crisis.

"He was going drinking, spending a lot of time at Jack of the Wood," she said, referring to his favorite local bar. "He got himself a new little girlfriend. We figured it'd just blow over. But it didn't blow over. It blew up."

"During the workday were you noticing anything strange?" Sarah asked. "Were patients saying anything?"

"No. I mean he still gave his undivided attention and time to each patient like always," Terri answered. "And what he done after work—he just done after work."

Kathy stayed for about a month before heading back to Alabama. Vince, for his part, was dumbfounded that she didn't want to stay on at Cane Creek.

"Really?" Sarah asked.

"I had to sit him down and explain it to him," Terri said.

Then Terri told us something that put me on the edge of my seat. Four or five months before his separation from Kathy, Vince had been in a bad car wreck. He was scheduled to take his medical boards—he was a licensed physician, but still needed to pass his Family Medicine Certification—and had significant test-taking anxiety. En route to the exam, he hit a telephone pole and flipped his truck. An ambulance took him to Mission Hospital in Asheville as a trauma patient. After regaining consciousness, he told the medics his name was Bobby Brown, and he didn't even recognize Kathy when she met him in the emergency room. His amnesia lasted for about twenty-four hours before he was discharged.

"It sounds like he had a severe concussion," I said. "Or worse, traumatic brain injury precipitating temporary global amnesia."

"Well, he really didn't like taking the boards," Terri said.

"Wait a second," Sarah said. "Are you saying the wreck was *intentional* so he could get out of taking the boards? Because that's crazy—like the riskiest behavior *ever*."

"I mean, he'd wanted a new truck," Terri said. "And he'd failed the test before."

I remembered what Tommy had told me, how Vince had been impulsive, free with money, even though he was in debt.

"Did the wreck ever come up in court?" I asked.

"No," Terri said. "I tried to tell one of Vince's lawyers, but he kind of blew me off. And then, you know, Vince fired him."

I knew that Vince had represented himself during the trial—and that it had been disastrous. What I didn't know was that Vince owed a lot of money to Broughton on his father's behalf—over two hundred thousand dollars, in fact. Vince, Terri told us, had been receiving his father's Social Security checks every month but not paying the hospital bills. The prosecution had jumped on this money and the medical debts as a primary motive for the killing, she said.

Terri told us that Vince had no satisfactory explanation for why he wasn't using Dalton's Social Security for his medical care—or for why he'd booked a flight to Alaska for the week after Dalton was found dead.

"Why was he going to Alaska?" Sarah asked.

"Vacation," Terri said. "That's what he said at the time. But now I think..."

She paused.

"He was going to get gone."

That first interview was exhausting for all of us, but particularly for Terri. Over the course of an hour, her voice dropped from its customary cheerful lilt to something quieter and sadder.

"I mean, Vince was my friend," she said. "We were family. He watched my kids. Even that last week after the murder—he treated my son for his asthma. Nothing seemed wrong."

"How do you feel about him now?" Sarah asked.

"I feel sorry for him," Terri said. "I can't help it. He ruined a lot of people's lives, but he was a good guy."

"What do you mean, ruined people's lives?" I asked.

"The clinic had to close," she said. "Kathy had to file for bankruptcy. A lot of people lost their jobs, me included. I lost my house."

Sarah asked, "So why do you feel sad for him?"

"Because we just lost money and things," she said. "He lost everything."

After the interview, Terri gave us a big bag of photos, newspapers, and personal letters related to Vince, his trial, and the killing. Two photos caught my eye. The first was benign: the entire Cane Creek office staff, posing outside of the clinic. Vince was kneeling, surrounded by five women, like a quarterback leading his team to battle. Dressed in a flannel shirt, jeans, and hiking shoes, he looked like he had just been on a mountain, not in an exam room.

The second was more grisly: a black-and-white image of Dalton Gilmer's swollen, unshaven face, with bruised lips and a red halo around his neck. Any novice *CSI* viewer could tell this was a man who had been strangled. I put the picture down. Traumatic brain injury or not, Vince had brutally killed his father. There was no doubt about that. He was guilty.

"It's hard to reconcile these two photographs," I said to Sarah as we debriefed. "The guy in the first one doesn't seem like the guy who could do . . . all of that."

"People snap," Sarah said, staring out the window. "What I'm curious about is the in-between time. If he was one guy before the murder, and one guy after it, when did the shift happen?"

Terri had repeated all the things I already knew about the week of the killing: how Vince had shown up to work like nothing was wrong, how he'd treated patients the same as always. But one moment in her story was new, and it stuck with me. On Wednesday, June 30, 2004, two days after killing Dalton, Vince had taken the whole staff out to lunch at Iannucci's, an Italian restaurant not far from Cane Creek. As they waited for their food to arrive, Vince received a call from a Buncombe County sheriff's deputy asking him to call a Detective Mike Martin in Virginia. When he did, Detective Martin informed Vince that his father's body had been found and that a homicide investigation had been opened.

At that moment, Vince handed the phone to Terri and lay down on his table's bench, like a young child lying on a pew during a Sunday service, resting his head in his mother's lap.

Detective Martin then emailed a photo of Dalton's body to Vince's phone so he could preliminarily identify the body. When it came, Terri was still holding the phone.

"I think this is him but you are going to have to look," she told Vince.

He looked.

"Yes, sir," he said into the phone.

What had been going through his head in that moment? And what had happened after that, to his mental state?

I hoped our interview with Tommy a few days later could fill me in. Tommy was, as before, both eager and slightly reluctant to talk. At first, everything was pretty normal. As with Terri, I could sense both intense loyalty to a dear friend and confusion about what Vince had done.

"Vince was an excellent doctor," he said. "He was deeply loved by his patients. The great thing about him and Kathy was their approaches complemented each other. Kathy was more to the point. But if you wanted a good ol' boy to shoot the breeze with, Vince was your guy. My job was to stand at the door and say, *Dr. Gilmer? Time for your next patient.* If you didn't do that, you'd walk into an exam room after an hour and he'd be sitting there telling fishing stories."

Guided by my questions, Tommy talked about the changes he'd noticed in his friend over the last year before the killing. He chivalrously declined to speak about Vince's marriage.

"Did you notice any cognitive changes in him?" I asked. "Terri told us about his car wreck."

"No," Tommy said. "But he did. I remember one time he said that it was hard for him to think. *I just can't form words in my mind,* he told me. *My brain is just slow.*"

Tommy told us a lot about the week of the murder. He was no longer working at Cane Creek by then, but he had actually been with him Wednesday night, hours after Vince had identified the body in person. When I asked Tommy if his friend seemed different that night, he said no.

"That was the last time he was Vince, to me," Tommy said. "He was the same guy that night. But after that—after that, he was somebody different."

"What did you two talk about?"

"We didn't talk at all," Tommy said. "We just sat on the porch for a couple hours, not saying a word."

"Did part of you know that he'd done it?" Sarah asked.

"Absolutely not," Tommy said. "I don't think *Vince* knew he'd done it."

Still, the police had identified him as a person of interest by that point, and three days later, they placed him under house arrest. On Saturday, unable to get ahold of him, Tommy assumed that Vince had been picked up for further questioning and was in jail. So he drove over to Vince's house to get Cav, Vince's dog, and take care of him for the time being. The house was empty. (He would later find out that Vince had heard him coming and, thinking that Tommy was a police officer, had hid in the basement.)

So Tommy grabbed the dog and headed out—only to be questioned by a deputy sheriff stationed at the end of the street.

He didn't want to talk about the ensuing interrogation. It clearly hadn't been pleasant.

Tommy had visited Vince in jail, had been in close contact with him during the trial, and had even served as a character witness in his defense.

"Did Vince ever admit to you that he'd done it?" Sarah asked.

"No," Tommy said. "At first, after he was in jail, he denied it. It was always, *I didn't do it.* But over time, the conversations changed. Eventually, he stopped trying to convince me he was innocent and instead just started talking about SSRI withdrawal. He was always convinced that he was one expert witness away from convincing everyone that it was real—if we could just get this expert to say this on the stand, or if the judge would just read this study—"

"And what did you say to that?" Sarah asked.

"I wanted to do whatever I could to help him," Tommy said. "He was my friend. But the guy who was around during all that . . ."

Tommy trailed off. He looked pained.

"That wasn't the same guy," he said. "Even when the judge was sentencing him, listing all the things he'd done—even then, I just found myself thinking, *That ain't Vince that he's talking about.*"

Over the course of our conversation, I kept noticing one word that Tommy used more than almost any other. It was "debt." He first used it when he was talking about the loan Vince had given him to start his berry farm. But later, when talking about visiting Vince in jail, or the trial, or the letters he wrote to him after he was transferred to Abingdon, he still used it. Tommy felt like he owed something to Vince: money, friendship, love. He was still deeply attached to his friend, and deeply conflicted about what that meant.

Tommy spoke about trying to lift Vince's spirits, early in his confinement, by going along with all of his plans to support him during trial. He also spoke candidly about how even though he wished none of it had ever happened, he didn't think that Vince should be released—not after years of deterioration, without help, without access to medical care.

Tommy, it was clear, was still struggling to reconcile the man he knew with the man sitting in state prison. Like me, looking at the photo of Dalton's mangled corpse, Tommy knew that Vince had killed his father—that wasn't in doubt. And yet he also knew that in some way, it hadn't been Vince who had strangled Dalton with the leash, or cut off his fingers, or dumped the body on the side of the road.

It was somebody else.

"Do you believe the SSRI stuff?" Sarah asked, near the end of the interview. "Or do you think he was faking?"

"I don't think what he is now is fakeable," Tommy said. "I think something happened in his brain. And I think . . . well, if it could happen to Vince, it could happen to all of us."

He paused.

"We're all just one step away."

Not everyone was as conflicted as Tommy. When we called Michael Martin, the lead detective on Vince's case, he was unequivocal: He believed Vince Gilmer had known exactly what he was doing.

"This guy is very intelligent," he said. "He's not being controlled by some demon."

Detective Martin had been the first to question Vince after the murder. The night after the body was found, he'd knocked on Vince's door to interview him. It wasn't quite an interrogation—there was no police station coffee, no swinging bright lamp—but it wasn't a friendly visit, either. Detective Martin already thought that something about Vince's boating story didn't add up. When he knocked on the door, he didn't know what to expect. What he encountered was an intelligent, well-presenting doctor who seemed not all that surprised by the news of his father's death.

"Did Vince know he was a suspect?" Sarah asked.

"He came to know it," Martin said. "Over the course of our conversation."

Vince told Detective Martin a completely different story than the one he'd told his co-workers at Cane Creek. He'd picked his father up at Broughton, he said, the two of them had eaten dinner at the Huddle House in Fletcher, and when they arrived home, he and Dalton had played a game of Frisbee in the yard. Then, when Vince wasn't looking, Dalton had wandered off.

Detective Martin's skepticism was obvious. Eventually, he told us, Vince sensed it.

"You don't believe what I'm telling you," he had told Detective Martin.

"No, I do not," he had said back.

"Why didn't you believe him?" Sarah asked now, over the telephone.

"Ma'am, I've been in law enforcement twenty-three years," Detective Martin said. He had a soft, gentle voice, but there was quiet authority in it. "There are questions people ask. Questions like, *Where did you find Daddy? Is Daddy dead? What happened to Daddy? When can I see him?*"

"And he didn't ask any of them?"

"Not a one."

Detective Martin told us he'd known that night that Vince had killed his father. Nothing that happened afterward made any dent in his belief about Vince's culpability. He didn't see Vince as someone whose brain had betrayed him. He saw Vince as a calculating, cold-blooded killer who had planned the whole thing ahead of time. He had a financial motive and a one-way ticket to Alaska. Vince had committed murder and then lied about it—in the jail and in the courtroom. Although he declined to speculate too much about Vince's psychology ("It's beyond me to say what the mind can or cannot do," he said), he told us that he perceived no remorse.

As for all of the symptoms of mental illness and distress Vince claimed to be experiencing: the bobbing head, the gnawing jaw, the constant hand movements? Detective Martin wasn't buying it.

"He was manipulative," Detective Martin said.

At the county jail, Detective Martin and the other police officers suspected that Vince was faking his symptoms. So they derived a test: They installed a camera in the jail, recording Vince without his knowledge. What they saw confirmed their suspicions. Vince exhibited symptoms only when in the presence of someone else: a guard, a police officer, a lawyer. Left to his own devices, he was fine, and even played basketball with the other inmates.

Detective Martin also recorded Vince's phone calls from jail and caught him saying that he was going to "play the doctor card" in order to receive more medical care. And Vince was observed instructing other inmates in how to exaggerate their symptoms, in order to get the medication they claimed to need.

Detective Martin said that he saw only one personality from Dr. Vince Gilmer: a manipulative, haughty liar who believed he could outsmart everyone.

"Let me just ask you straight up: Did you ever have any doubt that this was a premeditated murder?" Sarah asked, near the end of our interview.

"No, I did not," Detective Martin said, without any hesitation whatsoever.

Sarah and I got a lot done that week. But it was clear, by the end of it, that we were nowhere close to figuring this out. The story got more complicated with every person we interviewed.

Was Vince Gilmer a scheming sociopath, like Detective Martin believed? Was he someone who had been pushed to the brink by a traumatic brain injury and SSRI withdrawal? At the end of that first week, we were still asking ourselves the same question with which we'd begun: Was he a kindly country doctor or a brutal killer?

Some of these questions we could answer through diving into court transcripts. So the day before she left, Sarah and I drove up to Abingdon, Virginia, where the records from Vince's trial were held. It felt odd to be within fifty miles of Vince's prison cell, traversing some of the same government buildings we'd just heard about in our interviews. While we were there, waiting for photocopies of as many of the court documents as we could find, I tried to imagine walking the halls of the courthouse seven years earlier, when Vince's fate still hung in the balance, and he stood on the stand, alone.

On our way back to Asheville, Sarah and I discussed our next steps. She was going to make her way through the court transcripts, to try to put together a fuller picture of exactly how everything went wrong—and to gain some clarity on her biggest question: Why was Vince deemed competent to stand trial, given his claims of mental illness?

My task was to comb through the medical records from Terri's treasure trove. But first, I had to do something more pressing.

"You have to write Vince in prison," she said.

This shot a jolt of nervous energy down my spine. It was obvious that this was the next step, to confront Vince: Gilmer to Gilmer. But it still unnerved me, and Sarah could tell.

"You had to know this was coming, right? I mean, if we're going to do this story, you two are going to have to meet each other."

"I know," I said. "But it's still nerve-racking. I've never even been to the county jail."

I thought about my dream. The gun. The children.

Sarah explained that I had an opportunity to answer all the questions we'd been asking for myself. Everything up to now—our interviews, the stories I'd heard from patients—had been second-hand. But meeting Vince in person? That would give us the first-hand knowledge we didn't have. Kathy, his wife, was nowhere to be found. It was rumored that she was living in Australia somewhere.

"He's not going to talk to me," Sarah said that afternoon in the car. "But you? With you, he'll want to talk."

"That's what I'm afraid of," I said.

I put off writing that letter for weeks. I told myself it was because I had a practice to run, kids to raise. I'd taken a lot of time off to work with Sarah for the week and I was in a deep hole. Each day felt like an endless game of Whac-A-Mole.

But really, deep down, it was because I knew that once I contacted Vince, there was no going back. Once I wrote to him, he'd know where I was.

Every couple of days, I'd get an email from Sarah, back at her home in Pennsylvania.

> Did you write him yet?

And every couple of days, I'd say that I just hadn't gotten to it.

This went on for almost three weeks. But finally, I couldn't put it off any longer. So one night, after putting Kai and Luya to bed, I sat down at the desk at the back of our house. I brewed a mug of tea, opened my computer—and then walked back to the kitchen for that forgotten bottle of scotch.

Here's what I wrote:

> November 16th, 2012
> Dear Dr. Gilmer,
>
> My name is Benjamin Gilmer and I am currently one of the 2 practicing physicians at Cane Creek. I have thought about writing you for some time as I have been working at Cane Creek for 3 years now. It is likely that you didn't even know that there was another Dr. Gilmer at Cane Creek; I know that it is very ironic.
>
> My first intention in writing to you is to share that your patients loved you. To date, I have not encountered a patient that didn't cherish you as a physician. They describe you as a "kind, humble man who did everything for the community." Everyone was shocked by the event and many still deny that you did it. My experience at Cane Creek has been interesting. Firstly, it was my first job out of residency at MAHEC which, as you know, is challenging. Nearly daily, I am reminded of your legacy which has been confusing. At first, it was confusing for the patients who thought that you had returned and

then later confusing because the stories and image of you just didn't match up to newspapers or stories from the hearing.

I have spoken to Tommy and Terri and they of course have been affected by everything but miss you dearly. Tommy has not shared much but tells me that you were the type of guy who would give the shirt off his back to anyone and that you would never turn a patient away.

In many ways, I have inherited what you built at Cane Creek and thank you for all of your work and the good care that you gave to the community. You will always be remembered by many as a caring, dedicated physician. As a curious, compassionate person and physician, I have naturally wanted to figure out what happened to you leading up to the event. Your memory is still very palpable in the building and of course closer to me because we share the same name. Many people think that we are cousins or brothers even. I'm actually about the same age as you were when you left in 2004.

I have wanted to meet you in person but have also been fearful of this at the same time. For several months, I was somewhat obsessed about understanding just what happened and have heard a mosaic of patient stories about you leading up to that June day. I shelved this desire to meet you until recently when an NPR program, "This American Life," asked me to tell the story about my experience walking in your footsteps. At first, I told them no and felt very uncomfortable pursuing it as a physician. I later accepted because I thought that it might help me and the community to understand the truth in an effort to heal. I felt that if I didn't pursue knowing the truth, I would be haunted by the unknowing for the rest of my personal and professional life. I would also like to be able to tell our patients: Yes, I have seen him and he is well. If you allow me, I would like to come to the prison to meet you. I would like to ask you a few questions and also give you a chance to hear an update about Cane Creek. I'm not sure exactly how the process works, but I could be available to come see you potentially before Christmas.

You are welcome to communicate your response to:

MAHEC Family Health Center
c/o Benjamin Gilmer
1542 Cane Creek Rd
Fletcher, NC 28732

Sincerely,
Benjamin Gilmer, MD

The next morning, on the way to work, I dropped the letter off at the Cane Creek post office. I thought that maybe a postmark from his hometown would predispose him to some nostalgia. Fear had prevented me from putting my personal address on the envelope. A layer of separation still felt necessary, but as a family we had crossed the anonymous line.

He knew I was here.

Now, I told myself, the only thing to do was wait.

I waited for weeks. For the rest of November—through Thanksgiving and into the Christmas season—I checked the mail at the clinic twice a day: once when I got in, and once when I left. Laura got used to the sight of me, asking for letters. Eventually, we didn't even have to talk; she'd just shake her head at my approach.

By the time the MAHEC Christmas party had arrived, I was pessimistic about getting a reply. Standing in Dr. Coladonato's kitchen, eating tamales Laura had made and eyeing my second spicy margarita, Mike's holiday specialty, I tried to put Vince Gilmer out of my mind. But I couldn't concentrate—not on the discussions of that year's horrible flu season, not on the lighthearted ribbing Mike was directing at all of us. I couldn't even muster up much excitement about my favorite annual Cane Creek Christmas tradition, the "dirty Santa" gift exchange, even though I had a great gift that year.

I was heading to the kitchen for more of Robin's cheesy sausage balls when Laura stepped in front of me and cleared her throat.

"Dr. Gilmer, it came this afternoon."

I stood frozen for a moment.

"What?"

"He wrote back," Laura said.

The room had gone quiet. Laura handed me an envelope with my name on it and a return address of Wallens Ridge Facility, Big Stone Gap, VA. It felt light, maybe one page.

I would have preferred to open the letter at home, with Deirdre. But everyone had heard Laura, and now all eyes were on me. They had been waiting, too.

I tore open the envelope.

The letter was handwritten. It was short.

Dear Dr. Gilmer, it read,

> I know who you are. I appreciated your letter, but you
> have stolen everything from me. Cane Creek is still
> mine. When I get out of this hellhole, I will be coming
> after you. I will find you and you will pay.

Before I could say anything, I was running for the door, headed for refuge outside in the cold air. My body was shaking, my mind was racing. I didn't feel in control of anything.

"Honey, wait," Deirdre shouted after me. But I didn't stop.

Outside, I tried to regroup. I stared at the mountain behind the house, partially lit by a waning moon. I filled my lungs with cold, clean air. The letter I had written was so carefully crafted and non-threatening. I didn't understand how anyone could read it and want to hurt me.

The front door opened and Deirdre appeared.

"You okay?" she asked, putting her arms around me.

"No," I said. My voice sounded high, pinched. "I just introduced myself to a murderer. Now he fucking knows we're here. And he's not happy about it."

I handed Deirdre the letter, and she read it under a string of Christmas lights.

"Oh my god," she said.

"I know."

"He's never getting out," Deirdre said. "Right?"

I didn't know for sure. But after about ten minutes, I'd calmed down enough to go back inside.

"Maybe it's time for another margarita," Deirdre said.

We walked back into the house together. The Christmas music had been turned down and people were weirdly quiet. Drink in hand, I stared at the giant Christmas tree, which was covered in red ornaments and must have been at least eleven feet tall. Laura slowly inched her way over to me.

"Dr. Gilmer," she said, her voice trembling, "We wrote that letter. It was a joke. A bad one. I'm so, so sorry."

The color drained from my face. Before I could say anything, Mike stepped up.

"It wasn't just Laura," he said. "It was partly my idea. We thought it would be a funny practical joke but we really misjudged things. My bad. No hard feelings?"

"Sure," I stammered. "No hard feelings."

Everyone tried to laugh it off. But I was upset, and more than a little embarrassed. For me, the Christmas spirit had evaporated from the room, and I didn't see any point waiting for the gift exchange. So after a few minutes I gathered the family, politely wished everyone Merry Christmas, and then headed for the door, again.

"Some party," Deirdre said, once we were in the car.

"How could they imagine that would be okay?" I asked.

Deirdre put her hand on my shoulder. "Honey, you're the only one with skin in this game," she said. "You're the only one named Gilmer."

Eventually, I got over it. Mike called me to apologize again, a mortified Laura wrote me a sweet note and baked me a cake. It had just been a practical joke gone very wrong. No one involved had really understood how emotionally invested in the other Dr. Gilmer I'd become or how afraid I was. It wasn't really their fault—how could they understand?

After about a week, I could even laugh about it. I started to believe that maybe I'd never get a reply—that I'd have to content myself with interviewing Vince Gilmer's friends and former coworkers. I could read the hundreds of pages of trial transcripts. I could contact members of his family. I could get as close as humanly possible, without ever meeting the man in person. Maybe it was better that way, I reasoned. Maybe I could get some peace of mind, even if I never heard from him.

By New Year's, I'd almost convinced myself.

But then Vince Gilmer wrote me back.

7.

WALLENS RIDGE

Sarah and I drove up the mountain in the dead of winter, ascending through the dense fog that still blanketed the frigid Big Stone Gap valley. It reminded me of being lost in the clouds once while paragliding, dangerously losing all orientation except for the sun above that guided me to the west. As Sarah and I neared the crest of the ridge, we emerged into a glittering field of ice crystals and light, a scene so beautiful we had to pull the car off the road. I needed this pause to collect myself and embrace the unknown that awaited us. We both marveled at the beauty of the mountains and nature's light show glistening through the frozen trees.

Though reluctant to get back into the car, we eventually crept up the final stretch of the prison road. And there in the distance, high above the valley floor, carved into the very side of the mountain, appeared a hulking edifice, seven L-shaped buildings surrounding a central fortress like blades of a throwing star. It looked out of place, like someone had dropped the Pentagon directly into a national park.

Wallens Ridge is one of Virginia's most infamous prisons, a supermax facility like its sibling, Red Onion State Prison, thirty miles away in Pound. Wallens Ridge houses twelve hundred inmates, most of them behind bars for life, many of them carrying multiple life sentences. It is a famously bleak environment, a place designed less for rehabilitation than for extended punishment. And it looks like that, even from a distance. Austere and foreboding. The kind of place that makes you want to drive in the other direction—fast.

But Sarah and I were headed on a crash course toward it.

It was January 2013. Finally, after months of investigating, we were on the way to confront Vince Gilmer.

All that morning, I'd nervously folded and unfolded the same piece of thin notebook paper. By then, I'd read it so many times I practically had it memorized.

I'd carried Vince Gilmer's unopened letter to me around in my briefcase for a week before summoning up the courage to open it. Even then, it had taken a few stouts and the support of my friend Jay to get the image of a murderous, hulking Vince Gilmer, his face crumpled in rage, out of my head long enough to break the seal of the envelope.

But once I opened it, I couldn't stop reading Vince's letter. Even that morning, just hours before visiting him, sitting with Deirdre and Sarah in a diner in Big Stone Gap, Virginia, I'd taken it out of my wallet to read it again, as though I'd find something in there that would unlock the mystery of Vince Gilmer.

AGGRESSION, the letter began, in a handwriting I can only describe as a madman's scrawl, jagged and childlike, huge letters—some of them written backward—colliding with each other the same way that Kai's did.

VIOLENCE, it continued.

SEROTONIN DEPRIVED BRAIN

The handwriting got indecipherable for a while, three-

Vince Gilmer's letter

quarters of the way down the page. But it ended clearly, unambiguously:

PLEASE HELP

"You really buy the SSRI stuff?" Sarah said, snapping me back to the table, where my spoon was poised over an untouched cup of coffee. "When we talked to Gloria, she seemed to think that we wouldn't be able to get much out of him, that his brain was permanently damaged. You really think SSRI withdrawal would be that debilitating, ten years later?"

Gloria was Vince's mother. She lived in Alabama, and once a month she made the nine-hour drive up to Virginia to visit her son. She was heartbroken about him.

Gloria had had a hard life. She'd spent thirty challenging years with Dalton before their divorce. The years after Vietnam had not been kind to her husband. After Dalton served in Vietnam, Gloria told us that he had been volatile and often physically abusive. She still carried emotional scars from their marriage. She worked as a greeter at Walmart and didn't have much money. A deeply religious woman, she'd told us that we were instruments of God's will, sent by Jesus to help her son. She had been so effusively grateful for our interest in Vince's case, and had parroted Vince's lines about his "serotonin brain" so closely, that Sarah didn't seem to fully trust her.

I was more receptive, or perhaps more gullible. Gloria was a deeply southern woman like my mother. I saw her as a broken and desperate person whose life had been consumed by pain and loss. Vince was all she had left. And she believed him.

I watched Sarah wipe a trace of runny egg off the rim of her plate with a piece of toast while I tried to force the last bite of waffle down.

"Benjamin? You there?" Deirdre said, knocking on my skull with her knuckles.

"Sorry, what was the question?"

"The SSRI issue," Deirdre said. "It sounds like you think SSRI withdrawal explains some of what happened. But not all. You'd need a combination of things: the Lexapro, the concussion, maybe something else?"

I wasn't sure, and Sarah was skeptical that we would find some unifying theory that explained Vince's fall.

"I guess we'll just have to see," I said, finally.

As we finished eating and discussed our visit to the prison, Deirdre could tell I was nervous. She squeezed my leg, and when the check came, she took care of it, slapping down our exhausted Amex.

"You okay?" she asked as she signed.

"Yeah," I said. "Just a little nervous."

While Sarah and I were at the prison, Deirdre would spend the day at Sarah's hotel room in downtown Big Stone Gap. Vince was allowed only two visitors, and Deirdre was mostly moral support for me. I needed her.

"Good luck," she said in the parking lot.

"Thanks," Sarah said, unlocking her rental car. "Let's get this show on the road."

In the vast prison parking lot, Sarah and I took off our watches, removed our driver's licenses from our wallets, and grabbed our bag full of quarters for the vending machines. Then we locked the car and walked toward the entrance.

The check-in for the prison was a freestanding building outside the walls. Above and behind it, guard towers loomed, snipers pacing their balconies. There wasn't just one tall fence, crowned with razor wire—there were three, the last of which was electric. You could hear it humming from fifty yards away.

"This is dark," I said to Sarah.

She seemed less disturbed than I was. It wasn't her first time in a state prison. She had previously been a Baltimore crime reporter. She didn't even blink when the corrections officer in the check-in building scolded her for bringing her microphone inside. I would have been trembling and apologetic, but Sarah just shrugged and walked back out to the car. She'd stash her equipment there until we were done.

I remained in the waiting room, alone, and became hyperfocused on the state seal of Virginia, which took up most of one wall. It depicted a barefoot woman, sheathed sword in one hand and spear in the other, standing over a slain man, a crown, and the words *Sic Semper Tyrannis*. "Something-Always-Tyrants," I figured it meant—either a resounding message that tyranny had been over-

come, or the reverse. It was hard to imagine this as a message of
freedom.

The form we both had to sign asked for basic information: name,
date of birth, the inmate you were visiting, your relationship to that
inmate. It was the sort of form that should take less than thirty seconds to fill out. But standing in the cold waiting room, pen poised
over the form, something odd happened.

I couldn't write my name.

I gripped the pen between my fingers and willed myself to write.
But all that resulted was a shaky squiggle, somewhere above the
line where I needed to write *Benjamin Gilmer*. I gripped the pen
tighter but that only made it worse. I had lost the ability to write.

As a doctor, I know how to diagnose a panic attack. And it was
clear to me, even then, that that's what was happening to me. My
breathing was shallow, my face was tingling, and despite the chill in
the room, sweat was pooling in my armpits and along my forehead.

"You all right?" Sarah asked.

"I think so," I said, trying to conceal the pen shaking in my hand
and the clumsy block letters—about as legible as the other Dr.
Gilmer's—that I made once I could finally make my hand move
across the page.

No *Dr.*, no *Benjamin*—all you could read was *Gilmer.*

Sarah and I walked through the metal detectors, got our hands
stamped, then passed through a gate into an outdoor corridor, a no-
man's-land with high fences enshrouded by razor wire. When we
entered the prison proper, a guard examined our hands under a UV
light, then waved us forward. A heavy door slid open.

The visiting room was a vast, open space that smelled like a high
school cafeteria: body odor, industrial food production, and harsh
chemical cleaners. A series of long metal tables ran the length of
the room, each bisected by a six-inch divider, intended to prevent
any contact with the inmates. Visitors sat on one side, in uncom-

fortable chairs. Inmates sat on the other, watched over by burly corrections officers.

When Sarah and I stepped into the room, there were already several other visits in progress. To our left, a strikingly handsome inmate leaned forward toward his two visitors, his smile radiant. To our right, an inmate who couldn't have been older than twenty stared at the table, while two adults—his parents, I assumed—sat silently. Tattoos snaked up his arms and neck. He tried to make conversation but his shame was palpable, as thick as the room's odor of disinfectant.

It made me think about Kai, who was only six. I couldn't imagine shepherding a child through life, only to end up here. I tried to imagine what he might give up his life for: a stolen car, a bag of Oxy 10s, gang-related violence?

"I guess we're early," I said, trying to make small talk.

We sat there for about twenty minutes, scanning each new inmate who entered the room.

"Is that him?" I whispered to Sarah, again and again, as a parade of inmates entered: a bald man in his fifties, a guy with a fresh scar on his forearm, a man with a salt-and-pepper beard.

"Nope," Sarah said, after the third possible Gilmer. "Just relax, Benjamin."

Then an older gentleman, much older than every other inmate, appeared in the corner of my eye. He shuffled toward us, moving so slowly I thought his feet were shackled at first.

"Is that him?" I murmured to Sarah.

"Nope, can't be—way too old."

The man was nearly bald, with sharp, sunken facial features. He was very thin, his orange jumpsuit hanging off him, three sizes too large. He seemed unsteady on his feet, unsure of where to go, placidly guided toward us by a corrections officer. Sarah and I both assumed the man was visiting someone farther down our table.

Then he sat down across from us.

The old man was Dr. Vince Gilmer. He looked nothing like his picture, nothing like my nightmares.

I tried to hide my shock. I was used to doing this, with patients who were very ill or injured. I cleared my throat.

"Hi, I'm Benjamin Gilmer and this is Sarah Koenig," I said.

The man looked at both of us, taking us in. Then his face began to contort, his mouth opening and closing, his eyes deviating upward and to the left. I realized after a second or two that he was struggling to speak, to find the words to address us.

"I'm Vince," he finally said, in a voice barely louder than a whisper. He laid his hands down on the cold table, his fingers twitching uncontrollably. His mouth twitched, too, his lips curling up over his few remaining teeth. After every word, he halted, painfully trying to capture the next one.

"What's . . . the . . . word, what's . . . the . . . word?" he asked, each time gazing upward and away from us. He was trying to greet us, but every word was clearly a painful effort.

Sarah glanced at me. For the first time, even she seemed rattled. I could hear her unspoken thought: *What the hell is this?*

So I let my physician instincts take over. There was something obviously wrong with the person across the table from me, and my job was to figure out what it was.

"I want to thank you for all the work you did at Cane Creek," I said. It sounded absurd, here in this terrifying prison, to describe the gratitude his patients still felt for him, years later, back in North Carolina. It felt even more absurd to compare the healthy man I'd seen in pictures, kneeling in front of the clinic, to the hollowed-out husk of a human in front of me. But I did it. They were the same person.

I told Vince about the current state of the clinic, and even filled him in about a couple of his former patients.

"They ask about you often. Especially Mrs. Burton, Dr. Hamon next door, and of course Dr. Ed Reilly," I explained in the most soothing voice I could muster.

Hearing familiar names, Vince mustered up a smile. His twitching hands slowed, his face stopped twisting, and he seemed more at ease. We were connecting.

Sensing that Vince was opening up to us, Sarah abruptly dove in and asked him to tell us about the night of the killing. We didn't need a confession—he had already done that. We wanted to know what his state of mind looked like.

"I didn't want to kill my father," Vince said, his face twisted with emotion.

I thought he was going to cry, but no tears surfaced, only the twitching of his fingers again. His lips moved side to side, his face set into a writhing grimace.

"Voices-voices, w-were . . . *telling* . . . me . . . to . . . do . . . *it*. Let . . . me . . . see, let . . . me . . . see . . . J-jellyfish *stings*. S-serotonin. T-t-t-*torture*."

Vince then spent the next twenty minutes or so describing his "serotonin brain." The details of this monologue were familiar to me, but I was struck, listening to him speak, by how much effort he had to expend, just to get any words out. It was like listening to an aphasic stroke victim: halting, slow, with long, tortured pauses while he searched for words that often didn't come. It was clear that Vince had decided, before we'd even arrived, to tell us this about his brain, and that he'd attempted to organize his thoughts so that we would understand.

But the labor was exhausting him, and, by the end, Vince was slumping in his chair. As tired as he was, I could tell that he was still engaged. His eyes, though exhausted and deeply sad, had a calmness to them amid the chaos of his moving hands and spasming face—as though he had more to say.

He needed a break, and anticipating that Sarah was about to

launch into a barrage of questions, I played the good cop: I asked Vince if I could get him something from the vending machine.

"Please," he said.

We were allowed to walk together to the vending machines, so Vince and I made our way across the room. Vince's steps were unsteady and shuffling, as though years of being shackled had altered his gait. I paused and waited for him to catch up to me, trying to keep some distance between the two of us.

At the vending machine he told me he wanted two Cokes, two pizza pockets with pepperoni, one cheddar cheeseburger, and four Hostess Snoballs, a gas station treat I was forbidden to eat as a child.

It was about two days' worth of calories, and back at the table, he consumed it all in about ten minutes. He ate like a starving person, almost without chewing. Watching this meal was like watching a wild animal scavenge for food. He ate without any visible enjoyment, but with total rapacious need. Sarah and I tried to keep each other in our peripheral vision without being too obvious about our shared glances, shocked by this scene.

A caged animal, I thought. *This is a human being who has been reduced to his most animalistic nature.*

As bits of marshmallow and flecks of processed meat began to cover Vince's side of the table, Sarah fearlessly launched into her first round of questions: *Do you remember killing your father? Why did you do it? Was it premeditated? Why didn't you turn yourself in? Why did you fire your lawyers?* All the obvious questions that I didn't have the guts to ask, still busy trying to be the nonprovocative member of our duo.

But Vince wasn't offended. Slowly, between bites, he told us that although he remembered killing his father, he hadn't planned it ahead of time. Voices had told him to do it; his serotonin brain had failed him. He did remember wrapping Cav's leash, a rope, around his father's neck and pulling it tightly until Dalton stopped breathing. He also vaguely remembered using his pruning shears to dissect each of the fingers from the corpse—to better conceal the identity, he said.

But he was at a loss about so much of what happened that night, he said. Our conversation was filled with many long pauses, holes in his memory, as he tried to retrieve specific details. Looking us right in the eye, he would say, "Can't remember that." He was only 100 percent clear about one thing: He hadn't intended to kill his father.

What were we to make of this? Could he truly not remember? Was he just in denial about the details? Or was he intentionally hiding the story from us, as any deceptive sociopath would?

And if he was deceiving us, where did the deception end? It seemed hard to believe that the physical symptoms we were observing were all an elaborate con. But that's what so many people—like Detective Martin—had concluded.

Then Sarah asked about the one-way trip to Alaska.

"I just can't remember. What's the word? What's the word?" he repeated apologetically, bobbing his head, lips contorted, eyes scanning the ceiling, then the rest of the room.

What he could easily remember, though, was the way he was treated once he arrived at Wallens Ridge. The word he used was "torture." After he pronounced it, he pulled back his lips to show us his teeth, or the lack thereof. Most of them, he said, had been "beaten out of his head."

Vince told us that the guards mistreated him, that the other prisoners beat him, that he had often been kept in solitary isolation, confined to "the hole" for disruptive behavior—which he said was the result of his malfunctioning brain. He told us that prison officials frequently withheld his medicine, an SSRI, which he knew helped him. That when he didn't take it, he started to hear the voices again. That they only got worse in darkness, in silence, in a locked room with no human contact.

Vince could tell us a lot about prison. But he could not explain why he was there, or what had happened to him in the months before he killed his father. Why he had changed. He seemed just as perplexed as we were.

But for the second half of our visit, he was also finally awake. As the caloric barrage from the sugary Snoballs and Coke infused his brain, Vince's speech became more intelligible, his tremors noticeably improved, and his affect brightened. He was awakening, in a way that reminded me of neurologist Oliver Sacks's description of giving Parkinson's patients dopamine for the first time. Like those patients, Vince became cognitively enlivened, his eyes brighter, his words sharper.

Vince had an explanation for this: His calories had been restricted over the years and caffeine was not available to the inmates. Both, he said, were like drugs to him. In the weeks before his father's death, he told us, he had frequented the gas station next to Cane Creek, carb- and caffeine-loading every afternoon just to survive his clinical day.

I asked if that had been normal for him, and he said no. In fact, he'd been on a strict low-carb diet then. But the compulsion for sugar and caffeine was uncontrollable, he told me. He hadn't been able to survive a day in the clinic without it. He suspected it had something to do with what he referred to—again—as his "serotonin brain."

I found his inability to use medical terms or reasoning—even with another doctor—unsettling. Serotonin brain is not a diagnosis. A doctor would have said "serotonin discontinuation syndrome." And while "electrical shocks" or "jellyfish stings" is descriptive, most second-year medical students would be able to tell you that what he was experiencing were paresthesias or facial dyskinesias.

I wanted to ask him more about how he was feeling in the days leading up to the killing. But before I could, our time was up. The

CO—the corrections officer—had returned to our table and was standing behind Vince, his arms crossed.

"Time to go," he said.

"We'll call you tomorrow," I told him. "We have much more to talk about."

I wasn't sure if Vince had heard me—or, if he had, if he'd understood.

But then, as he gripped the table, pushing himself to his feet, he looked me in the eyes.

"Please," he begged. "Help me."

Twenty minutes later, Sarah and I were outside the prison walls, sitting in the icebox of her rental car. Only three hours had passed since we'd arrived, and yet it felt like we had been transported to a completely different world from the one we'd been in that morning.

"Well?" Sarah asked.

"That was intense," I said.

"What do you think?" Sarah positioned the microphone in front of me.

I knew, staring at the black foam tip of the mike, that I was entering the audible record, becoming part of the story. But I didn't have it in me to self-edit just then. What I felt was so powerful, so instinctive, that there was no hiding it.

"I think he's telling the truth," I said.

"You don't think he's faking?"

"I don't think you can fake that," I said. "I mean, you saw him. Did that guy look fifty to you?"

"He looked at least seventy-five," Sarah said.

"And his mouth! And his hands!"

"The way he shuffled away was so strange," Sarah said. "At first, I thought he was shackled. But he wasn't."

"Any one of those symptoms, sure," I said. "You could fake it. But all of them, together like that? He said it himself: What reason would he have to lie to us?"

Sarah tilted her head and squinted. "I mean, I can think of a few," she said. "He wants a new trial. He wants you to contact some expert witnesses about SSRIs. There are plenty of reasons for him to lie to us."

"Maybe I'm gullible," I answered. "But I can usually tell when someone is faking, medically speaking. And that . . . that seemed totally real."

"You're convinced?"

"I don't know about *convinced*," I said. "But before today, I believed that he *could* have premeditated that murder. That he *could* have planned it. Now I'm not so sure. I don't think so."

We were silent for a while. I couldn't stop thinking about Vince, sitting somewhere deep within the belly of the prison in front of us. We had been face-to-face for hours, but how many barriers—how many fences, doors, plates of reinforced glass—separated us now?

"I guess the question is pretty simple," Sarah said, watching two crows chattering on the high fence of the prison in front of us. "Is he crazy?"

She paused, and the crows took off from the fence, rising into the fading sun like tattered black balloons.

"Or is he crazy like a fox?"

8.

WHAT HAPPENED

The first thing I did when I got home was read through Vince's trial transcripts, from the very beginning to the very end.

I had seen bits and pieces before, of course. Sarah had been reading them for weeks, from start to finish, every so often calling me to read a bit of testimony aloud.

"Isn't this crazy?" she'd say. "Are you reading this shit?"

I was shocked by the highlights Sarah shared. But between Cane Creek, teaching duties, and my own efforts to reach out to Vince, I'd never had the time to read the whole thing.

After meeting Vince, though, I had to read it for myself. How had the frail, obviously sick person I had just met ever represented himself in a trial? What was going on with him?

The answer, I thought, might be buried somewhere deep in the transcripts. So I blocked off a weekend, sent the kids to their grandparents', and locked myself in my office with a stack of photocopied pages the size of the medical tome *Gray's Anatomy*.

In the end, it took me about a week to read everything. The trial had been four days long, which translated to hundreds of pages of transcriptions. It was packed with dense legal argument and arcane procedure. But even through the legalese, it was easy for me to see that this had been no ordinary trial.

It had been a disaster from the start. Before the start, even—before anyone stepped foot into the Washington County Courthouse.

I'd already learned from news reports that Vince had been extradited to Virginia after seeding confusion about where the murder actually happened. On the night in question, Vince had been driving with Dalton near three state borders—North Carolina, Tennessee, and Virginia—and in his confessions, he at various times claimed to have killed Dalton in each of those states. No one disputed where the body finally rested: Washington County, Virginia. But none of the detectives could determine with any degree of certainty which of Vince's stories was the correct one. There were no fingers, no bloodstains, no signs of struggle at the scene of the crime—just a body.

Steve Lindsay, Vince's lawyer in Asheville, was unable to cross state lines and could not legally represent him in Virginia. But from letters in Terri's bag of Vince material, I had learned that he thought Vince should plead not guilty by reason of insanity, and that a trial in Virginia could offer some benefits. Jurors there didn't know Vince Gilmer. There would be less media coverage, less emotional attachment. Also, there was a higher probability that the crime would not be a capital offense there.

Was this the reason why Vince seemed unable to remember where, precisely, he'd killed Dalton? I wasn't sure. But his counsel might have had something to do with it. Mr. Lindsay, a seasoned litigator, had strategized extensively for an NGRI (not guilty by reason of insanity) defense. As part of his plan to present Vince as a remorseful killer whose brain had betrayed him the night of the killing, he had proactively asked Vince to surrender his medical license on day one—an indication that Vince recognized, as part of an insanity plea, that he would never practice medicine again. And he'd had him examined by Dr. Tony Sciara, a veteran forensic psychologist in town who had an affinity for evaluating psycho-

paths. Curiously, I couldn't find the results of that evaluation anywhere.

Vince had a good lawyer in North Carolina. But as I learned
from pretrial hearing transcripts, his defense went downhill the
moment he was extradited to Virginia. He battled with his new
lawyers from his prison cell in ways that only hindered their ability
to help him.

In the weeks before the trial, Vince's new lawyers, Wayne Austin
and Joshua Cumbow, very sensibly wanted to call expert witnesses
to corroborate his claims that he was suffering from SSRI withdrawal, and to prove to a jury that SSRI discontinuation syndrome
was a real medical condition, one that might bolster an insanity
plea. The court itself even offered to pay for the expert witnesses.

But doing so would take some time, and by then Vince had spent
fifteen months in a series of jails and prisons in North Carolina and
Virginia, awaiting trial. He was so impatient for the trial to begin,
and so confident that he would win, that he elected to fire Austin
and Cumbow, represent himself, pro se, and file a motion with the
court to establish *himself* as an expert witness—despite having no
qualifications in the field of psychology, psychiatry, or neurosci-
ence, nor any relevant publications in those fields.

He was an innocent man, he told the judge at a pretrial hearing,
and he'd been sitting in solitary confinement for a year and three
months. All he needed to do was tell the jury what happened, and
they'd realize the truth. All of the procedural delays from the prosecution just showed how obvious it was they had no case.

"Basically, the District Attorney wants to lose this trial later
rather than sooner," Vince said.

Vince's confidence in the pretrial hearings was bizarre to me—
and, seemingly, to everyone else. As a brutal cross-examination by
one of the prosecutors, Nicole Price, made clear, Vince was not an
expert witness—he was just a doctor who'd been taking an SSRI.
He was most certainly not a lawyer, and his decision to fire his

counsel—who later attended the trial on standby, sitting behind him and occasionally giving Vince advice—was such a bad one that even the judge, the Honorable Randall C. Lowe, tried to talk him out of it.

"You know you'll be facing a jury on Monday," he said. "You'll be required to follow the rules of evidence and the procedures of the court. Again, I advise you to reconsider representing yourself. You had competent counsel. I'd again encourage you to consider allowing them to represent you and to have sufficient time to obtain any experts necessary."

But Vince refused, believing he could do a better job. And as the trial transcripts made clear, it was the second-worst decision he ever made.

To Nicole Price and David Godfrey, the experienced prosecutors representing the Commonwealth of Virginia, the case was clear: Vince Gilmer was a lying, manipulative sociopath who had planned, executed, and then tried to cover up the murder of his father.

Over the course of the four-day trial, they provided a motive (Dalton's $272,000 in unpaid bills at Broughton), evidence of pre-meditation (ropes in the front seat of Vince's truck, gardening shears in the bed, a canoe to help transport the corpse at the lake), and expert witnesses who could attest to Vince's sanity at the time of the killing—all of which supported a charge of murder in the first degree.

Vince's defense was harder to follow. In page after page of ram-bling monologues, meandering examinations of witnesses, and counterproductive outbursts, he insisted that he was hearing voices and legally insane at the time of the killing, due to the cessation of his SSRI. Constantly interrupted by the prosecution's refrain of "Objection!" he led witnesses, testified instead of asking questions, and ran afoul of proper courtroom procedures. He spent more time apologizing to the judge, jury, and even the prosecution for procedural missteps than he did proving his case. It was a farce, and it would have been comical if the stakes were not so high.

"I'm sorry," he said on the second day of the trial, to a forensic scientist from the state crime laboratory who had analyzed DNA from the crime scene. "I'm not a good questioner."

"I'm sorry. I'm sorry. I'm sorry," he said on the third day, when Nicole Price objected to the way he was using questions to testify. At one point, Vince started hearing phantom objections from the prosecution and began apologizing before any had been raised.

Even the prosecutors seemed to feel bad about how often they had to interrupt him on issues of proper procedure.

"I don't want him to feel that I'm unloading on him because he's unrepresented," David Godfrey said on the fourth day of the trial.

"It sure feels that way from over here," Vince replied.

As the trial went on, Vince seemed less and less sure of himself. He quickly grew more exhausted and disorganized, and seemed unable to put sensible sentences together. During days three and four of the trial, when he was laying out his defense, he often leaned on the judge and his standby counsel for guidance. He didn't seem to understand at first that he had to ask witnesses to state their names and professions for the court—and then, once he did, he often spent an inordinate amount of time on it, confident that there, at least, he was on solid ground. He didn't know how to lay a foundation for questioning by asking a series of specific questions that could then allow the witness to make a broader point in his defense. Instead, he either clumsily bludgeoned the witness with leading questions, shoehorned his own testimony into the examinations, or launched scattershot queries leading in multiple, inconclusive directions. Hammered by objections, he went in circles. His strategy eventually seemed limited to asking whichever questions he thought the prosecution wouldn't object to—not the ones that would actually help his defense.

At one point, during a procedural dispute about recordings of calls Vince made in prison, he asked the judge a series of questions that seemed to confuse them both.

"I don't know what you're asking me," the judge said.

"I don't, either," Vince replied.

As I read through the trial, I got a sinking feeling in my stomach. I didn't know if Vince was telling the truth, but I did know that he wasn't capable of convincing the jury of anything. Apart from his guilt, innocence, or insanity, his defense was so incompetent that he was destined to lose the trial. He seemed lost, desperate, at times incoherent. He didn't speak the language of the law.

Despite all that, Vince's insanity plea wasn't totally without merit. There was, I knew, a precedent for SSRI discontinuation syndrome and NGRI pleas—my friend's father had gotten a shorter prison sentence after mounting a successful defense on those lines.

But to have even a shot of proving his case, Vince needed two things: an evaluation from a psychiatrist showing he was insane at the time of the killing, and acknowledgment from an expert witness that there was credible scientific evidence that SSRI withdrawal could cause someone to hear voices.

And, in the end, he had neither.

After his motion to serve as his own expert witness was denied, Vince had no one who could prove to a jury that SSRI discontinuation syndrome was real. He had to rely on Dr. Jeffrey Feix, the forensic psychologist who had examined him at Central State Hospital in Virginia as part of a court-ordered psychiatric evaluation, to corroborate his claims. The problem was, Dr. Feix had already judged Vince to be sane—both in the prison and on the night of the murder. In fact, he was an adverse witness—one the prosecution was using to prove the exact *opposite* of what Vince was claiming.

When Vince questioned him, Feix seemed totally unreceptive to the scientific articles Vince provided in support of his SSRI withdrawal theory. Vince had found them on the internet, and though some were from apparently legitimate medical journals—*The American Journal of Pharmacology, The Consultant Pharmacist*—there were pages missing from the printouts. Asking Feix to assess their validity, in real time, on the stand, using incomplete documents, was an extremely risky move, even if Feix were predisposed to Vince's theory.

And he wasn't.

"Would this published article be acceptable in my field?" Feix said, presented with one of Vince's exhibits and asked about its contents. "I wouldn't base a recommendation, a conclusion, and psychological report on the basis of a web search."

"Why are you not accepting that?" Vince asked, a few minutes later, about a second article.

"Because I do not know if this is a peer-reviewed article accepted by the scientific community at all," Feix replied.

"If we could get it in its entirety then you would see that it is," Vince said.

A competent lawyer would have made sure that Vince's exhibits were complete, thorough, and credible. An expert witness—like the one Vince's lawyers had wanted—would have testified to the veracity of Vince's claims regarding SSRI withdrawal. But Vince was trying to get the very psychologist who had deemed him sane and competent to admit that he might have been wrong.

And on cross-examination, the prosecution pounced.

"Is any of his behavior in and around the time of this offense consistent with being influenced by symptoms of mental illness?" they asked.

"No, I don't believe it is," Feix replied.

"Does he appear to suffer from a mental illness?"

"No, I don't think he does."

Under further questioning, Feix stated that he believed Vince's behavior in prison—his shuffling, his facial tics, his constant arm movements, his claims about hearing voices—to be consistent with malingering, or faking his symptoms.

In other words, the only person who could have proven to a jury that Vince Gilmer was not guilty by reason of insanity instead became a tool for the prosecution to prove that not only was Vince sane—he was a fraud.

Of course, the only person who knew what happened that night was Vince—and the trial showed that even he wasn't so sure about all of it.

Vince called himself as a witness to tell the story. But his narrative of that night—and the weeks following—had already been summarized in a document he'd handwritten in the Washington County jail, then given to a psychiatric nurse friend to disseminate to doctors and friends who might be able to help him.

Titled "What Happened," it began graphically, describing something I'd only heard hints of before:

> My faggot Dad started sexually molesting my sister and I
> when we were three and seven. The things I remember
> worst is his Old Spice aftershave and that when he would
> get a hard-on he would hum "Baa Baa Black Sheep."

In the letter, Vince claimed that on the night of the killing, he had been off his Lexapro for two days, and had started hearing voices.

> When the voices come it happens like this. The voices
> start with just voices in my head. Sometimes I can pace
> them away or eat food and make them go away. If I
> couldn't get them to calm down, the next step is a pressure
> in the front of my head. This is when the voices become a
> compulsion.

In the truck with Dalton, Vince wrote, Dalton had sexually assaulted him, and the voices urged him to kill.

*I was fighting the compulsion to kill my faggot Dad. I got
some Arby's food. We pulled into the parking lot. I ate a
sandwich. He was humming "Baa Baa Black Sheep." He
said he had a hard-on, did I want to suck it like I used to?
The compulsion took over. It loved killing my faggot dad.*

There were no details about how Vince killed his father. In his
telling, he didn't even commit the act—"it" did. It was as though
Vince were entirely absent from the scene, only to reawaken once
Dalton was dead.

In the trial, too, Vince often seemed at a loss concerning the
events of the night in question. Early in the trial, the prosecution
called the medical examiner to testify to the nature of the death,
asphyxia by strangulation. During cross-examination, Vince asked
him, "I'm sorry this is hard. I'm trying to—some of the things you
said helped me to figure out what happened that night—is there any
evidence to show that the ligature marks were not caused by one
rope that was placed three times?"

It was as though Vince were using the questioning to figure out
for himself what had happened that night—as though he himself
didn't even know. He said as much, later in the trial, after he'd called
himself as a witness on the third day of the trial.

"That's one of the good things about this—in the process of getting everything ready to come here, you figure things out. . . . I still
don't have it all figured out. But I'm now better at saying it today."

When Vince called himself as a witness, he went into unsettling
detail about the abuse he claimed he and his sister had experienced.
He alleged that after Dalton returned from Vietnam, he was a
changed person—someone who could feel pleasure only by causing
other people pain. He'd started abusing Vince when he was six or

seven, and his sister when she was three. He'd drugged and tortured Vince's mother and sister, then had taken photographs of it. He'd peeped through a hole in the bathroom wall while Vince, his sister, and his mother were using the toilet.

"He—he preferred me to my sister because he said he liked it because I was—I was so muscular," Vince said.

> [He] would—he would—then he would take—he would
> take me by the back of my head and force his penis into
> my mouth and he would hold it there and he would—he
> would see how far I could take it in. And he would—the
> pleasure he got out of it he said was—was—when he was
> holding it in in there and I didn't—he wouldn't—not let-
> ting me up for air was how he—that's the pleasure he got
> from it was when he was holding me down there forever
> and forever and ever. And then when he was done with
> that he would use the—he would use me in any way.

Eventually, Vince claimed, Dalton started forcing Vince and his sister to have sex with each other while he took photographs.

This abuse was hard to read about and even harder for Vince to speak about on the witness stand. His testimony was filled with self-interruptions like "Oh my god" and "I'm sorry." Sometimes the judge had to ask him to speak up so the jury could hear.

The abuse, according to Vince, was one of the defining incidents of his life. He said it was the reason he left home at sixteen, and one of the reasons he worked so hard in college and in medical school. He wanted to escape, and also to help people. He didn't want anyone to suffer the way he had. He was also afraid to have his own children because of it.

When asked about the abuse on the stand, Vince's mother, Gloria, corroborated Dalton's extreme personality changes after Vietnam.

"It was almost like he was a different person. They put him on medication, and with that, my husband was normal, just like you or I. But when he come off it, it was like I didn't even know him."

Dalton, she said, had often been violent with her. More than once she'd taken refuge in battered women's shelters, and had even landed in the hospital after being beaten. But Gloria claimed to have not known about any sexual abuse of her children as it was happening. It wasn't until Vince was arrested, she said, that he had told her about it.

"If I had known about the abuse," she said, "I would have killed him myself."

The only person who could corroborate Vince's claims about the sexual abuse was Diane, his sister. But on the day she was supposed to testify at his trial, she didn't show up. No one knew where she was.

Which left Vince alone, with only Gloria's descriptions of Dalton's violence and instability to lend credence to his portrait of a sexually abusive father and a family plagued by dysfunction. At one point, Vince asked his mother if there was a history of mental illness in the family—but the prosecution objected, and the judge sustained it, scratching the question from the record.

"There is not a proper foundation for that question," Judge Lowe said.

At first, I scratched my head: Why wouldn't mental illness be relevant to Vince's story? It was core to any psychiatric evaluation, and Vince's defense was based on his mental health. But the prosecution, of course, wasn't interested in a clinical diagnosis. What they wanted to do was build a case on what they saw as Vince's malice and premeditation.

And they were winning.

The prosecution was able to write off Vince's claims about sexual abuse as more lies, a horrific story meant to retroactively excuse the murder and garner sympathy from the jury. And I admit that when I first read Vince's testimony, I wasn't sure what to make of it. It was so lurid, Dalton's actions so monstrous, that my initial instinct was total disgust and disbelief.

But what if he was telling the truth?

If Vince had really been sexually abused as a child, it could be reasonable to add PTSD to the mix of afflictions Vince's brain was suffering on the night of the killing. If Vince was a survivor of sexual abuse, and—as Vince claimed at the trial—his father began molesting him in the truck that night, pulling his head toward his lap, it seemed possible that he might snap.

And it could be true that under this perfect storm of neurological insults—PTSD, SSRI withdrawal, and a recent traumatic brain injury—Vince really was incapacitated, as he said over and over in his testimony and the "What Happened" letter.

After I got control back, my brain was not working right, Vince wrote.

> *It was as if I was mentally retarded. I had no idea what to do. I started driving. Highways to smaller roads. At one point I moved the body to the bed.*

> *My brain was not working right. I came up with the plan that I would drop the body on the side of the road, not in a field or bury it. I cut the fingers off to hide the identity but left the name tags on his clothes.*

Throughout the letter, Vince kept repeating one key phrase: *My brain was not working right.* It was a kind of mantra, an explanation for why the killing had been so impulsive, the cover-up so haphazard. The paper towels detectives found in his truck, stained with blood? The Arby's bag, the plastic sack from Walmart with a receipt for hydrogen peroxide?

If my brain had been working, he wrote, *those things would have been gone.*

The shoes he'd worn that night, the bloodstains in the bed of his truck, the glove he'd worn, whose match was found near Dalton's body?

If my brain had been working right at all those items would have been gone.

As he put it at the trial to Nicole Price: "An eight-year-old could have concealed it better."

"Are you telling the jury," Price answered, "that since you're a smart person, a person who's become a medical doctor, since you're smart . . . Must have been that your brain wasn't working right or you wouldn't have made those mistakes that allowed the police to go right to you? Is that what you're telling them?"

"Yeah," Vince answered. "That would be true."

The prosecution didn't buy it, maintaining that just because a murder was committed sloppily, that didn't mean the murderer was insane.

A fair point, I thought. But by the same logic, just because an innocent person defended himself poorly, that didn't mean he was guilty of premeditating his father's murder.

Vince did not deny that he had killed his father. But his entire defense rested on his ability to convince the jury that he was legally insane at the time of the killing.

And that was proving to be difficult.

Vince's descriptions of his mindset after the killing were bizarre. In the letter and on the stand at the trial, he described the days after—filing a fraudulent missing-person report on Wednesday, fielding visits from detectives on Thursday and Friday, the interrogations at his house after a warrant had been placed for his arrest—as filled with alternating calm and confusion. At times it was unclear whether he understood that he'd killed his father, or if he honestly believed that Dalton had just gone missing. It was as though he'd disassociated from whatever had happened that night in the truck.

And at first, everything was normal. He told everyone he was innocent. He showed up to work and treated patients without incident. The morning after killing Dalton, he treated Terri's son, who was having an asthma attack, then went driving with a friend to look for the man he had killed less than twelve hours before.

But as the week went on, disordered thinking led him to act erratically, without much forethought. On Saturday, July 3, after a round of police interrogations, he was in his basement when he heard someone—Tommy, it turned out, coming to rescue the dog—entering the house. Without a second thought, Vince impulsively grabbed his black and blue Lowe's backpack, with almost no supplies, and absconded out the back door. As the sun fell behind the Burney Mountain ridge, he headed toward the clinic to retrieve some Lexapro samples from Cane Creek. Never mind that he already had a supply of Lexapro in his backpack that he had forgotten—he never made it inside.

As I approached the practice I could see police lights there, he wrote in the "What Happened" letter.

> *I hid in bushes until 1:00 then I walked 7 miles to a house that was for sale. I had very little water, no food, no medicine.*

> *I thought the house would be deserted but there were caregivers. I hid under a large deck. I was very close to discovery all day. Without the Ambien I could not sleep. I waited until dusk then I went to Subway and called a cab to take me into town. I stopped at a Motel 6. Again, since I*

*didn't have any Ambien I couldn't sleep. No Lexapro so
my brain was not working right.*

*The next day it was hot so I caught a cab to the mall. I was
starting to come up with what to do. It was the worst place
in the world for the most wanted man in Asheville to go. I
saw several people and one of them saw me and called my
name.*

*I came up with my plan. I would get some camping gear
and go hiking until I figured out what to do. The voices
had come back pretty good. . . . I called Tommy Ledbetter.
He told me everybody's lines were tapped and that I
should turn myself in.*

Vince called a woman he had been seeing, instructing her to pick up a note in a cup by an ATM. When he showed up to drop his note off, a police officer was waiting for him. He ran, turning downhill on Tunnel Road, then jumped into the woods behind Lowe's and crossed a creek. The canine team quickly had his track. Exhausted, Vince lay down, chest in the dirt, holding on to the earth, his only stable ground. When he looked up, the dogs were nearly upon him.

Nothing about this escape plan made any sense: the trip to replenish a medicine supply that was not yet exhausted, the seven-mile walk without supplies, the day (and night) hiding under a neighbor's porch, the communication with friends, though he knew their phones to be bugged. And why head straight for a populated shopping mall, when Vince's backyard had a beautiful view of the Southeast's largest wilderness area, a perfect escape route? Less than a mile from Vince's house, a mountain ridge led to Pisgah National Forest. He wouldn't have been the first fugitive to take refuge in the Appalachian wilderness. Just the summer before, Eric Rudolph—popularly known as the Olympic Park Bomber—

had been captured after hiding in the woods of North Carolina for nearly six years.

In Vince's story, the escape didn't proceed from a plan—it was the product of panic. As for whether it was due to SSRI withdrawal or remnants of a traumatic brain injury, I couldn't be certain. But in Vince's telling, something was certainly wrong—and it continued to be wrong at the Buncombe County jail. Without Lexapro, without sleep, confined initially to the drunk tank, his mental state declined precipitously.

It was different than the voices, he wrote.

> *It was like my brain was filled with sludge. I started pacing. I really paced hard. It got harder and harder to keep my balance. I laid down on the drunk tank floor.*

> *It was then that the seizures started. I never had one before. I didn't know what was happening. I peed on myself. Someone called the guards. Six of them came and "subdued" me. They dragged me down the hall and threw me in a room with nothing in it. Then because my mouth got on the leather boot they all started kicking me while I was having the seizure. I had seizure after seizure that night. In between I was thinking how easy it would be to stop this in the ER. When a seizure leaves it takes away some brain function. I could barely walk, barely talk. I couldn't remember things.*

The morning after his arrest, Vince couldn't recognize his attorney, Stephen Lindsay, whom he had met a mere twelve hours before. Despite a judge's orders, his lawyer's efforts, and his own frequent requests, Vince neither received psychiatric care nor saw a doctor. The only care he got was from a nurse, who gave him an antibiotic for his dog bites.

Meanwhile, he claimed, the voices were coming back. Vince tried to pace and chant them away, repeating *I will not kill I will not kill I will not kill.* Again, he referred to the "compulsion" as an "it": *I walked around to each of the other inmates and pictured how to kill them. Just allowing the thought made it happy and it would let off the pressure just a little.*

Eventually, seeming to realize that Vince was a danger to himself and others, guards moved him to a private cell. But in Vince's account, he wasn't treated well. He was mocked by guards and denied access to his medication; his mental state continued to deteriorate. He described *anxiety storms, like jellyfish stinging my brain.* He wrote about how the voices were getting worse and worse: *I could not recover. I kept getting dumber and dumber.*

No doctor in Asheville would come to see him, not even the doctors who knew him. According to Vince, he didn't see a medical doctor until he'd been extradited to Virginia and had been in the Washington County jail for two months. He didn't receive an SSRI again until December of that year, when he was prescribed citalopram—conveniently, just before his competency evaluation with Dr. Feix.

In the "What Happened" letter and at the trial, Vince's account of the killing and the aftermath emphasized his suffering: at the hands of his father, cruel prison guards, and his own compromised brain. When he called himself as a witness, and in his closing argument, he took great pains to tell the jury about how good a doctor he was— how much he cared for Cane Creek and his patients there, how he had led a nonviolent life. He was an honorable veteran, a devoted son, and a committed advocate for his community as a family doctor.

"I've been a terrible, terrible lawyer," he told the jury at the end of the trial. "But I was a good doctor."

Rambling, stumbling, and disheveled, in his closing he futilely attempted to respond to each of the prosecution's arguments in turn, claiming that his evidence—the papers on SSRI withdrawal—was being suppressed. Eventually, defeated, he presented himself as naïve and duly chastened by the entire process of the trial.

"I really, really thought that if I were able to come in here and tell you all what happened then you would understand," he said.

The prosecution, by contrast, painted Vince in their closing as a manipulative liar, changing his story when it suited him. They hammered Vince over shifting details in his account of the night in question, details like where, exactly, the killing took place—an Arby's parking lot in North Carolina? Somewhere in Virginia? They argued that he had conveniently changed his narrative to exploit differences in state sentencing guidelines. They posited that he invented the sexual abuse history, pointing out slight discrepancies in the way he told the story in his "What Happened" letter and the way he related it to prison psychiatric evaluators. They reinforced Dr. Feix's conclusion that he was malingering, that he was faking it all. They dismissed his SSRI withdrawal claims as overblown—and, bizarrely, even insinuated that he had *planned* to go off Lexapro for the very night he was picking Dalton up, so that he would be more likely to commit violence. He'd brought along his canoe not because he wanted to take his father boating, but because he wanted to use it to dump Dalton's corpse in South Holston Lake after murdering him.

Something had gone wrong, and he'd dumped the body on the side of the road. His plan went awry. But Vince wasn't insane, the prosecution alleged. He was just bad at carrying out his plans.

"He's manipulative, he's controlling, and he's calculating," Nicole Price said in her closing statement. "And that's not crazy, unless it's crazy like a fox."

The jury agreed. After four days of argument, it took them only forty-five minutes to return a verdict of guilty.

———

Just before the sentencing hearing the next day, Vince threw a Hail Mary:

He moved for the trial to be thrown out, explaining that he had not been able to participate mentally because of his SSRI withdrawal. He revealed new evidence: a 1996 article from *The New England Journal of Medicine,* one of the most well-respected medical journals in the world, that showed proof for SSRI discontinuation syndrome.

"I told you it was going on and nobody believed me, but it turns out what I've been saying all along is totally true," he said. "But nobody, nobody believed me. . . . Please, please get me some experts to read my research, examine me and they will tell you that there is no way I can function in this trial. I'm sorry, Your Honor."

His motion was denied. So at the sentencing, Vince's only recourse was to call witnesses to attest to his character. And he couldn't even get through that.

"I'm sorry," he said just a few questions in with his mother. "Your Honor, I can't do this."

Vince then asked for his standby counsel to take over during the sentencing phase of the trial. The prosecution was livid—if he'd been competent to stand trial and act as his own attorney for three days, they argued, he was competent now. The judge agreed.

"I am asking to be mentally evaluated right now," Vince pleaded.

"I've denied that," said Judge Lowe. "I'm proceeding. Do you want to call a witness or not?"

He did, ineffectively questioning Gloria and a few other character witnesses before retiring, so that Godfrey could take the stand one last time, look the jury in the eye, and describe him as a "deceitful, manipulative, selfish and self-centered liar who is clearly without a conscience and is capable of the atrocious crime of premeditated murder of his own father in a horribly cruel manner."

Malice. Premeditation. Murder in the first degree.

All of it pointed to a harsh sentence.

Here is how the Honorable Judge Lowe summed things up:

> I, like the jury, listened to the evidence. We watched
> your behavior at trial and realized that it was an act. You
> have researched, you picked up these symptoms from
> the internet and you have tried to tailor your behavior to
> fit that diagnosis without any factual basis.
>
> What concerns me the most about this entire event,
> what this entire event misses is any truthful show of re-
> morse. It's all about Vince Gilmer. Never a thought, con-
> cern or one ounce of remorse to the murder of Dalton
> Gilmer. Mr. Gilmer, the jury found you to be a cold-
> blooded killer. I think the evidence supports that find-
> ing. They imposed the largest sentence they could,
> which was life in prison. I think that sentence is correct.
> I sentence you to serve life in prison.

After reading through the whole trial, I wasn't sure what to believe. It was obvious to me that Vince Gilmer had done a terrible
job of defending himself, that he'd faced a competent prosecution,
and that he had killed his father.

But I wasn't so certain that he'd premeditatedly killed his father.
The prosecution's arguments for premeditation seemed flimsy to
me—it seemed absurd to argue that Vince, knowing that he might
become violent off his Lexapro, had intentionally stopped taking it
two days before picking Dalton up.

I also wasn't convinced there was a motive. As Vince pointed out
multiple times in the trial, there was no financial reason for him to
kill his father. If, as the prosecution alleged, he was stealing his father's Social Security checks, then those checks would cease upon
Dalton's death. And if, as Vince claimed in the trial, he was not re-

sponsible for Dalton's medical costs at Broughton—since Dalton was a veteran, the U.S. Army was—he wouldn't be escaping massive debt, either. (Even if Vince was wrong about this, the fact that he believed it would still eliminate a motive.)

The only motive that made sense for the killing was the sexual abuse Vince claimed to have suffered at Dalton's hand—and the prosecution didn't seem to believe that had ever happened, the same way they didn't believe that Vince was suffering from SSRI withdrawal or any mental disease.

The prosecution had done a perfect job of disproving Vince's defense. They'd made Vince look dishonest, ill-prepared, and inconsistent. They'd poked enough holes in his case to sink a battleship. But it seemed to me they still didn't have a coherent explanation of their own about what had happened on the night of June 28, 2004. If Vince was a cold-blooded killer with a one-way ticket to Alaska, able to choreograph an elaborate defense predicated on shifting, baroque explanations for his behavior, then why was the murder itself so haphazard? Which was he—a master manipulator or an incompetent murderer? Did it really make sense for him to be both?

Vince, for his part, did himself no favors in the trial. He was disorganized, often confused, and inarticulate. He never even mentioned that he had a serious concussion, a possible brain injury, prior to the event. Rather than describing, as a doctor would, that he had sequelae from lifelong generalized anxiety disorder, he talked about "jellyfish stings" to his brain.

Vince's grandiosity didn't endear him to the jury—or the judge. He fell apart under cross-examination. And he was a clumsy questioner, unable to heed the most basic lawyer commandment: *Never ask a question to which you don't already know the answer.*

But I was struck by how often he apologized in the trial. He said the word "sorry" hundreds of times. He seemed to understand that he was flailing, and frequently apologized to the judge, jury, and even the prosecution about the ineptitude of his defense. This, I thought, was not in line with my understanding of sociopathy. Sociopaths don't apologize.

The prosecution painted him as a bloodthirsty killer, someone you should be afraid of. But I didn't fear Vince Gilmer when I read his trial transcripts. I pitied him. He was so obviously in over his head, unprepared in the most pivotal moment of his life. He seemed to only belatedly understand what was happening to him, and he was frustrated by his inability to tell his story in a way that made sense.

I felt, reading his trial, that he was earnestly trying to tell the truth. But sometimes, it didn't seem like even he knew what the whole truth was.

I was particularly struck by an exchange Vince and Nicole Price had, late in the trial, that seemed, instead, to touch on something larger: the nature of truth itself, and how stories capture it. More important, how telling a story helps the *teller* capture it.

Nicole Price was cross-examining Vince about how many times he claimed Dalton had tried to force Vince's head into his crotch. Vince had sometimes claimed this had happened once, sometimes three times.

NP: Did you or did you not tell Dr. Feix that it only happened once?

VG: . . . I can't say for certain. Each time you tell this you cannot get everything in. You have little parts and so if I didn't—I don't know if I told him every single part. It took five times of telling him to get—there were some different parts that got left out each time and there were parts that—so I don't know. That's how it's worked. Every time I've told this story it doesn't have everything in it. You have to add—add a little—yes, sir.

NP: Isn't it true that you crafted the story that was told to Dr. Feix in order to attempt to get the result that you wanted?

VG: In no way, shape or form was any of this crafted. All of this happened to me. There's nothing about this year that I crafted in any way, shape, or form. When I—none. It wasn't crafted. This happened.

[...]

VG: I—each time you say it I come—you can't say it the same way every single time. I'm sorry.

NP: Isn't it true the truth doesn't change?

VG: This grows into the truth. Each time a little bit more and more of the truth—little parts of the truth get added in each time. You have to take the whole story. There's little parts that get left out each time this is told. You've got to take them all.

You have to take the whole story, I read, again and again.

Maybe Vince was right. Maybe the discrepancies in his stories weren't lies; maybe they were evidence of his dogged effort to tell the truth. The whole truth, all of it. Maybe the whole truth just didn't make much sense. And maybe Vince was trying, even as he was on trial for first-degree murder, even as his brain malfunctioned, to figure out exactly why. To figure out exactly what had happened to him and Dalton that night.

Even after twelve hundred pages of trial transcripts, I still didn't think I'd gotten the whole story. The prosecution and Vince had told two competing stories at the trial, but neither of them added up to anything satisfying. I felt like I was missing something. My clinical intuition told me he was not a psychopath, but my gut was still uncertain.

I wanted to take another trip up to Wallens Ridge—this time, with a psychiatrist.

So I called Dr. Steve Buie.

9.

REVELATION

Dr. Steve Buie was on faculty with me at the new UNC medical school in Asheville. Tall and thin, with a salt-and-pepper beard, he is the consummate Asheville psychiatrist: an active man in his midsixties who pairs his elbow-patched tweed coats with sturdy Merrell hiking shoes. I had always admired his calm, soft-spoken demeanor and his devotion to the community.

So when we met for coffee at the Chocolate Lounge in downtown Asheville, I was happy to spend an hour picking his brain about sociopathy, psychopathy, and the psychiatric effects of childhood abuse. I learned a lot in that conversation. And toward the end of it, I made my big ask: Would he drive to Virginia with me to spend the day in a supermax prison, talking to a possible psychopath, on a weekend?

I figured he'd say no, claim a prior engagement. But he surprised me.

"Sure," he said. "How early you wanna leave?"

Three days later, after I'd called the prison and asked Vince if we could visit him, we made the two-hour drive from Asheville to Wallens Ridge in my all-wheel-drive Subaru, prepared for snow. Along the way, I measured our progress with familiar landmarks: the peak of Mount Mitchell through the passenger window, the verdant walnut and hickory trees of the Cherokee National Forest, the flattened hilltops outside Clinchport where mines had once been so plentiful.

It was no accident that Wallens Ridge and its sister facility, Red Onion, were out here in coal country. When the mines shut down, the rural communities needed a source of income. Building prisons on cheap land far from urban centers, then selling them to the government, had been a way to survive. The logic was that the prisons would pump tax money into the local economy while also providing jobs to locals who, a generation before, would have been underground, mining coal like their fathers. But it was unclear just how much of an effect the prison had on local commerce, and the citizens newly employed as corrections officers and workers still made barely more than minimum wage.

I didn't need to explain any of this to Steve. As a longtime practitioner in Appalachia, he knew the struggle many small towns—and the people in them—went through just to survive. In particular, he knew about the lack of access to psychiatric care down in the hollers and over the ridges. At the time, there were only two psychiatrists in the region outside of Asheville, and they had to serve sixteen counties. It was as if our healthcare system didn't believe mental illness existed in the country.

Today, I needed Steve to help me understand how sane Vince Gilmer was—whether he was psychotic, sociopathic, or somewhere in between. Sarah and I had been discussing this over the phone, and after meeting him, reading his trial transcripts, and interviewing dozens of people, neither of us really thought that Vince was a born sociopath—which, in our layman's terms, was the sort of person who harbored negative, violent, or antisocial attitudes about other people. He had dedicated his life to helping people heal, after all, and prior to the night he killed his father, had never demonstrated antisocial tendencies.

Maybe, Sarah had postulated the day before, he had undergone some kind of psychotic episode or break. Maybe Vince was following in his father's schizophrenic footsteps?

"I mean you can have psychosis with schizophrenia, obviously—exacerbated by landing on your head in your truck," I'd told her. "I'm not a psychiatrist, but he had lots of reasons to be moving toward psychosis."

"But someone who is experiencing psychosis . . . could they come to work and see patients and tell a story about how they had the fire department out looking for their dad?" I could imagine Sarah cocking her head, giving me her bullshit detector look. "Is that really psychosis?"

"Yeah, that sounds more sociopathic. And I think it would be hard to perform your duties as a physician in full-blown psychosis," I said. "Impossible, really."

Getting through a day in clinic with all of my faculties, a pot of coffee, and a competent nurse was hard enough. I couldn't imagine surviving a day treating patients after killing my father while being surrounded by psychotic voices.

But both of us also found it hard to believe that Vince was purely sociopathic, either. Vince knew the difference between right and wrong. Sarah and I were confused: about psychosis, about competency, about the devolution of sanity. And after reading the trial transcripts, we couldn't understand how Dr. Feix had deemed him both competent and sane.

So as the mountains and valleys of what had once been coal country opened before us, I asked Dr. Buie about the process by which a clinician determined someone's competency to stand trial and their sanity at the time of an alleged offense. I'd already told him about the results of Dr. Feix's examination, but I wasn't quite sure how he'd come to his conclusions.

"Typically, a psychiatrist will meet for a few hours with a patient," he said. "Everyone's different, but I would say ninety-five percent of the time, you spend the first half of the consultation getting a baseline read on their current psychiatric condition: Is this person competent to stand trial now?"

"How do you tell?"

"Sometimes it's obvious," he said. "If a patient is experiencing hallucinations, unable to express himself coherently, does not seem to understand the charges that have been brought against him—those are red flags. If it's not clear they could communicate with their counsel, or understand basic issues related to their situation, they might not be competent."

He paused.

"But competency to stand trial is a pretty low bar to clear," he said. "There's a lot of wiggle room. And it's definitely possible for someone who doesn't *fully* understand the charges against them, their general situation, to be deemed competent."

"What about a brain injury? Or mental illness?"

Steve and I had already spoken to some degree about my theory that Vince incurred a traumatic brain injury from rolling his truck. Both of us knew even mild trauma could cause memory issues and radical personality changes. I'd told him that Vince struggled with amnesia, remembering new things (anterograde) as well as old memories (retrograde). When Sarah and I met him, he struggled to remember even his cell number, which we observed he had written down on the back of his left hand.

"A serious brain injury could make someone incompetent, absolutely," Steve said. "But a patient can be mentally ill and still competent to stand trial. You can be a schizophrenic and still be able to stand trial."

"So," I said, "say you commit a crime because of a mental illness . . ."

"It's a separate issue," Steve interrupted. "As a clinician, you have to decide if the patient is competent to stand trial *now*, and also make a judgment about whether or not the patient was mentally ill at the time of the offense."

"Part of that is up to the jury, right?"

"Sure," he said. "You could have a defendant pleading tempo-rary insanity, despite a court-ordered psych eval deeming them sane at the time of the offense."

"That's what happened with Vince," I said.

"In that case, usually, the defendant will then try to establish how and why the court-ordered psychiatric evaluation is wrong," Buie said. "He might call another psychiatrist as an expert witness, or introduce information that complicates the initial judgment."

"Vince tried to call one," I said. "An expert in SSRIs."

"Who was it?"

"Himself," I said. "Needless to say, it didn't go well."

Steve shook his head.

"Wouldn't that signal, to you, that he wasn't all there, mentally?" I asked. "That maybe he wasn't competent to stand trial? A guy with no relevant expertise, who believes going off his SSRI made him kill his father, refusing a court-provided expert witness in the subject, and instead saying he could do it?"

"Maybe," Steve said. "But making horrible legal decisions doesn't necessarily make you insane. And being insane doesn't necessarily make you incompetent. You can be legally insane and competent to stand trial. That's what a *not guilty by reason of insanity* plea is for."

"What about being a psychopath?"

Steve nodded. "That still wouldn't make him incompetent," he said. "But it would make a big difference for understanding the *how* and *why* in the trial."

From his backpack, Steve took out a sheet of paper with a list of bullet points. It was a psychopathy checklist, a set of twenty behav-ioral characteristics common to people suffering from psycho-pathic mental disorders. Steve told me the list had been developed by Robert Hare, a Canadian psychologist known for his work with criminals and prison inmates. For each trait or behavior, a patient scored a 0, 1, or 2, for a maximum possible score of 40. Anything over 30 was clinically psychopathic.

"It's not an exact science," Steve said. "But it's a useful metric. Ted Bundy was a thirty-nine. Someone in the twenties or higher probably merits further evaluation."

"The defense painted him as a sociopath at the trial," I said. "But I don't know if I buy it. He expressed some remorse, some self-awareness, he apologized to the jury."

Dr. Buie took a bite of one of the Krispy Kreme doughnuts I'd bought that morning for the drive, then wiped his mouth with the back of his hand.

"Well, sociopaths can show remarkable self-awareness," he said.

"What about psychopaths?"

He shook his head.

"Could he have become a psychopath later in life? After a car wreck?"

Steve shook his head and finished his doughnut. "You don't acquire psychopathy late in life. You're either born with it or acquire it at a very young age. But sociopathy can be learned, or it can result from changes in the brain."

For the next forty-five minutes, Steve took me through the checklist, asking questions about Vince's behavior and background. It reminded me of the ACE (Adverse Childhood Experiences) score questionnaire we used for patients in clinic. ACE scores are a way of quantifying childhood trauma, to better predict adverse health outcomes in adulthood. Patients who, like Vince, experience significant childhood trauma—an alcoholic parent, periods of homelessness, sexual abuse—are more at risk for certain physical and mental health problems later in life. An accurate ACE score helps us to understand the spectrum of why people respond so differently to the same adverse stimulus.

Everyone has their own buffering capacity, or resiliency zone, as Deirdre would remind me. Through her work in the public school system, she had learned that ACE scores could help predict whether a kindergartner might throw a book across the room, call their teacher stupid, or sit quietly and raise their hand. As a new physician, I was beginning to understand that everyone had their own tipping point, beyond which they became mentally or emotionally vulnerable.

We knew what Vince's tipping point was, but I wondered what his ACE score would be. As Steve made notes on his printout of the Hare checklist, he asked me about each trait in turn.

Was Vince *glib* and superficially *charming*? (No—people liked him because he seemed down-to-earth and earnest.)

Was he *grandiose*, with *an inflated sense of self*? (Not before the killing—but during the trial, he had often come across as boastful and superior, calling himself a "savant" in medical school even though his grades suggested otherwise.)

Was he *prone to boredom, in need of constant stimulation*? (Yes, but he also had ADHD.)

It was perplexing. Vince was a strong match for some of the characteristics, and a complete miss for others.

He lacked *self-discipline*, but not *empathy*.

He didn't live a *parasitic lifestyle*, mooching off friends or relatives, but he did have poor *impulse control*.

He wasn't *irresponsible*—the morning after killing his father, he'd gone in to work—but after his separation from Kathy, he *had* become sexually promiscuous, hitting the bars and, according to one person I interviewed, developing something of a porn addiction.

He was *impulsive*, but he didn't *lack long-term goals*. As he'd repeated, over and over during his trial, he'd had one goal in life: to run his own practice and serve a rural community. And he'd done it.

Vince didn't have a *shallow affect*. He had not been a *juvenile delinquent*, nor had he been a part of multiple short-term marital relationships. Killing his father was the first criminal act he'd ever committed.

"Next is *pathological lying*," Steve said. "In the moderate form, they will be shrewd, crafty, cunning, sly, clever. In the extreme form, they will be deceptive, deceitful, underhanded, unscrupulous, manipulative, dishonest."

"I don't think anybody, any of his friends, would describe him that way," I said. "But we're really stuck on what happened after he killed Dalton—he came back in total normalcy and practiced medicine for a whole week without anybody having any idea that something was going on. To be able to pull that off requires incredible—"

"Deceitfulness!" Steve beat me to the punch.

Vince had been widely regarded as an honest man in Fletcher. But at his trial, he was accused of lying about pretty much everything that had happened since June 28, 2004. And what was malingering, which he'd been accused of for years, other than a manipulative, pathological lie?

"I just don't see any reason to keep up the pretense of all of his symptoms," I told Steve, watching the prison rise in front of us, wreathed in morning mist. "It's been nine years. You don't have SSRI discontinuation syndrome for that long. Concussive symptoms from a single incident resolve in a few months, most of the time. You'd think that if he was faking all of that, he would have stopped by now. It would be exhausting to keep up the charade of the convulsions, the shuffling, the twitching for so many years. He doesn't just do it when we're there. According to the COs, he does it all the time. In public areas, in his cell—everywhere."

Steve looked thoughtful as we pulled into the prison. "Sometimes, people get attached to their delusions," he said. "A lie becomes indistinguishable from the truth."

"Or he just isn't faking," I said. "What do you think his Hare score is?"

"I'd have to examine him," Steve said. "But based on what you've said, he seems in the twenties. Not necessarily psychopath level, but close."

I didn't want to jump to any conclusions. But I couldn't help but think that if Vince wasn't a psychopath, or didn't have a traumatic brain injury, there might be something very deeply wrong with him that we hadn't even considered yet.

He was either a complete psychopath, or he was even sicker than we thought.

My second visit with Vince was, in many ways, much like the first: the same bleak visiting room, the same divided table. The visitors on either side of me were different, and the inmates were, too. But Vince seemed largely unchanged. He still shuffled out to meet us, slow as a man his father's age. His eyes still rolled around his orbits, as though searching for something in the ceiling. His hands still writhed in front of us, his speech still halting.

"Wow," I heard Steve mutter under his breath as Vince approached.

Vince remembered me and greeted me warmly. He seemed more at ease this visit, more sure of himself. I felt slightly more relaxed myself. Vince and I had a history now, as short as it was, and I was somewhat sensitized to the bleakness of Wallens Ridge. It was also slightly bolstering to be showing another doctor the ropes, instead of nervously following Sarah's lead.

"This is Dr. Steve Buie," I told Vince. "He's a psychiatrist in Asheville. He knows a lot about SSRIs. He also recognizes that stopping them can adversely affect your brain. I brought him here to talk to you so you could explain what you think happened, doctor to doctor."

"Nice ... to meet you," Vince managed.

I again gave Vince greetings from his patients at Cane Creek—Donna Burton, specifically. After my first visit, she'd called me to ask how things had gone, and to again express her best wishes to Vince. I was moved that a little old lady in her late eighties with plenty of health problems of her own was taking so much time to ask about her old doctor in prison—and I could tell Vince was, too. With all her years of wisdom, she still couldn't explain what had happened to her doctor, someone she trusted with her life. He nodded his head, smiling, clearly happy to be reminded of the clinic he had loved so much, and the patients who needed him.

But he looked tired and scarily thin—atrophic, even. Remembering the effect food had made on his cognitive bearing during our last visit, I asked what he'd like from the vending machines. And while Steve started to ask Vince questions, I walked over and took out my plastic bag full of quarters. The machine was out of Snoballs, but I compensated with several pepperoni pizza pockets, a pack of peanut butter crackers, and two twenty-ounce Mountain Dews.

Vince stopped everything he was doing when I arrived with his snacks. He ripped open the pizza pockets, finishing each in two bites, then washed it all down with half a bottle of soda. The effects were almost instantaneous. His twitching slowed, his eyes became more focused. And the narrative he'd been giving Steve about SSRIs and his serotonin brain acquired a new fluency, as though he'd just had a shot of espresso.

"Can you talk about that night, Dr. Gilmer?" I asked Vince. I had made the conscious decision to call him by his professional title on our visits, as a way to give back some of the dignity that he wasn't usually afforded in prison. It seemed to lift his spirits. For his part, he never called me Benjamin. I was "Dr. Gilmer," too, a fact which seemed to delight him.

"What's the word . . . what's the word . . . don't . . . remember . . . everything," Vince said apologetically, again giving a hazy description of picking Dalton up, hearing voices, and "losing it" when Dalton assaulted him in the Arby's parking lot.

"What was your relationship with your father like, as a child?" Dr. Buie asked.

I could practically hear Vince's mind whirring, shifting into gear. By now I'd come to realize that his brain seemed to have three or four buttons—push them, and Vince could get on a roll, tell a coherent narrative. I'd also come to realize that he enjoyed having an audience. He had prepared for our visit, thought of things he wanted to tell us, and now that we'd asked him the right questions, he felt a kind of pressure to perform. I was acutely aware that this man had had very few visitors over the past eight years, and that none of those visitors were in any position to actually help him.

"Dad molested me," Vince began. "Growing up was hell."

Then he calmly, clearly summarized the abuse he'd described at the trial. He didn't go into the same level of horrifying detail, but the basic story hadn't changed at all. His voice broke as he told us about the abuse he'd suffered at the hands of his father. This was the first time I'd heard him talk about it, and any doubts I'd had about the veracity of his claims during the trial evaporated. I knew he wasn't making it up. It was too raw, too painful, and yet also too consistent.

Out of the corner of my eye, I watched for any reaction from Steve. But psychiatrists are trained to keep a poker face, and Steve was unflappable. I couldn't tell if he was buying it.

"Did you ever have any trouble with pets?" he asked. "Did you ever light fires or get into fights?"

These were classic hallmarks of childhood psychopathy, and Vince knew it.

"I'm not . . . crazy, Doc," Vince said slowly. "At least . . . not like that."

When Vince had finished the second Mountain Dew I went back to the vending machines for another, along with a Snickers bar. As I made my way back to the table, I asked one of the corrections officers supervising the room, a tall, thick man with a receding hairline, if he had any observations about Dr. Gilmer.

"You mean besides faking those weird symptoms and walking funny?" he said, in a deep southern accent. "He's always complaining about stuff, but usually he treats us politely. Has a short fuse, though, that can be unpredictable."

"So you don't think something's seriously wrong with him?" I asked.

"No," the CO said. "Guys here, they'll do anything they can to get you to treat 'em different."

Back at the table, as Vince ripped into the candy bar, I asked how he'd been getting along with the guards.

He paused, rolled his eyes upward, grunted, and said one word: "Torture."

Vince told us that they weren't giving him his meds, that he'd been thrown in the hole too many times to count, and that he wasn't getting enough food.

"Not enough calories. My brain . . . not enough calories."

Eventually, between bites, Vince explained that over the past few years, he'd come to the conclusion that he needed at least 2,500 calories per day to achieve normal brain function. The prison allegedly ran on a 1,500-calorie diet—a sufficient amount for most people—but Vince was convinced that the prisoners only got 1,200. To agitate for more calories, Vince had undertaken several hunger strikes before Sarah and I had visited him. He'd ended the last one after being sent to solitary confinement.

"That's why you look so thin," I said.

"And you think the voices and the confusion were related to SSRI discontinuation?" Steve asked.

Vince nodded. "That is the holy truth," he said. "Before . . . before the . . . event, I couldn't stop . . . eating. Why I went to Arby's. The voices went away if I took my Lexapro but also if I ate enough."

"And they came back when you were hungry again?"

Vince nodded.

"They always . . . came back," he said.

He'd finished the Snickers bar by then, and our time was up. The CO I'd spoken to was at our table, telling Vince to stand up.

"Time's up," he grunted.

"I'll call you soon, Dr. Gilmer," I said.

Vince nodded, his eyes heavy, as he turned to go. Steve was about to turn around, too, but I grabbed his arm, made sure he saw the way Vince walked away. It was more than reluctance that made him drag his feet. There was something seriously wrong with his gait. It was cautious and shuffling, like the movement of someone with Parkinson's.

"You see that?" I whispered.

Steve nodded.

We waited until Vince was gone, then made our way back to the exit. We were silent, and I refrained from asking Steve what his impressions were. I wanted to give him time to collect his thoughts, without prejudicing him toward my own views. We had a two-hour car ride ahead of us, and I thought we'd probably spend most of it discussing our clinical impressions.

I did ask him one question, though.

"Do you think he's a malingerer?"

"No way in hell," Steve replied, without any hesitation.

To exit the visitors' room, you have to step into a kind of air lock, a space between two locked doors. One door slams shut behind you, then, after an uncomfortable pause, the door in front of you opens. During that moment you are in a dead, silenced zone, locked between worlds: inside and outside, imprisoned and free.

Steve turned to me as soon as the lock clicked behind us. The air was stagnant.

"Do you think he has Huntington's?" he asked.

A shiver of recognition ran through me. In a flash I saw it: the writhing hands, the uncontrollable facial twitches, the anxiety, the gait disturbances, the tiny paragraph of text in a long-forgotten medical school textbook on inherited neurologic disorders.

Of course, I thought.

Then, before I could answer, the door in front of us slid open, and a wave of ice-cold air hit me like a slap in the face.

10.

SICK

Steve and I marched back to the car, trying to conjure up distant memories of Huntington's. I had never seen an actual patient suffering from the disease, but I had studied it as a medical student and could still easily recall its genetic defect, the famed CAG repeat. As soon as we made it to the car, I grabbed my phone and ran through a checklist of symptoms on one of my medical apps.

"Motor symptoms such as chorea and bradykinesia," I called out to Steve.

"Yes."

"Psychiatric symptoms—depression, anxiety, irritability, paranoia, delusions, and psychosis."

"Check, had them all."

"Cognitive impairment—executive function impairment, impulsivity, inability to switch from one task or cognitive goal to another, lack of awareness of self or impairment, memory deficits."

"Check. Check. That was clear from the trial."

"Gait disturbance, weight loss, and seizures."

"Check. Check. Check."

The list went on. Steve and I sat for a moment in shock, still shrouded by the razor wire and watchtowers behind us. A pang of nausea gripped me.

Everyone had gotten it wrong. The judge, the jury, even Sarah and I—we'd all been wrong about Vince.

And now a seriously ill person was behind bars.

I started the car so we could warm up. Silence surrounded us as we slowly headed down the mountain. Nearing Big Stone Gap, I finally spoke again.

"Steve, if this diagnosis is true—"

Steve interrupted me.

"Then he needs immediate medical care."

On the way back to Asheville, I couldn't stop talking. It was the only thing keeping my anxiety for Vince at bay. I told Steve about Dr. Feix's psychiatric evaluation. I told him about Detective Martin's hidden-camera "test" while Vince was in county jail. I even told Steve about a very interesting conversation I'd had with Sarah Lee Guthrie after she performed in our backyard. After the show, she had reminded me that her grandfather, Woody Guthrie, had suffered from Huntington's. The disease had landed him in a psychiatric hospital after he became essentially destitute—and it had eventually killed him.

I couldn't believe that I hadn't made the connection between Woody's and Vince's mysterious symptoms. It was so obvious! But at the time, it just didn't register. Like most people, I'd thought of Woody Guthrie as an iconic American songwriter, not a withered patient in a psych ward. But that's exactly what he was when Bob Dylan made his famous 1961 pilgrimage from Minnesota to New Jersey's Greystone Park Psychiatric Hospital to visit his hero. I'd listened to "Song to Woody," the tune Dylan wrote after that visit, hundreds of times—but I'd never realized the pain that must have been behind it, seeing a hero laid low.

And I'd never realized the extent to which the disease had haunted the Guthrie family. Huntington's is the quintessential example of an autosomal dominant genetic disease. If one parent carries the gene, each offspring has a fifty-fifty chance of inheriting it. Sarah Lee's father, Arlo, didn't receive the genetic mutation that causes the disease from his father, so he never developed Huntington's. That meant Sarah Lee had little to no chance of inheriting it herself.

"The Huntington's lineage stopped with her, fortunately," I said to Steve. "She just inherited the songwriting genius."

"Some people aren't so lucky," Steve said.

Huntington's resembles the worst of Parkinson's and Alzheimer's diseases. A devastating neurological illness, it usually manifests in the third or fourth decade of a patient's life. There is no cure.

The disease is named for George Huntington, a physician in the late nineteenth century. In 1872, he published a paper describing a condition he had observed in several families in East Hampton, New York, where, like his father and grandfather before him, he practiced medicine. Here's how he described it:

> The disease commonly begins by slight twitchings in the muscles of the face, which gradually increase in violence and variety. The eyelids are kept winking, the brows are corrugated, and then elevated, the nose is screwed first to the one side and then to the other, and the mouth is drawn in various directions, giving the patient the most ludicrous appearance imaginable. The upper extremities may be the first affected, or both simultaneously. . . .
> As the disease progresses the mind becomes more or less impaired, in many amounting to insanity, while in others mind and body gradually fail until death relieves them of their suffering.

By comparing notes with his father and grandfather, Dr. Huntington observed that the disease—which he simply called *chorea*—

had presented in the area for decades, and ran in several families within the community. In fact, he was able to trace it back to one man, an immigrant from England named Jeffrey Francis, who had relocated to the area in 1634.

Though Huntington noted that parents tended to pass on the condition to half of their children, he published his paper thirty years before the rediscovery of classical genetics—and eighty years before James Watson and Francis Crick discovered DNA's double helix. It wasn't until 1983 that scientists were able to really study Huntington's, after discovering two remote Venezuelan mountain villages where more than eighteen thousand people, many of them related, showed symptoms. It took until 1993 for molecular biologists to identify the precise gene associated with the disease: 4p16.3.

Huntington's disease stems from a mutation of the HTT gene, which everyone carries. Its DNA sequence (cytosine, adenine, and guanine) repeats itself over and over. In normal HTT genes, this sequence (CAG-CAG-CAG) repeats fewer than 35 times, coding for a protein called huntingtin. In people with Huntington's disease, however, the gene can sometimes repeat the genetic chain up to 250 times. This leads to the accumulation of undigestible cellular debris inside the nerve cell, preventing its normal function—a subtle balance between perfection and pathology.

Huntington's disease is an insidious and genetically ingenious aberration that slowly destroys the brain—but not too early to prevent its host from producing offspring. Most carriers don't know they have the disease until after they pass it on to their children, and each successive generation is more and more likely to inherit it, as the destructive CAG chain grows.

Huntington's affects the basal ganglia, a part of the brain's subcortex that helps govern movement. In a normally functioning brain, the basal ganglia keeps our voluntary movements voluntary—it prevents us, say, from raising our arms or arching our eyebrows *unless* another part of the brain indicates that's what we want to do.

In a brain affected by Huntington's disease, however, the withering basal ganglia can no longer coordinate movements, which then become involuntary and uncontrollable—classically called chorea.

Patients with Huntington's typically notice mild musculoskeletal symptoms first, usually after the age of thirty. They might initially report increasing restlessness or clumsiness, or rapid involuntary eye movements. Eventually, their physical symptoms become overwhelming: constant facial tics, jerky arm movements, and other chorea. Patients with Huntington's often walk with a shuffling gait and exhibit a twisted or deformed posture. As the disease progresses, speech becomes difficult, as does chewing and swallowing.

On its march through the brain, Huntington's decimates cells in the cerebral cortex, the hippocampus, and the thalamus. That means it has a wide range of effects on behavior and mental health. Patients with Huntington's don't only exhibit involuntary movements—they can also have involuntary, impulsive thoughts, delusions, and even seizures. It can lead to an increase in compulsive behavior: gambling, sexual promiscuity, alcoholism, or drug addiction. Depression and anxiety are common, as is a reduced emotional palette and grandiose thinking. The disease lays waste to the prefrontal cortex, diminishing its executive functions—the ability to plan, to understand social boundaries, to monitor behavior and emotions, to think abstractly. Memory, both short- and long-term, weakens over time, until dementia sets in.

Because its symptoms are so vast and can mimic many other diseases, Huntington's is difficult to diagnose. It is also rare enough—affecting only about five people per one hundred thousand in the United States, Europe, and Australia—that it often doesn't even occur to doctors as a possibility. Someone experiencing early symptoms of the disease might just appear to be a drug addict, or depressed, or experiencing a nervous tic.

What's more, Huntington's doesn't always look the same, patient to patient. The penetrance of the disease, the severity of its symptoms, are dependent on the number of CAG repeats. Someone with a lower number of repeats, say thirty-six, will have a totally different expression of the disease compared to someone with seventy-five. This doesn't even take into account the vast complexity of the human brain, which can respond so variably when under attack. A failing brain is not as predictable as a heart after a heart attack or kidneys after acute failure. Symptom onset may vary by a decade, and the severity of the disease can be wildly different from person to person. Some Huntington's patients have no doubt been misdiagnosed as schizophrenics. Even in later stages—and especially in older patients—the disease might just look like dementia or Alzheimer's, coupled with physical frailty and other maladies.

Patients usually die within fifteen to twenty years of the onset of symptoms. And it can take years for the full complement—cognitive disorders, physical impairment, dementia—to assert themselves in a way that would be obvious to a physician.

That means that by the time Huntington's is diagnosed, it has often already been running its course, undetected, for years.

Steve and I explored the possibility of a Huntington's diagnosis all the way home from Wallens Ridge. It explained so much about Vince—but it also could shed some light on Dalton. If Vince had Huntington's, he would have received it from his father—his mother had no symptoms and was well into her seventh decade. Was it possible that Dalton's schizophrenia and dementia had actually been part of a larger constellation of symptoms that had never been diagnosed as Huntington's—and that he had passed that disease on to his son and daughter? If Dalton had Huntington's, then Vince and his sister both had a fifty-fifty chance themselves.

"The thing is," Steve said in the car, "I don't recall that Huntington's usually correlates with violence, although suicide is definitely more prevalent. It's only a killer disease for the people who have it."

"That's true," I said. "But if Vince has it—and a brain injury, and PTSD, and SSRI discontinuation syndrome . . ."

Steve nodded. "It's not a reason for killing someone. It's an explanation of what happened. A piece of the puzzle."

"A big piece," I said.

I thought back to all those moments in the trial when Vince pleaded to be reevaluated by a clinical psychiatrist, a medical doctor. His repeating loop of *My brain's not working right.* The jellyfish stings, the seizures, the profound anxiety—Vince had known all along that something was wrong, he just didn't know what it was and, strangely, couldn't describe his mental experience in medical terms. A Huntington's diagnosis would support his repeated claims, which had fallen on deaf ears throughout the trial and his imprisonment, that he needed medical attention.

It would also mean he wasn't lying or faking his symptoms.

It would mean that a catastrophically sick man was in prison.

And it would mean that his trial was a major miscarriage of justice. Because if Vince had Huntington's, and the jury and judge had known it, he would never have been branded a malingerer. The jury may have had more empathy toward him because he was mentally and physically ill. They might have been more inclined to believe his horrifying abuse allegations. They would have seen him as a victim of a fallible, sick brain, and extended him compassion. Any half-witted lawyer would have landed him in a secure hospital where he could receive continuous medical care.

We would need a genetic test to know for sure. In the meantime, I wanted to explore this diagnosis with someone who knew Huntington's disease well, a neurologist. The first person I thought of was Dr. Reid Taylor, a respected neurologist at Mission Hospital in Asheville. If anyone in town would be familiar with the disease, it would be him.

I looped Sarah in, as well. She was intrigued but still suspicious of any single unifying explanation that would tie the whole mystery together. But I think she could also hear in my voice that I believed Huntington's was a real possibility, and that we might be approaching a major breakthrough.

"This story," she said. "Good god. It keeps getting stranger."

Ira Glass, the host and producer of *This American Life,* had been patiently waiting for us to wrap this up, after about six months of our investigation. Every time we thought we were getting to the end, another clue would propagate our search. At this point, with or without a diagnosis, the story was going to be aired.

Sarah thought my conversation with Dr. Taylor would be interesting to record for *This American Life.* So, I arranged for the two of us along with Dr. Buie to meet at the Asheville NPR studio, with Sarah patching in from a separate line in Pennsylvania. I wanted to challenge Dr. Taylor to arrive at the diagnosis on his own, and then have a roundtable discussion.

This was my journalistic baptism, since Sarah was not there to facilitate things in person. I could hear her voice in my head: *Don't ask leading questions; help them to describe specific scenes.*

I had grown to enjoy the journalistic adventure and being Sarah's sidekick. I realized that interviewing someone for the radio was not much different from talking to a patient. The goal was the same: enable someone to tell their own story. Over years of practicing medicine I had learned that patients normally held the key to unlocking their diagnosis—you just had to listen.

A few days after my trip to Wallens Ridge, we convened downtown at the WCQS studio. The three of us sat in a soundproof studio, around a desk designed for four to five guests. The walls were padded except for a large window that allowed people to peer in past the microphones that hovered in front of our faces. With my headphones over my ears and my notebook open, I tried to channel Terry Gross.

"Fifty-year-old male," I began, "currently imprisoned for the murder of his father..."

I thoroughly described Vince's symptoms, his physical exam, and his clinical history, just like I teach my medical students to present to me. Since I didn't have any video or sound recordings from the prison, I had to act out the dyskinesias, demonstrate the gait instability, and imitate his speech.

After all the hours at Wallens Ridge, it felt ridiculous to be sitting in a public radio station, pretending to be Vince. But I kept the editorializing to myself. I simply described him as best I could, then sat back and waited for Dr. Taylor to proffer a diagnosis.

It didn't come immediately.

"He could be a schizophrenic," Dr. Taylor said. "That would explain the auditory hallucinations, perhaps the grandiosity and lack of remorse."

"He expresses remorse now," I said. "The prosecutors just didn't buy it at the trial."

"There's still the issue of the chorea," Dr. Taylor said. "A sociopath would keep that up only as long as it could possibly benefit them, though. And you say he's been like this ever since the trial?"

I nodded. "Before it, too."

"Hmmm," Dr. Taylor said. "Has he been tested for Parkinson's?"

For the next twenty minutes or so, we went through a range of possible diagnoses: Parkinson's, early onset Alzheimer's, Creutzfeldt-Jakob disease, spinocerebellar degeneration, Friedreich's ataxia. Bipolar disorder with psychosis, carbon monoxide poisoning, traumatic brain injury, PTSD, sociopathy. Dr. Taylor asked detailed questions about Dr. Gilmer's medical history, the medications he took, and his family. Steve chimed in to corroborate my presentation and bolster my descriptions of Vince's psychiatric symptoms.

Then there was a silence so long I knew Sarah would have to cut it in half if we ever used the tape. I was about to break in when Dr. Taylor spoke up.

After about twenty-five minutes of clinical musing, he said, "This would be a long shot, but have you considered it might be Huntington's disease?"

The next day I pulled Laura Cone, our astute medical student, aside at Cane Creek.

"Pop quiz," I said, then did the same thing with her as I had with Dr. Taylor. I acted out his physical symptoms, gave a brief medical history, outlined Vince's story. I very pointedly did not mention Dr. Gilmer's name.

Laura was a third-year medical student. She wasn't yet qualified to see patients on her own. She had just finished her classwork and had two years of clinical rotations before embarking on residency. I assumed she had probably never seen a case of Huntington's, but I knew that every medical student is taught that it is one of the primordial inherited diseases. Most can regurgitate the CAG repeat pathology, but few know that Huntington's first presents as a psychiatric disease. I didn't know how long it would take for her to drill down to a diagnosis, but she asked the perfect questions.

"Age of symptom presentation?"

"Vague symptoms around thirty, more fulminant symptoms around forty."

"Family history?"

"Father had similar symptoms."

"Uncontrollable movements, dyskinesias?"

"Yes, mostly in his face and arms with some gait instability."

It took her less than five minutes.

The more I learned about Huntington's disease, the more it explained Vince's story. There were so many odd aspects to Vince's behavior, both before and after the killing. And now that I had a neurologic explanation for them, everything started to make more sense.

There was, for instance, the story of Brenda McCormick, a patient of mine—and a former patient of Vince's. The week of the killing, she told me, she'd needed a refill on a prescription. The clinic was closed, but when she called Vince at home, he told her to just head on over to his house—he'd come out to her car and write a prescription for her.

In a small town like Fletcher, at a clinic like Vince's, this wasn't unusual. But Vince's behavior when Brenda arrived at his house struck her as bizarre. He had the prescription ready, but after he gave it to her, he invited her inside. He wanted to show her something, he said.

That something was a gleaming, three-foot-long, machete-like knife. In his living room, Vince brandished the blade and talked about his knife to his confused patient.

Why is he showing me this? she remembered thinking.

Something felt wrong. She made her excuses quickly, thanked Vince for the prescription, and left.

What had led Vince to such a bizarre, impulsive interaction? Huntington's, I knew, impaired the brain's executive functions—its ability to regulate behavior in accordance with social norms. Perhaps that night with Brenda was a kind of blip. It made no sense—if you had just days earlier killed your father, and were trying to avoid becoming a suspect, why would you threateningly display a medieval weapon to someone in your home?

Most of the stories about that week were about how normal Vince seemed. Maybe, I thought, that week was when the damage to his prefrontal cortex crossed a certain neurologic threshold. Maybe Vince's behavior in that period—the violence against his father, the bizarre interaction with Brenda, the otherwise normal behavior at the clinic—could be explained by a brain whose prefrontal cortex was under attack, and just starting to flagrantly reveal how destabilized it was.

I had so many questions:

Would Huntington's have allowed him to believe his own lies about Dalton going missing, so that he could continue life more or less as he had before the killing?

Could it shed some light on Vince's bizarre flight from his house, his retreat under the neighbors' porch, his inability to sleep, his ill-fated camping trip near the Asheville mall?

Could this evolving disease allow us to see the events of that week in 2004 in a new way, a way that made sense?

Vince was fifty years old now. His symptoms were pronounced and hard to ignore. Perhaps nine years earlier, they had been less noticeable. The only physical symptoms he'd shown in the weeks before the killing were promiscuity, ravenous hunger, and—according to one of his square-dancing friends—a newfound clumsiness, a tendency to step on his partners' feet. The change in behavior could have easily been mistaken for other things: anxiety, depression, minor alcoholism. A midlife crisis.

Fortunately, Huntington's was a disease that could be confirmed by a genetic test. But when Sarah called Wallens Ridge the week after Steve and I visited to plan a follow-up call and discuss this clinical suspicion with Vince, she got some shocking news.

Vince was no longer incarcerated there.

He had threatened suicide.

Dr. Colin Angliker was a voluble Irishman in his seventies with the bedside manner of a southern doctor and the tongue of a Gaelic sailor. When he called me at the clinic, the day after I'd gotten the news about Vince's plan to harm himself, I had no idea where he was from.

"Belfast," he said, then laughed. "By way of McGill in Canada, then Virginia."

Angliker was the chief forensic psychiatrist at Marion Correctional Treatment Center, the prison in western Virginia where Vince had been transferred. Despite its massive size and an inmate population in excess of one thousand, Wallens Ridge had no permanent psychiatrist on staff—which meant that suicidal patients often were transferred to Marion, which was better equipped to handle them.

"Are you kidding me?" I asked. "A prison that large, and there's no one like you there?"

"Sadly, no."

"What happened?" I asked.

"Apparently, he was planning to cut himself," Angliker said. "They found a knife hidden in his bed and a threatening note intimating that he was going to sever an artery. Because he certainly knew how to do it, it was a credible enough threat to take action."

"I feel awful," I said. "Steve and I were the last people to see him. Is he safe?"

"Oh, sure," he said. "They found the knife before he had a chance to use it. He was totally unharmed."

"That's such a relief," I said. "I'm so glad he's okay."

"Well, he's not really okay," Angliker said. "He's a wreck. That's why I'm calling, actually."

When Sarah called Wallens Ridge, she had serendipitously landed on the social worker facilitating Vince's transfer. Sarah had mentioned to her that I suspected Vince might be suffering from Huntington's, and the social worker had included that information—and my phone number—on the transfer documents. That was why Dr. Angliker was reaching out, he said. He was interested in Vince's case. He was skeptical about his malingering diagnosis.

"As soon as I heard we were getting a malingerer, I knew it was bullshit," he said. "I've been working in prisons for forty years and I haven't met one yet who could pull this off."

"You don't think he's faking?"

"Hell, no," Dr. Angliker said. "I don't know what's wrong with him, but whatever it is, he's not making it up."

I told Dr. Angliker about my visits with Vince and the symptoms I had observed. All of it, Angliker said, was flagrantly apparent at Marion. I told him about the clinical hypotheses—traumatic brain injury, SSRI discontinuation, sociopathy, temporary psychosis—that Sarah and I had entertained, as well as our hunch about Huntington's. Dr. Angliker listened to every word I said, as any good physician would while taking a history.

I even told him about the dispiriting trip I'd taken the previous afternoon to the bowels of Mission Hospital, where the radiology reading room was located. The week after Steve and I returned, I had wanted to see if a CT or MRI had been taken after Vince's truck accident. I was looking for evidence of a traumatic brain injury, but also for any indication that Huntington's had started to affect Vince's brain in ways that would be visible radiologically.

The radiology reading room was cavelike and quiet, with a couple of radiologists reading acute scans. That morning, one of the founders of the practice had been there. I recognized him by his cowboy boots and laid-back southern swagger.

"Do you mind pulling up a scan for me? Name—Vince Gilmer. Date of scan—July tenth, 2003."

A CT of the head had, indeed, been performed on that date. When the radiologist brought it up, I calmly asked him if he could take a look at the midbrain, mentioning that I was concerned about a TBI and possibly Huntington's.

He paused before scrolling through the slices of Vince's brain, not engaging my line of sight. After a cursory glance at the black-and-white pixels of Vince Gilmer's brain, he turned away from the screen and looked me squarely in the eyes.

"Vince Gilmer is a murderer. I don't see anything wrong with his brain."

"Can you look more closely at the basal ganglia?" I asked, somewhat bewildered. "Do you see anything concerning in the globus pallidus? The caudate nucleus and putamen?"

I was listing specific brain sites to establish my bona fides. But the radiologist wasn't taking the scan—or me—very seriously.

"Nope, don't see anything there," he said, with the most cursory glance at the images. "He doesn't have Huntington's. He's a murderer."

"How do you know?"

"I've been a volunteer deputy sheriff for many years, and I was on duty the week of the manhunt," he said. "I've seen a lot of killers. And Vince Gilmer? Son, that's a cold-blooded murderer."

Only in Appalachia, I'd thought as I left the office, *can a radiologist also be a deputy sheriff on the weekends.* I was angry, frustrated that he couldn't see past his preconceptions. At the same time, he was there. He saw Vince Gilmer around the time of the arrest. My own doubts that Vince Gilmer was a grand manipulator started to creep back in, so eventually I asked a different radiologist to take a look at the scans.

Now I relayed those results to Dr. Angliker. "He said the basal ganglia looked questionably abnormal," I told him. "But we can't really know anything for sure unless we get him a genetic test and an MRI. A CT scan is not ideal for looking at the key structures."

There was a pause on the end of the line. I was expecting a polite demurral—for Dr. Angliker to apologize and say that there was no way. That there were insurmountable legal hurdles, or administrative obstacles, that all he could do was provide Vince with basic psychiatric care and—at long last—a prescription for Lexapro.

But Dr. Angliker surprised me.

"It's gonna be a struggle," he said. "But I'll see what I can do."

11

MY AMERICAN LIFE

Getting Vince tested for Huntington's wouldn't be easy. A genetic test would require more than a simple blood draw—it would mean an expensive DNA test and countless hoops to jump through. For a hospital, this is easy: There are procedures and mechanisms to obtain any diagnostic. But for a prison, it would be a logistical nightmare.

It was also a big ask. To gain approval for Vince's genetic test, Dr. Angliker would have to appeal directly not only to the warden of the Marion Correctional Treatment Center—but to the head of the entire Virginia Department of Corrections in Richmond.

It would require, as Dr. Angliker expressed it, "putting my ass on the line."

I gathered that the prison system wouldn't be too excited about opening up this can of worms. Expense and hassle aside, the justice system had very little to gain were Vince to be diagnosed with Huntington's. A diagnosis of that magnitude would cast doubt on his whole trial—not to mention his continued incarceration, with only minimal access to the medical care normally afforded to a patient with his condition.

Still, I was happy to know that at least now, Vince Gilmer was in a facility where he could be treated by a staff psychiatrist, one who seemed to be curious and interested. He had his first shepherd in Dr. Angliker, someone who actually listened to him without bias, who was invested in understanding Vince's psychiatric behavior. Colin Angliker had been doing forensics in the prison system for five decades. He was no fledgling physician like me, and had never forgotten his oath "to do no harm." In the early sixties, he had moved from Belfast, Northern Ireland, to Montreal to pursue a residency in psychiatry and specialize in forensics under the mentorship of Dr. Bruno Cormier, considered the father of Canadian forensics. Inspired by Dr. Cormier, and deeply intrigued by the question of why people kill, Dr. Angliker became a devoted student of homicide. His philosophy was to instill humanity in the prison system: to treat the inmates, not punish them. The system itself was already doing that.

Within a few days of Vince's arrival at Marion, Dr. Angliker had him on 40 mg of citalopram, the SSRI that he had been requesting since the day of the arrest. I was shocked how quickly the SSRI took effect. Within days, Vince's symptoms of anxiety, and even the tremors to some degree, began to improve. He was getting enough to eat, and his impulsive outbursts against guards and other inmates quieted. The hunger strikes and periods in isolation seemed to be over—at least for the time being.

While Dr. Angliker petitioned for a Huntington's test, Sarah and I continued work on finalizing the *This American Life* piece. The pressure was on. What was supposed to be a fifteen-minute segment had evolved into something much stranger and deeper, and now consumed the entire hour-long episode. Sarah and I joked that we could fill multiple episodes—a serial.

"We are so close to having an ending. I can feel it," I told her sometime in early March of 2013. "We're so close to finally understanding what happened that night."

"What, just because he might have Huntington's?" Sarah replied.

"Sure," I said. "If he has it, that changes everything. It means he should get a new trial. It means he should be in a hospital. It means—"

But Sarah cut me off.

"We don't know yet," she said. "Let's see what the test says."

I could tell Sarah was a little stressed. We had devoted over six months to this story, and she was anxious that we would never find an answer. It was hard for her to buy my gut instinct that something was really wrong with him, that his mind was potentially a victim of something much deeper. My theories explained his behavior changes, but they were still ambiguous. Sarah was a journalist. She needed proof—a solid, unifying theory filled with cold, hard facts to bring it all together. At the same time, we were torn about what such a diagnosis would bring.

"You're right," I said. "I hope he doesn't have it. I don't know what's worse—life in prison, or dying prematurely and painfully from this disease."

We'd told Vince about our hunch, and although as a physician he knew about Huntington's, it wasn't clear to me how much he actually understood. He was still wedded to the idea of his "serotonin brain"—or he simply could not face the magnitude of a possible terminal diagnosis. Either way, Sarah and I figured it wasn't a good idea to talk about it too much with him until we had test results. After his planned suicide attempt, we didn't want to run the risk of him harming himself.

Vince's stubborn attachment to his "serotonin brain" theory made me think about the role preconceptions play in diagnoses. In medical school, doctors are taught to take an evidence-based approach to diagnosis—to observe and trust in their physical exam, while also listening to the patient's own insight about their body. But to make sense of this data, doctors must cultivate a kind of clinical intuition. Over years of clinical practice and thousands of patients, they learn to recognize patterns. Their brains begin to build models for different illnesses and treatments—preconceptions that allow them to efficiently process billions of memories in real time.

Preconceptions are the brain's necessary shortcuts. We could not think at high speeds without them. They are designed to help us by making our cognitive choices much easier. They help everyone—not just doctors—be more efficient. We perceive the world according to the unique way that each of us has trained our brain.

And they can be useful in medicine. But sometimes they just become biases that blind us to the truth. You can be sure that a thirty-five-year-old man complaining about a swollen lymph node is just getting over a virus, when in fact he has Hodgkin's lymphoma. You can be blinded by the shining smile and sunny disposition of a straight-A high school student, and miss the chronic depression under the façade.

Vince knew he was suffering from SSRI withdrawal, but he didn't understand that it could be something much worse.

I'd already seen the role preconceptions had played at Vince's trial. From the very beginning, everyone's minds were made up. The judge, the prosecution, and eventually the jury had entered the courtroom with a set of preconceptions about Vince, aided and abetted by the law enforcement officers, court-appointed psychologists, and news media reports about the case.

Even my own approach to Vince's case was based on a set of preconceptions. For most of the previous year, I'd operated under the strong hunch that Vince's behavior was mostly due to a traumatic brain injury from his truck accident, combined with SSRI discontinuation and—once I found out about it—PTSD from childhood abuse. But how much of my interpretation of Vince's health was based on my own preconceptions about the brain? Did these things actually explain Vince Gilmer's behavior? Or did I just think they did, because I'd written my master's thesis on how to save dying neurons after brain trauma?

To a hammer, everything looks like a nail. Maybe to a doctor with an MS in neurotoxicology, everything looks like a brain injury.

But if Vince turned out to have Huntington's disease, his brain's health was not a question for subjective analysis. It would be a cold scientific fact, and it would upend everything we knew about his case. It would mean that all of those preconceptions were flawed. It would mean that the gut reaction of nearly everyone who encountered Vince Gilmer after he killed Dalton—everyone who was not already his friend or his family—was wrong.

My medical training had taught me to recognize the essential fallibility of the human brain. It's a remarkable organ, one whose complexity surprises researchers every day. But it's still matter, an organ, made up of cells. And every organ can fail.

And that made me think: If Vince's brain was fallible, wasn't everybody's?

What was keeping any one of us away from our own personal June 28?

Was I really that different from him?

One brain's fallibility was particularly on my mind that spring: my own.

For most of my life, I'd had trouble paying attention. Or, to put it more accurately: It wasn't hard for me to pay attention, but it was supremely difficult to focus that attention on only one thing at a time. Left to my own devices, I'd multitask. As a college student, I'd write research papers while watching Atlanta Braves baseball and simultaneously brainstorming weekend plans with my roommate. In medical school, I had to lock myself in a dark room in the library, with only one textbook at a time, to ensure I didn't work on all of my assignments at once. And at home as a young father, I'd often leave the yard half-mowed, and Deirdre would find Kai and me lying on the trampoline trying to identify animals in the clouds.

Family medicine was perfect for me. It required me to be infinitely curious. Each day was a succession of new things to concentrate on: fifteen to twenty patient visits, each of them twenty minutes long, each of them presenting a new set of symptoms, a new face to greet, a new person to help. For distinct bursts, I could hyperfocus on one person, finding multiple solutions for an expanding number of problems. Family medicine rewarded the curiosities of a generalist: It left no organ system behind. As a family medicine doctor, I reveled in tackling someone's acute depression, heart failure, and knee pain in one visit.

But that spring of 2013, as I juggled working on the *This American Life* story with Sarah, teaching family medicine residents at MAHEC, leading medical student didactics at UNC, keeping Cane Creek afloat, and maintaining family life, I found the surplus of tasks more exhausting than invigorating. It became impossible to train my full attention on each segment of my life in turn—and when I did, I could no longer marshal all of my cognitive strength.

I was falling behind in clinic, battling to answer fifty emails a day, and struggling to make it to coach Kai's soccer practices. One day, I forgot to pick Luya up from daycare. As any parent knows, there is no worse feeling than answering a phone call from a daycare worker asking if you're still planning to pick up your child.

My split attention affected my marriage, as well. By the time we fed the kids and read them a bedtime story, the day was over for Deirdre and me. We were already low on quality time together, and during the little time we had, I was unable to make her my singular focus. I knew that she felt neglected, that she needed me to be more present for her. But I didn't know how to close the gap between us, or why it took me so long to see it. There was something inside me, I thought, something wrong. But I didn't know what it was.

It all came to a head one day when a man about my age visited the clinic. During his thirties, he had excelled in every way—his boss, his kids, *and* his wife had adored him. By age forty, though, I had spent years climbing the professional ladder, inheriting more and more responsibility at work, and things had turned bad at home. His marriage was failing, he felt isolated from his kids, and he limped through each day with an aura of defeat. Rarely did he receive positive feedback from anyone at work or from his family. He was just surviving and putting out fires. He told me that his brain was constantly overwhelmed, that he was physically exhausted by life.

I felt like I was seeing myself in the mirror.

I rocked forward, looked him in the eye, and said, "I hear you."

Of course, he was depressed. Rather than spewing a long list of clinical solutions at him, a hug felt much more appropriate. I told him he was not alone, that many of us feel this way.

I certainly did. In fact, his symptoms sounded akin to my own: forgetfulness, difficulty completing tasks, inability to focus—or, conversely, a tendency to *hyperfocus* until everyone else in the room just disappeared. When I printed off an adult ADHD diagnostic test for him, I printed one out for myself, as well.

That night, after the kids went to the bed, Deirdre read the questions aloud to me at the kitchen table.

How often do you have difficulty concentrating on what people say to you, even when they are speaking to you directly?

How often do you have difficulty unwinding and relaxing when you have time to yourself?

How often do you put things off to the last minute?

Do you depend on others to keep your life in order and attend to details?

I answered honestly:

Sometimes.

Often.

Always.

Often.

By the halfway point of the test, Deirdre was laughing out loud. It was already pretty obvious to both of us. I was undoubtedly on the ADHD spectrum. It was one of those punctuated moments where you start to make sense of your life: The middle school tests that took longer than they should, the impulsive behavior, the seemingly impossible task of not fidgeting. The feeling of a crowded brain, barraged by stimuli competing for attention.

Attention deficit hyperactivity disorder isn't just a psychological label. Nor is it merely a behavioral problem, dependent on social situations and relationships. Behavioral psychologists think of it as pathology, or a syndrome to be fixed. I think of it more as an inherited state of mind. Sometimes it is a superpower that renders you capable of noticing things that others can't see: a single apple that survived the fate of a dying tree, a spider spinning a web on the outside of a twentieth-story window. It enables one to see the world unfiltered, with wonder, curiosity, and delight. In the clinic, it allowed me to solve problems through a macroscopic lens, by thinking outside of the box.

But it can also be overwhelming. Without a cognitive filter to limit the constant influx of stimuli competing for the brain's attention, ADHD can paralyze your thinking. I have seen countless examples of patients who arrive at their third or fourth decade completely exhausted from their mental marathons. They struggle at work, with self-esteem, and in their relationships. Some battle depression, anxiety, and addiction, unable to calm the perpetual chaos in their head.

Now that I'd diagnosed myself—and had my suspicions confirmed by my own physician—I saw ADHD everywhere: in my patients, in my family, in Kai's friends at soccer practice. It might explain my mother's playfully impulsive behavior and constant activity, my cousin's anxiety.

It certainly explained me. And it gave me surprising new insight into Vince's—and really everyone's—neurological plight.

ADHD is not Huntington's. It isn't fatal, it's treatable, and it's relatively common, affecting 4 to 5 percent of the population. But even a disorder as relatively minor as ADHD makes one thing very clear: The world is full of unique brains, each of them with their own individual thresholds for attention, for stress, and for pain. And each of us has a cognitive threshold where we cross the lines of resiliency into pathology. A manic episode from lack of sleep; delirium from being in the hospital; or extreme agitation from the stress of two jobs, four children, and bottomless financial burdens—any of these things can take us to the edge of what our brain can handle. Add childhood trauma or inherited mental illness, and that threshold decreases even further.

None of us know how close we are to that edge, or when we might cross over it.

Until it's almost too late.

For me, it was my first year out of residency, soon after starting at Cane Creek. Luya was a baby, crying incessantly, and, after two nights on call, I hadn't slept for about forty-eight hours. Each of Luya's cries was like a stabbing migraine, each scream an ice pick in my forehead, and after an hour of trying to calm her, I had the sudden urge, involuntary and awful, to grab her by the shoulders and shake her until she was quiet.

No parent ever thinks they'll find themselves about to harm their child. As a doctor, I'd advised hundreds of new mothers and fathers about how to safely hold their newborns, and had rolled my eyes at the corny "shaken baby" video the hospital required all new parents to watch before taking their infant home. I never thought I'd be like the man in that video, angrily shaking a realistic-looking doll. And yet there I was, at three o'clock in the morning, in my daughter's nursery, gripping Luya tightly at arm's length, sobbing. I had arrived at my precipice, and when I stared over the edge, what

I saw was horrible: myself, shaking Luya to sleep, maybe to death, as thousands of parents unintentionally do every year.

That snapped me out of it. I placed Luya in her crib, still crying, and woke Deirdre up.

That night taught me something valuable: Every brain has a breaking point. And when we cross it, it's easy to fall over the edge.

Vince certainly had. And that spring, as we waited for a definitive diagnosis for him, one that might explain his neurological crisis, I knew that I needed to take steps to address the ways my own brain was failing me. I got a prescription for Ritalin. With Deirdre's help, I started to meditate every morning and beefed up my midday mindfulness exercises. I tried to approach my work and my time with family with clear intention, writing out weekly goals for myself to guide my behavior in the office and in our home. And I tried to limit my intake of caffeine and other stimulants. I silenced my phone, eliminated screen time, made a rule to stop working at ten P.M. so that I would have an easier time getting to sleep. All of this was an attempt to return my brain to its baseline, to give my nervous system a rest.

It worked. The drug had immediate effects, but the non-chemical interventions were helpful, too. Where I was previously substituting sheer activity for sustained accomplishment, I now found a sense of purpose in reminding myself of my long-term intentions. And simply knowing that my brain had a particular malady made me more aware of the ways it affected my behavior.

It also made me wonder what a Huntington's diagnosis might do for Vince Gilmer. If he turned out to have Huntington's, it would be a far more devastating blow than an adult ADHD diagnosis. But maybe knowing that he had it would give him some peace: He could finally understand why he experienced a "serotonin deprived brain" for so long. It might allow him to strategize ways to live with the disease and encourage the corrections officers to relate to him differently—as a patient, not a prisoner.

Or maybe knowing it would terrify him, the way it would terrify me.

All we could do was wait and see.

One morning at Cane Creek, about six weeks after Steve and I visited Vince, I got an email from Dr. Angliker.

> DATE: 3-28-13
>
> SUBJ: Results
>
> Vince's lab work has come back positive for HD: Huntington allele 1 = 43 CAG repeats. The allele 2 was normal = 17 CAG repeats. Now, I'm going to proceed with plan "B" and get an MRI.
>
> Colin Angliker

I sprung from the chair and ran out into the backyard near Vince's fishpond. Forty-three CAG repeats was a definitive result. Anything thirty-six or more was unequivocally abnormal. Vince was positive for Huntington's. This was not a subjective analysis, dependent on the biases or preconceptions of the observer. This was unambiguous genetic proof that explained why Vince's brain had changed.

Steam rose from my breath, and my heart raced with a strange, frenetic energy that I struggled to identify at first. Was it excitement or despair?

On the one hand, we had done it. We had found a unifying answer that explained so many of Vince's strange behaviors.

On the other, we'd uncovered a diagnosis more devastating and condemning than prison: death.

Dr. Buie's hunch was right: Vince Gilmer—and, by deduction, Dalton Gilmer, as well—were plagued by Huntington's disease.

It was still early, about seven in the morning, but I called Sarah immediately. She was shocked, and I could hear the nervous disbelief in her voice. But she wasn't entirely satisfied.

"Huntington's may have contributed, but it didn't make him kill his dad."

"Right. It doesn't usually make people violent. But it was part of what was going on in his brain," I said. "It's part of the answer, not the whole thing. And . . ."

I choked up. I could barely speak. In my mind's eye, all I could see was Vince, sitting alone in his cell after our last visit to Wallens Ridge, fashioning a homemade knife out of a piece of plastic, desperate to end his suffering. This was no longer about a radio show or a medical mystery. It wasn't about Ira Glass or Sarah Koenig. It wasn't about me.

It was about another human being: A terminally ill man with my name, rotting in prison in Virginia. Someone who was being punished for being sick, for receiving a genetic glitch from his dead father.

A man whom no one had believed. A patient who had received no care.

First, Vince's brain had failed him, then the justice system, whose job was to convict, and it succeeded.

But at that moment, on the phone with Sarah, I realized I had a different mission. The penal system had no interest in healing, but as a physician, it was my life's work. This is what I had signed up to do. I had learned that in every story of violence, pain, or suffering, there was an opportunity for healing.

"This changes everything," I said.

Dr. Angliker visited Vince in his cell to give him the news. Sarah and I scheduled a call for a few days later, to regroup with Vince and discuss his diagnosis. It would be our last conversation with him for the story, and we would be recording it. We wanted to make sure that listeners heard the voice of the person at the center of the story. Heard Vince.

But two days before the call, my father had a heart attack. He'd had one before, so he recognized the signs early and called his cardiologist, who immediately sent him for a test to determine the extent of blockage in his heart. The heart attack had been minor, but the findings were decidedly serious: He had five blocked arteries. He'd need a quintuple bypass, fast.

It was a risky surgery under any circumstances, made riskier by my father's age. I was on the phone instantly, asking about his lab work, inquiring about the plan of care—advocating for him as both a doctor and a son. But it quickly became clear that wasn't really necessary. Dad had excellent insurance and access to the best hospital in Tennessee. He was in very capable hands.

Still, it was a major health crisis, and I dropped everything to drive to Nashville when I heard the news. And as I made my way west through the Great Smoky Mountains, I was surprised at how often I found myself thinking about Vince. He popped into my thoughts completely unbidden—his face, his missing teeth and patchy beard. All throughout that drive, I thought about the differences between my father's access to medicine and Vince's. Here I was, nervously double-checking every stage of my father's care, even though I had full confidence in his doctors—all just because I loved him and wanted to call in any favor necessary to make the slightest difference.

In the meantime, Vince had spent almost ten years in a maximum-security prison, alone, exhibiting symptoms that nobody believed were real. He'd been locked in a cell by himself, denied even the most basic of psychiatric medications. He'd been languishing for years with a terminal diagnosis, given little more than ibuprofen to help him through it—all because he had no one, not a single person other than his mother, advocating for him.

Gloria loved him, but she wasn't a doctor, nor a lawyer. She felt defeated and beaten down by the system. One day she told me: "Once you get in, you don't get out."

Vince's situation, I was learning, was sadly indicative of the plight of most incarcerated people in the country. If Wallens Ridge, one of the largest prisons in Virginia—a facility built and maintained at great taxpayer expense—couldn't even keep a staff psychiatrist on the premises, despite the probability that half of its inmates suffer from some mental illness, what else were the people behind bars there lacking?

My father's precarious health that spring also brought to light the sad emotional truth of Vince's fractured, dysfunctional family. I was a child of divorce, but I never doubted that both my parents cared about me, that they would always provide me with a safe and warm home. I was worried sick about my father. But that worry was the product of decades of love and trust. I knew he would be there for me.

Where had that love been for Vince? What must it have been like to grow up with a father like Dalton—abusive, unpredictable, damaged?

I couldn't imagine it. Then again, after all of that, Vince had still felt an obligation to care for the man who had traumatized him the most. He'd brought him into his home when the rest of the family couldn't. He'd decided to move him into a facility close by. And the night everything changed, he was bringing him even closer.

Something happened that night, something dark and violent. Something horrible. But despite all of it, Vince had also felt a son's love for his father.

And that broke my heart.

Sarah and I taped our final audio for *This American Life* as my father awaited surgery. I recorded in my brother Nate's office on the Vanderbilt campus—he worked as in-house counsel for the university—jogging the half mile from the hospital during a brief break. It felt surreal to be describing the inside of a very sick person's brain to Sarah—explaining in layman's terms what Huntington's disease was, how it might have affected Vince the night of the killing, and what he could expect from it in the years to come—while my father lay in a hospital bed a short walk away, awaiting his fate.

Sarah and I had just spoken to Dr. Angliker, who had shared his experience telling Vince he had Huntington's.

"I was nervous, because it's more or less a death sentence," he said. "But much to my surprise and personal relief, he's taken it very well."

"Why do you think that is?" asked Sarah.

"Well, I think he had been trying to prove a point for some considerable time, that there was something wrong with him, and nobody was paying any attention," Angliker answered. "They thought that oh, it's all fake and he's putting it on, and that wasn't the case."

"To me, what's been so difficult to understand is that after two visits with him, it was clear that he had a neurologic illness," I said. "There was obviously something going on. So, it's very hard for me to appreciate that that could have been missed, after numerous, numerous evaluations."

"We're supposed to listen," Dr. Angliker said. "But I have found that often people don't listen to what patients are saying. They don't. They have a preconceived idea as to what's going on, and that's it. They are as inflexible sometimes as the system in which they find work. They have a stereotype of what an inmate is and they won't budge beyond that."

"Do you think that's what happened in Vince's case?" Sarah asked.

"I'm afraid so. It was really horrendous," Dr. Angliker said. "It just blows my mind how things went for him. To me, it's a travesty. He should never have been put in a prison."

Sarah and I had a call with Vince scheduled for the day after my dad's surgery.

"I'm just so curious about how he's processing this," Sarah said. "What do you think he's going to say? What do you think he's going to do?"

"I don't know," I said, opening and closing the top drawer of my brother's desk. There was nothing in it that I needed: business cards, letter openers, paper clips. I was just nervously fidgeting. My father had told me that afternoon that he was terrified about having his ribs cracked open, the interior cavity of his chest exposed to the world so the surgeon could repair his failing coronary arteries. As a minister and a chaplain, he'd helped many people over the years face the possibility of their lives ending—but now that he was the one on the way to the operating table, he truly understood their terror.

"I'll be fine," he'd said to me that afternoon. But I could see in his eyes that he was scared, that he knew this might be it. The image of his face just before surgery had been in my mind all afternoon, even as Sarah and I wrapped up our audio recording.

"I'll talk to you tomorrow," Sarah said. "And, Benjamin?"

"Yeah?"

"Wish your father good luck for me," she said.

My father's surgery was eight hours long and went off without a hitch. After he was released from the OR, the whole family visited him in his room, where he would recuperate for about five days before being sent home. I hugged my stepmother, Jo. She was a nurse and understood that Dad had a long road ahead of him. This was just the beginning. I promised to come back later to stay with Dad overnight.

Then I went back to Nate's office to record our call with Vince.

Sarah had arranged for both of us to call the prison at Marion at the same time. Vince would patch in from a prison telephone, and the three of us would speak over a kind of party line, Sarah recording the whole thing.

When I dialed the number at the appointed time, Sarah was already there. We said our hellos and awaited the telltale beep, indicating that Vince was joining. Then I heard his shaky voice.

"Hello, Benjamin."

"How are you, Dr. Gilmer?"

"I am ridiculously doing so much better, it's not even funny. I really and truly, I mean, right now, I am so close to being back to normal."

I knew that couldn't be true, but his voice was stronger, his mood was brighter, and he was laughing. Before this, Sarah and I couldn't even imagine he was capable of laughter. He sounded like a completely different person now—his speech quicker, less labored, easier to understand.

I told him that I was so glad to hear he was doing better.

"My brain is getting better," Vince said. "After all these years of hell, having the DNA diagnosis that can't be argued with—it's just a miracle all the way around. And it's going to work out for the best."

"I know this diagnosis is terrifying—" I began.

"I'm not terrified about it," Vince said. "To me, it was . . . it was a relief."

I was surprised that Vince's reaction to his diagnosis was so positive. I thought he might not have understood the gravity and seriousness of his disease, so I explained that there was no actual cure for Huntington's, just symptomatic treatments like the citalopram for his anxiety and depression. I told him there was nothing that could actually reverse the course of the disease. The damage to his brain was done. He would only continue to worsen.

But Vince didn't want to talk about that. He kept turning the conversation to our shared love for medicine, our mutual patients, and our passion for the outdoors. And eventually, as the conversation went on, and Sarah described the way that the radio story would reach people around the country, it hit me: It wasn't that Vince didn't understand the severity of a Huntington's diagnosis. He understood it perfectly well. He was feeling good because someone had finally believed him—and not only that, someone had been able to prove that there actually was something wrong with his brain.

He had known it all along, perhaps his whole life. He had always carried with him a deep-seated feeling that something wasn't right. He could sense that he was impulsive and prone to anxiety but hadn't ever been able to pinpoint a reason. He had instinctively known that he didn't want children, but had never quite understood why—was it only because he was afraid of becoming an abuser like his father? Did he fear passing along something else in his genes to his offspring? Did he somehow know there was something to inherit?

Vince had been telling the truth. He wasn't a liar, a faker, or a malingerer. His brain really wasn't "working right."

So the Huntington's diagnosis was a kind of vindication. Yes, the disease was serious. It was progressive. It was a death sentence.

But for the moment, Vince was calm.

He was, against all odds, at peace.

12.

AFTERMATH

When "Dr. Gilmer and Mr. Hyde," the *This American Life* episode Sarah and I had labored over, finally aired in mid-April 2013, Deirdre and I missed it. We were in the middle of feeding Kai and Luya after returning from a hike, and by the time we realized the story was being broadcast to thousands of people across the country, it was too late. We had to wait for the second airing later that night, listening to the clock radio in our bedroom, tuned low so it wouldn't wake up the kids.

Neither of us said much during the episode. It was the culmination of six months of work, boiled down to fifty tight minutes, and I was proud of what Sarah and I had accomplished together. But satisfaction wasn't the primary emotion I felt that night. I felt something closer to grief. Hearing the story from beginning to end, hearing the voices of Terri and Dr. Angliker and, at the end of the episode, Vince himself, all I could think about was the tragedy of what we'd uncovered. The tragedy of Dalton's death and Vince's childhood; the tragedy of the justice system that had failed him; the tragedy of curdled familial love and generations of abuse. The tragedy of inheriting a cruel disease for which there was no cure.

When the episode was over, Deirdre and I both wept.

Then, propped up on a pillow, dabbing her eyes with the sheet, Deirdre asked me the same question as Sarah had, after our first visit to the prison.

"So what do we do now?"

I didn't know how to answer Deirdre at first. Up to this point, I'd had a singular goal: get to the bottom of whatever had happened to Vince Gilmer, then tell the story in the most straightforward, impactful way possible.

I'd had Sarah as a partner in this journey. But I knew, long before April, that once the story aired, her job was done. She was a journalist, not an activist. And she didn't live in North Carolina, with a convicted murderer's name. She had already started working on her next assignment, a long-form investigative piece about the murder of a Baltimore high school student. It would be called *Serial*.

I was sad to see Sarah go, grateful for the experience and friendship we'd shared.

"We did this together, Benjamin," Sarah said, the week after the episode aired. "But now it's yours. Where you take it is up to you."

Stories, Sarah told me, had lives of their own. It was a journalist's task to capture them, to tell them truthfully, honestly, and transparently—but once you released a story into the world, it mutated. It evolved without your control. And so, Sarah had warned me, did your own relationship with it.

That certainly happened to me in the weeks after the episode aired. When Sarah and I first started reporting together, I had conceived of the story being about a community (Cane Creek) and an individual (me) confronting an act of incongruous violence committed by my double (Vince Gilmer). We were trying to answer two questions: What had happened to push a man to kill his father? And how could I—and the rest of Cane Creek—reconcile the good man I heard about every day at the clinic with the man in prison?

After I met Vince, the story became more of a medical mystery: Something was clearly wrong with this person, but what?

But now that we had a neurologic diagnosis, and now that we'd released the truth into the world, the narrative had changed under my feet once more. My involvement was no longer born of personal curiosity or medical interest. It was moral. And the question guiding me was simple:

How can I help him?

I wasn't sure yet, but I knew I couldn't abandon Vince now. Doing so would be abandoning the fabric of my own morality. Turning my back on him, as the system and many others had done, was not an option. He was counting on me. And so was his family.

After the episode aired, I called Gloria, Vince's mother. I wasn't sure how she'd respond. Although our intention was to portray her and her family with care, preserving their dignity—and although Gloria had been cooperative during the production, letting us interview her and paving the way for our meetings with Vince—Sarah had warned me that sometimes people's reactions to hearing their own stories were unpredictable. Especially when the stories revealed family dysfunction.

But Gloria wasn't angry when I called her. She was in tears.

"Thank you," she said. "Thank you for telling my baby's story. This was no coincidence. We both know that God put you in Vince's path to help him."

"We just want what's best for Vince," I said, taken aback.

At first, I didn't know how to accept Gloria's gratitude. Its intensity—and her implication of some divine intervention—overwhelmed me. I may have been a chaplain's son, but I didn't think I was an instrument of God's divine will. I was just a concerned family doctor who saw a sick man who needed help. This was the oath I took.

But the more I talked to Gloria that day, the more I realized that for her, believing in divine intervention was the most comforting way to approach what had happened to her and her family. Her life had been filled with so much pain: Dalton's beatings, his illness, his death at the hand of her son, and the disappearance of her daughter. Vince had been one of the lone bright spots in her life, the dutiful son who had escaped a childhood of abuse and dedicated his life to helping people. When even that was taken away, her faith was her only recourse. She had to believe that God would have mercy on her.

"I knew Jesus would not abandon us," she told me. "My Bible study just read this verse in Hebrews that I want to quote to you: *And without faith it is impossible to please God, because anyone who comes to him must believe that he exists and that he rewards those who earnestly seek him.*"

Gloria, it was clear to me, had never been rewarded for her faith. Her life, for much of the past twenty years, had been filled with one tragedy after another. It wasn't just Vince, either. That day on the telephone, she told me a truly horrifying story about Diane, Vince's sister. She had been missing for nearly a decade.

"I know she was murdered," Gloria said.

She told me Diane had been in an abusive relationship in Mobile, Alabama. Her boyfriend was an unstable sadist and, a year before Vince's trial, had kidnapped her and beaten her so badly that he'd broken several of her ribs and her eye socket.

"That's awful," I said.

"You don't know the half of it," Gloria said quietly. "When he was hitting her, he'd call me and make me listen. I'd hear my baby in the background screaming for help, but there was nothing I could do. It was like talking to Vince on the phone in prison, when he's telling me about the guards hitting him. But worse, because at least with Vince, I knew where to go. With Diane, I didn't know where she was."

Eventually, Diane was found by the FBI, still alive. She had needed weeks in a hospital to recover, and during that time her boyfriend went on the run. The boyfriend had eventually been captured and imprisoned. But unlike Diane, he came from wealth, and his family had been able to finagle his way out of prison. Soon after his release, his parents had died, leaving him millions in inheritance.

"And that's when she went missing," Gloria said. "I haven't heard from her now in nine years."

"Is this why she didn't show up to the trial to corroborate Vince's story?"

"Yes," Gloria said. "All of my babies. Sweet lord. All of them have just been so tortured. Dalton by his crazy brain. Diane by that man. Vince by the prison system."

Talking to Gloria made me angry. Not at her—but at the hand she'd been dealt. I couldn't change Vince's diagnosis, or Dalton's abuse, or Diane's disappearance. But I could help Vince get the treatment and care that he deserved. I could be—or at least attempt to be—what Gloria thought I was: proof that the world still held some joy, some justice, and some humanity.

"We're going to get him out," I told Gloria.

But after I hung up the phone, I kept asking myself the same question:

How?

Help came from an unexpected source: the U.S. Postal Service.

Within a week, I started receiving letters at Cane Creek. They weren't about how well produced the episode was, or how much they'd enjoyed Sarah's narration. They weren't about how gripping or well paced the story was.

They were about Vince.

People wrote to ask how they could help him. To ask if he was still in prison. To ask if he was getting better, if they could contribute money. They felt the injustice that had been done to him, and also were saddened that Dalton had lived a misunderstood life, ravaged by a disease he didn't even know he had.

Many of the letters inspired me. There were people who didn't know anything about medicine, anything about law, asking if there was anything they could do. There were people asking if Vince had a legal defense fund to which they could contribute. There were people who offered to visit him in prison.

> I was stunned and humbled after hearing the story of how you helped Dr. Vince and effectively ended his years of suffering. I became a nurse nearly 20 years ago because of the burning desire to ensure that the concerns of others are heard above prejudice and preconception. Is there an opportunity to volunteer at your office and help?

Some of the letters informed me. There were letters from doctors, sharing stories about diagnosing their own Huntington's cases and giving advice for treatment. Letters from scientists, filling me in on the latest drug therapies. Letters from lawyers and doctors decrying a system that could put a man that sick anywhere but a hospital.

> Dr. Gilmer, I am a family medicine doctor and I just heard your story on TAL. Your story is one of the greatest testimonials I've ever heard to the value of really listening, and maintaining your curiosity. It is a moral travesty that, as clinicians, we have allowed the system to continue locking up the mentally ill. We can do better.

Some of the letters broke my heart. There were letters from old friends of Vince's who hadn't known what had happened, and who heard about it all for the first time on the radio. There were letters from his medical school classmates and military brothers-in-arms, sharing stories about him from the old days, stories about Vince's compassion, his kindness, his mischievous sense of humor.

> Vince and I went to med school together and I was shocked to hear his story. I still can't comprehend it. He was so devoted, so giving to others. Please let me know if there is anything I can do to help his cause.

And there were letters—so many of them—from people who had personal experience with neurodegenerative diseases.

> I just listened to your episode of *This American Life* and want to thank you. The entire time I was listening, I was thinking about my dad. In 2007, my father took an unexplained fall down a flight of stairs, a month later he was arrested for possession of child pornography. It came as a great shock to our family, but I knew from the start we were dealing with more than just the crime. My parents divorced when I was 4 and I hadn't grown up with my dad but this didn't fit with everything I knew of him. The court felt he did not pose a threat to the community but even so, he faced six to ten years in federal prison. . . .
>
> No one suggested he see a neurologist. I set about showing the court they were not dealing with a well man. The evaluator found he was malingering. As soon as I heard "malingering" as Dr. Vince Gilmer's diagnosis, I knew this would be a story about a neurological disorder. . . .
>
> I am not a doctor, but I proposed he had Lewy Body Dementia. The evaluators told me they had no reason to believe my father suffered from it. Fortunately, the fed-

eral court system is slow which allowed me to take my father to a neurologist who agreed that he had a neurologic process, like Lewy Body dementia or Alzheimers or Huntingtons. Armed with a diagnosis, I was able to get him Medicaid and postpone the sentencing until he died a year later.

As you know, prisons are not equipped to deal with someone in his position, the courts have no mechanism for alternative sentencing, and NO ONE I spoke with had ever come across anything like this. How could all of these professionals in different disciplines, in the legal system, not think to test for neurological disorders as a rule?

Our prisons are full of mentally ill people. Knowing how many people like Dr. Vince and my dad are locked away without consideration of their condition is outrageous. It is an unacceptable situation in our country to knowingly level punitive sentences upon populations with rapidly degenerative conditions and no hope of rehabilitation.

Thank you for your compassion towards your fellow man and sharing your story.

I didn't have time to answer every letter, many of which were from children of people with Huntington's, asking me directly if they should be tested for the disease. I couldn't diagnose anyone by mail. All I could do was counsel them, clearing up any misconceptions they had about the brain or Huntington's and outlining the ethical complexities of testing. I recommended that they contact their doctor.

Since the disease is ultimately fatal and there is no cure, counseling patients to get tested is very complicated. On the one hand, the knowledge of a positive result can allow patients to prepare for the ravaging road that awaits them, and help them make informed decisions about whether they want children. On the other hand, it can instill immense anxiety, leaving them wondering about when symptoms will present.

Not knowing can be just as anxiety inducing. Few want to live a life of perpetual fear, always wondering if they carry a ticking time bomb in their genes. Ultimately, only about half of children born to a parent with HD get tested.

"What would you do?" Deirdre asked me, when I described the complexities of the testing decision.

"I'd want to know," I told her. "I'd want to plan the rest of my life. How about you?"

"I'm not sure. You know that dementia runs in my family," Deirdre said, frowning. "If there was a test for it, I don't think I would want to know my destiny so early."

Vince already knew his destiny. So the question I faced that spring was how to help him face the rest of his life.

Every week, Laura added letters to a growing folder on my desk. And the more I read, the more I started to understand where the next chapter in Vince's and my evolving story lay: the legal system. Vince had been sentenced because he was perceived to be faking symptoms that were now known to be related to Huntington's. Was there some legal remedy to his plight?

One day in late April, I received a fax from a lawyer in Texas named Jennifer Brevorka. A former journalist, she'd been fascinated by the story.

> Dr. Gilmer's story caught my attention for two reasons. I
> lived in Asheville in 2002–2004 while working as a
> crime reporter at the *Citizen-Times* so I am familiar
> with the Cane Creek area. I also worked as a federal dis-

trict court law clerk in Abingdon, Virginia, where Dr. Gilmer was tried.

I write to offer my assistance to you, or any other attorneys with whom you are working, in pursuing the release of Dr. Gilmer from prison. I have some familiarity with the federal habeas corpus proceedings due to my work as a federal law clerk. I would be happy to help with any legal research, document drafting or court appearance on a pro bono basis.

Thanks again for your persistence and hard work.

I called her that afternoon, and after a few minutes of pleasantries, Jenny told me she was buying a plane ticket to North Carolina to see family; she'd be stopping by Asheville, too.

"A much-needed vacation," Jenny said. "I went to Duke Law and love that part of the country, and my husband and I have been thinking about taking a long weekend away."

Four weeks later, May had arrived, and spring was at its height, the magnolias and dogwoods in full bloom. Walking through downtown Asheville on the way to dinner, Jenny said she missed this part of the country—but she didn't miss the old boys' club of its political and legal worlds.

"I have a lot of questions about the trial," she said. "I'm curious about whether or not Vince still had counsel when he declined to use the court-appointed funds to appoint an expert in SSRIs. It's egregious if counsel was representing him when he was awarded this money and they didn't use it."

Jenny also brought up the issue of an "irresistible impulse" defense. Similar to an insanity defense, it would claim that Vince had not been able to resist his thoughts or control his actions in the truck with Dalton, and was thus not guilty of malice. Virginia was one of the few states that allowed it.

Jenny was a slightly intimidating presence. Thin, with shoulder-length black hair and large, observant eyes, she had the brisk decisiveness and authority of the crew captain she'd once been at Yale. Her friendliness belied a steely intelligence. She could speak naturally to any southern Virginian, or blend in with any Ivy League crowd.

My first thought, meeting her, was *This woman could kick some ass.* I could tell that she would have relished the opportunity to go toe-to-toe with Nicole Price in the courtroom.

But for the moment, all she could do was give me a much-needed legal education.

"I think your first step should be a habeas corpus case," she said, as we sat at a restaurant in Asheville's River Arts District.

"I went to med school, not law," I said. "This is a foreign language."

"Latin for 'show me the body,'" Jenny said. "A writ of habeas corpus protects against unlawful imprisonment. Basically, it forces the state to give an imprisoned person a hearing, at which the state has to provide reasons for continued incarceration."

"How's that different from an appeal?"

Jenny nodded over her glass of sparkling water.

"You appeal a verdict," she said. "From what I can tell, Vince has already done that a number of times, and it hasn't worked. He's either failed or missed the relevant deadlines. Habeas corpus is a little different."

Jenny explained that a habeas case didn't seek to overturn a jury's findings. In fact, it made no judgment about the defendant's guilt or innocence. It just allowed the prisoner to make a case for why their imprisonment was unlawful. In Vince's case, that would be because he was seriously ill, and had been since before the trial.

"So he'd still be guilty."

"Yes," Jenny answered. "But a habeas corpus case could allege that there were irredeemable mistakes or errors in the trial—for example, that he was deemed competent and sane, able to represent himself, even though he was in the throes of severe mental illness—and that these mistakes led to unlawful imprisonment."

"As opposed to?"

"Well, institutionalization, for example," Jenny answered.

It felt strange to be discussing an ill man's legal fate over wine and ten-dollar appetizers. When the paella arrived, I felt a pang of guilt, thinking of Vince in the visiting room, where the finest delicacy was a Snoball and his most prized beverage, a lukewarm twenty-ounce Mountain Dew. I took a sip of wine, reminding myself that empathy and visits alone wouldn't change Vince's situation—it would take legal power.

In other words, it would take money. It would take dinners like these.

"I see," I said. "Habeas corpus wouldn't be arguing that he should be freed. It would just be arguing that the right place for him was a mental hospital, not a prison."

Jenny nodded. "It's often used for the mentally ill," she said. "Although more recently it's been in the news for the detainees at Guantánamo Bay."

"Will it work?" I asked.

"Probably not," Jenny said matter-of-factly.

"What happens then?"

"You go directly to the governor," Jenny said. "But to do that, you really need to exhaust every judicial possibility first. You have to show that you've tried everything else, that you've done your due diligence. Then you go for broke, appeal for clemency or a pardon."

"A Hail Mary," I said.

"Right," Jenny said. "And you have to throw it on fourth-and-long."

Over the next few weeks, Jenny started putting together a legal plan for Vince. It wouldn't be easy, she said. Nor would it be cheap.

"Typically, a case like this costs about half a million dollars," she said.

I laughed out loud. Numbers like this were so far beyond my pay grade—beyond *years* of my salary—that they didn't even register as real. That summer, we'd applied for a car loan and, in the process of working out my family's finances, I had come to realize that I'd be paying off my medical school debt until I was fifty. I didn't even want to think about the house.

"That's a lot of money," I said.

"I know," Jenny told me. "And I also know that Vince doesn't have any assets."

"Taking payment in garden vegetables will do that to you," I said.

"I wish I could do that," she said. "But it will be uphill sledding from Texas. You're going to need more people than just me. You need a Virginia law firm."

Jenny said we needed people on the ground in Virginia: people working with justice nonprofits, people allied with established, white-shoe firms, people with the ear of the governor.

She put me in contact with an old friend of hers, a lawyer named Dawn Davison, who was an attorney for the Virginia Capital Representation Resource Center. Dawn's life's work was in providing competent defense for people convicted on capital charges—the death penalty. It was underpaid, underappreciated work. You did it for the love, not the money—just like family medicine.

I called her one morning on my way to the clinic, my voice periodically drowned out by the wind through my open windows. The air conditioner in my Subaru was out again, and it was already hot in North Carolina. I could have the windows closed for only a few minutes at a time, and I tried to time those minutes for when Dawn was speaking. I wanted to be able to hear her. "So you're a public defender?" I yelled over the sounds of traffic and road noise.

"Sort of," she said. "The difference is I only work capital cases. Also, I'm not by myself. Our entire organization is dedicated to making sure people facing the possibility of execution get the best counsel possible. If the stakes are high, the representation should be excellent."

"Vince didn't do himself any favors on that front."

"I know," she said. "Jenny explained the case to me. And of course I listened to the NPR story. What happened to him is a legal travesty. I'd have to read the full transcripts, but if what you're saying about his medical condition is true, there is no way he should be in a prison. It seems like he should be in an institution."

"That's what I'd like for him," I told her. "But I'm not a lawyer, and Jenny is in Texas doing this on her own time. And Vince wasn't a capital case—he got life. So it sounds like you'll be limited in how much you can do."

"Well, I can't work on it by myself," she said. But her work often put her in partnership with other organizations, like the Innocence Project. "They could help us build a legal team."

I rolled up the window to make sure I'd heard her right.

"Us?"

Dawn laughed.

"What, did you think you were going to do this alone?"

13.

FAMILY THANKSGIVING

One of the first people we added to our team was Deirdre Enright, director of the UVA School of Law's Innocence Project Clinic. Forceful, well connected, and a natural problem solver, Deirdre was a passionate advocate for criminal justice reform and a fierce opponent of the death penalty. She'd represented many people on Virginia's death row.

"Vince's case is interesting," she said the first time we spoke. "This is a guy who doesn't dispute killing his father. He's not like many of our clients, who truly had nothing to do with the crimes for which they're imprisoned." The Innocence Project, a national nonprofit, works only to exonerate the wrongly convicted—people who are wholly innocent of the charges brought against them.

"Right," I said. "*Not guilty by reason of insanity* is a lot different than *not guilty.*"

"But he still has rights," Deirdre said. "Chief among them the right to a fair trial. And I don't think he got one. The fact that no one believed he was mentally ill—either at the time of the killing or during the trial—means that the whole thing is based on a flawed assumption of mental capacity."

Although Vince's case couldn't be taken on by the Innocence Project since he did not deny killing Dalton, Deirdre saw the injustice in it immediately and wanted to help enlist legal counsel who could intervene. She offered herself up more or less as a gatekeeper—someone who could help assemble a team.

"We've got to come up with a game plan," Deirdre said. "You're going to need many advocates and a strategy to have any shot of getting him out."

In mid-November 2013, Deirdre, Dawn, and I met in Richmond to do just that. The Virginia Bar Association had heard about Vince's case through Deirdre and had invited me to give a lecture at their symposium on capital punishment. I made the trek up from Asheville, eager to meet the growing legal team and nervous about giving a speech to a bunch of lawyers.

Luckily, I wouldn't be alone onstage. Dr. Angliker drove up from Marion to be a part of the presentation. I would go first, walking the assembled lawyers through the case, then demonstrating how cognitive preconceptions hardened into bias before and during Vince's trial. Then Dr. Angliker would explore the forensic errors of the case.

"Warm up the crowd for me," he said, as we waited to go on.

The conference was in a hotel, and the speeches were given in an older ballroom that felt more historic than the typical wedding venue. I'd spent my fair share of time at medical conferences like this, sitting at the same long, narrow rectangular tables, with the starched napkins, endlessly refilled water glasses, and watered-down coffee, waiting impatiently for the end of a lecture so that I could go get dinner somewhere interesting.

But this was not my crowd. Lawyers wore suits. I was wearing one, too—but it was the one I'd bought in 1990 for my grandfather's funeral, the only one I had. I felt nervous standing in the wings, looking out at the crowd. I was a doctor, not a lawyer, and for a moment I had a flashback to Vince in the courtroom, running afoul of proper protocol.

I was thankful someone handed me a glass of beer before my

talk. When I got to the lectern, I took a deep breath. I looked down at my notes.

"Maybe I should have been a lawyer," I told the crowd. "They don't serve beer at family medicine conferences."

The crowd laughed politely and my nerves calmed enough for me to start showing slides.

My first was a picture of Dr. Albert Schweitzer, playing the organ with his bushy mustache on full display. Since the beginning of my medical training, I told them, I had been inspired by his fundamental philosophy: Reverence for Life, which posits that "*good consists in maintaining, assisting, and enhancing life, and to destroy, to harm, or to hinder life is evil.*"

"I have a simple question for everyone in this room," I continued. "What is advocacy?"

At first there was silence. I could hear the tines of a fork scraping a plate, a muffled cough from somewhere stage left.

Then a young man in the front row chimed in.

"Advocacy is speaking for those who have no voice."

I nodded, then clicked through the next four slides:

A snapshot of Vince behind bars, staring blankly through them.

A panorama of the cornfields and cows behind Cane Creek.

A sepia-toned print of Broughton Hospital, back at the turn of the century.

A photo of me in Gabon, on June 28, 2004, treating patients in the bush, on the day that Dalton Gilmer died.

This collage of images depicted the trajectory of Vince's and my colliding paths.

"When I first met Vince Gilmer," I said, "I was terrified of him. I didn't want to speak for him—I wanted to be as far away from him as possible. I had my own preconceptions about who he was, what he did, and why. And that's precisely the problem with the way we treat the mentally ill in our courtrooms and prisons."

Each of the next slides had a line of dialogue from someone attempting to explain what had happened that night in 2004. There were quotes from Detective Martin, Dr. Feix, Nicole Price, Judge Lowe, Dr. Buie, me—and, finally, from Vince himself.

"It's like *Rashomon*," I told the crowd of lawyers. "Each of us is looking at the same story through an entirely different lens. We all think we are doing our respective jobs."

I showed them my job as a doctor working through a differential diagnosis for Vince. I listed dozens of possibilities in turn, methodically crossing off diagnoses, one at a time, and explaining why they didn't quite fit.

"Eventually," I explained, "I had to work to overturn my most basic preconception: that there was only one explanation for what happened to Vince that night. In the end, it wasn't just a traumatic brain injury, or PTSD, or Huntington's disease—it was all of those things. A trifecta."

Vince's case, I argued, was one of compounding errors, all of them stemming from an initial preconception. No one thought to test him for Huntington's, because they had already assumed he was faking his symptoms. Because they assumed he was faking his symptoms, he was deemed mentally competent to stand trial. Because he was deemed competent to stand trial, he was allowed to represent himself—despite being in the midst of delusions and a mental breakdown.

And because he represented himself, he never stood a chance.

"If this could happen to Vince," I said, "it could happen to any of us. We have a shared neurological fallibility, and I believe that means we have a shared responsibility, as well—to other people and their fragile brains."

My last slide was another picture of Schweitzer above a quotation that I'd come to cherish:

It's not enough to merely exist. You must do something more . . . You must give something to your fellowman.

Even if it's a little thing . . . something for which you get
no pay but the privilege of doing it.

Reading Schweitzer's words aloud, I realized that all of us in that
room, lit by cheap chandeliers, were on the same page. Many of the
lawyers opposed the death penalty and were doing everything they
could to abolish it. I was trying to keep a terminally ill man from
dying in prison.

We were not simply lawyers and doctors: We were advocates.
We were all trying to do something more.

When I was finished, Dr. Angliker slowly made his way to the
podium in his oversized suit. The room was quiet in anticipation of
what he might say. Never before had a forensic psychiatrist from
inside the Department of Corrections dared to show up to a conference like this. I introduced him as a seasoned veteran of the prison
system who had never lost sight of his original commitment to treat
his patients with dignity.

In a gravelly voice, Colin spoke plainly, describing what had
happened to Vince as a forensic travesty. He showed the lawyers
how a combination of bias, preconceptions, and oversight led to
Vince's inaccurate diagnosis as a malingerer. He didn't demonize
anyone for missing Huntington's in 2004, but he did argue that it
was the state's responsibility to rectify mistakes.

"If we find a wrong in the system," he said, "we must call it
out."

I had assumed Dr. Angliker's part of the presentation would be a
relatively dry forensic analysis. But as his speech went on, emotion
crept into his voice. By the end, he was gripping the lectern, his
knuckles white, like the fire-and-brimstone preachers I sometimes
encountered in the rural Tennessee of my youth.

"I have worked in the prison system for over forty years," Colin
thundered. "I know it well. Vince and his illness cannot be treated

there, because our prisons have failed. They have failed because we have stopped listening: to the incarcerated, to the sick, to each other."

He paused, wiping his brow with his hand. I could see regret on his face.

Also fury.

"For decades, we have treated the mentally ill in our prisons like statistics," he said. "But that has to change. We have to remember our purpose as physicians."

He stopped, cleared his throat, leaned forward.

"We have to treat them like patients. That means that first, we have to do no harm."

When he sat down, applause filled the room.

That night, four of us—Dr. Angliker, Dawn, another lawyer from UVA, and myself—crowded around a table at a restaurant in downtown Richmond. It was the first time we'd all been in the same room, and our agenda was simple: decide on a strategy to get Vince out.

We wanted Vince moved out of the general prison population and into a secure hospital, a nursing home with a dementia unit, or a facility dedicated to the treatment of Huntington's disease—in short, somewhere he could receive appropriate medical treatment. This, in itself, would be a form of justice.

But we also hoped to emphasize to the judicial system a key fact: that if Vince's Huntington's diagnosis had been made before the trial, *he never would have been condemned to the prison system at all.* He would have been treated appropriately well before firing his lawyers and making his disastrous attempt to represent himself. With a competent lawyer, it was highly likely that a jury would have found him not guilty by reason of insanity. Plus, had Vince been diagnosed with Huntington's before the trial, the allegations of malingering—a key focus in the prosecution's case—would never have stuck.

We wanted justice for Vince. But we also wanted to make sure that what happened to him never happened to anyone else.

What was the best way to accomplish these two objectives?

"Look," Dawn said. "He was saying over and over during that trial that his brain wasn't working. He asked for his counsel to step back in on day five. He *begged* to be evaluated again. If anyone had taken him seriously, he would have had a proper diagnosis—and a very different trial."

"We all agree on that," I said. "He didn't get a fair trial, but it appeared to be constitutional, which is a low bar. The question really is, clemency versus habeas?"

A habeas corpus case would essentially mean pursuing justice through the courts, a process that could take years. Clemency meant petitioning the governor directly for a conditional pardon. It wouldn't strike Vince's conviction from the record, but it would allow him to be moved out of the prison system and into a secure treatment center.

"It's really an issue of time," Dawn said. "How long did you say he had, Dr. Angliker?"

Dr. Angliker had been very quiet—unusual for him. But in response to the question he just shook his head.

"It's hard to say," he answered. "I'm getting a crash course in Huntington's disease myself. Benjamin?"

"Typically patients with Huntington's live for about fifteen, maybe twenty years after the acute onset of symptoms," I said. "He's been symptomatic for more than ten years already."

I thought of an odd story one of Vince's residency professors had told me a few weeks earlier, about how Vince, in the late nineties, had occasionally exhibited bizarre behavior. Once, he had ripped an intercom off the wall during hospital rounds, then cut its cord with a pocketknife, because its constant buzzing annoyed him. Then he calmly sat down as though nothing had happened.

"So we could pursue a habeas case for years, only to have him die before he was out," Dawn said.

Dr. Angliker nodded.

The four of us went back and forth. Morally and ethically, we all wanted him to get his day in court—not only to achieve justice for himself, but to show the judicial system how to correct the errors of the first trial, so they wouldn't happen again. But all of us worried that we might be setting Vince up for an expensive, time-consuming, exhausting battle—one that he might not survive.

"Jenny was right to say that we should exhaust all judicial approaches," Dawn said. "Under normal circumstances, we would. But we're up against the clock here already. Vince doesn't have much time. Clemency is our best bet to get him out of prison alive."

It was decided: If Vince agreed, we would pursue clemency. We stacked hands like a football team and decided we were going for the Hail Mary.

With a captive audience of legal experts, I needed to clarify an important point.

"So we're asking the state for mercy, right?" I asked. "Not justice?"

"Mercy is just," Dawn said. "Especially in this case."

But was it?

Later that night, unable to sleep, I put on my running shoes and walked down Broad Street to the governor's executive mansion. The lights were still on and the gates still open, so I walked in, meandering throughout the back gardens before stumbling onto a walkway that headed straight to the back of the illuminated white house. As I neared the window, I could see inside. I could even hear a television. Startled by how close I was, my mind wandered into fantasy: I imagined knocking on the door and asking the governor to have a word with me. If only I had ten minutes inside to talk to him, I thought, I could easily convince him that Vince deserved to be released.

But who was I kidding? The current occupant of that house, Governor Bob McDonnell, was a Republican with national—even presidential—aspirations, and he had spent years building a reputation for being "tough on crime." Even in my fantasy, he wasn't the sort of politician who would open the door to a stranger in the night—much less grant clemency to a convicted killer serving a life term.

Peering into that window, through the darkness of a cold November evening, it hit me. Vince's case was not just a medical question, nor was it solely a moral one. Now that we were appealing for clemency, it was all about politics.

This was how justice was so often served in America: at the whims of politicians, depending on their political goals and aspirations. I had been so wrapped up in thinking about the medical and legal aspects of Vince's case, so consumed by the immorality of locking up the mentally ill, that I hadn't even seen the real hurdle: the politicians themselves.

McDonnell was nearing the end of his term. We would be bringing our clemency petition to a new governor: Terry McAuliffe, who had won his election a couple of weeks earlier. A former businessman with a long career in Democratic Party politics, he would likely be a much friendlier audience for Vince's clemency petition.

But why should justice depend on who happens to be in office when a wrong needs to be righted?

It was clear to me now that Vince's case didn't hinge on making a moral argument, or demonstrating that a sick man received an unfair trial, or that we are all fragile humans. No, this was going to be about making a persuasive argument that would enable a governor to make a decision that would not hurt him politically.

A hundred miles away, Vince slept in a cold concrete room. On the other side of the window, the governor was sitting on his couch, comfortably watching the evening news. And there I was in the shadows, on the edge of the mansion's bright security lights—an outsider, looking in.

A week later, I was driving to Marion with papers for Vince to sign, authorizing the release of his medical records. Our minivan was full of laughter and anxious questions.

"Are we there yet?"

Kai had been strapped into his booster seat for most of the two-hour ride, but somewhere near the Virginia state line, he'd pulled a Houdini and unbuckled his seatbelt. Now he was leaning forward from the back seat, his head between Deirdre's and my shoulders.

"We're close," Deirdre told him, gently pushing him back toward the safety of the back seat. "Sit on your bottom, honey. Put on your seatbelt, please! Play with your sister."

Luya was singing "Happy Birthday" to herself in her car seat, playfully wrapping herself in the blue "blankie" that accompanied her everywhere. Kai looked at her for a moment but quickly lost interest.

"Why aren't we going to Meme and Papoo's?" he asked, for the fifth time that day.

"Because someone else needs a family today," I told him. "We'll see your grandparents next week. Today I want you to be nice to Daddy's friend, Dr. Vince. Treat him like he's part of our family."

Luya nodded. "And we get ice cream after?"

"Sure can," I said, exiting the highway and scoping out locations—McDonald's, Hardee's, a seemingly derelict TCBY—for later in the day. After the desolate grandeur of Wallens Ridge, it was odd to see normal businesses within walking distance of a prison. I'd grown accustomed to the forested approach, the bleak fortress on the other side of the valley. There had been something medieval about it, angular and harsh.

But now we were driving down the main drag of Marion, Virginia. It was Thanksgiving, which was also Luya's birthday—and the Gilmer family was on its way to its first holiday behind bars.

After a few days of wrangling, I'd managed to get clearance for my whole family to visit Vince in prison. Prison rules meant that we couldn't bring a turkey with us, so there was no enormous platter with a freshly carved bird filling the car with its delicious aroma. There was no stuffing in the back seat, no pumpkin pie in the trunk, no tiny dish of cranberry sauce for us to balance in the cupholders. All we could bring inside was a pocketful of quarters for the vending machines and another release for him to sign.

"Do you think they'll be able to handle this?" Deirdre said under her breath, while Kai and Luya gazed out the passenger-side window at the high fences of the prison.

"I think so," I said. I'd already explained to Kai, as best as I could, why my friend Dr. Vince had to stay in a little room by himself, and why I wanted to get him out of it. I'd told him that Vince was very sick and needed a doctor like me. I'd told him—and Luya—that he needed friends right now.

But there is no way to tell how a six-year-old and a four-year-old will respond to a state prison—and I had no idea how Vince would respond to them. Would he frighten them? Would they make him uneasy? Would they remind him of everything he had lost in the last nine years?

And what would they think of the bars, the barbed wire, and the shackles? How would they react to the fact that we lock people up in a cell for life?

I wasn't sure. All I knew was that Vince needed company. More than that, I knew that he needed to feel like he still had a family, that there were people in the outside world who loved him and were working hard to make his life better.

"You're a Gilmer," Vince's mother had told me on the phone

when I mentioned my plan to her. "You should visit him whenever you want. As far as I'm concerned, you're part of the family now."

Vince's real family was across the country, or missing, or no longer alive. Gloria could afford to make the trip up from Alabama only once every few months. In the meantime, Vince was alone.

This Thanksgiving, there was just us. And as I pulled the car into the razor-wired parking lot of the prison, I hoped it would be enough.

"Daddy, up," Luya said in the waiting room at Marion, opening her arms and looking up at me, her eyes imploring. Luya still didn't quite understand why visiting a prison had become her big birthday outing. We hadn't been allowed to bring in our usual bag full of distractions—books, noisemaking toys, snacks—and an undistracted toddler can quickly become a terror. Deirdre and I were doing everything we could to appease her. Neither of us wanted a meltdown in the middle of a prison.

So I lifted her to my shoulders, letting her sit up high, her little feet kicking me in the chest. The CO approached us and asked all of us to take our shoes off so she could inspect them. Both Kai and Luya thought this was funny. Then she made us all hold our arms up so she could search us. When Deirdre and I struck the pose, the kids started doing jumping jacks. They were curious, alert, and, surprisingly, not at all scared.

As we walked into the prison, Kai mentioned that it was like going into Willy Wonka's Chocolate Factory. I was surprised—the high fences and razor wire sparkled, but there was nothing quirky about it. And when the large door slammed shut behind us, he seemed to change his mind.

"Dad, I don't think this is a very friendly place," he said.

Escorted by one of the COs, we entered the visitation room. The kids started feeling more comfortable and thought it was funny to see everyone with orange jumpsuits. They studied the decorations on the walls: a mural by one of the inmates depicting a nature scene at nearby Hungry Mother State Park, and another painting of an eagle standing proud.

"Daddy, you think Vince ever goes hiking in that park?" asked Luya.

"Don't think so, baby. Dr. Vince can't leave his home here."

We had explained that Vince lived at the prison, but the kids clearly still did not really understand what that meant. Neither, Deirdre confided in me, had she. It was her first visit, and she was surprised at how unsafe she felt, how foreign it all was.

"I'm glad you're here with me," I said, squeezing her hand.

Then the door opened.

"Is that him?" Deirdre asked.

Vince was standing in the doorway to the visiting room, a CO by his side. When he saw the four of us, he broke into a wide smile.

"Hello, Dr. Gilmer," he stuttered.

"Hi, Dr. Gilmer," I said back. "This is my family: Deirdre, Kai, and Luya. Say hi, everybody."

At first I worried that Vince's appearance—his grizzled beard, his missing teeth, his oscillating eyes—might alarm the kids. But the citalopram Dr. Angliker had prescribed was working to calm some of his more obvious anxiety symptoms, and the gap-toothed grin he was shooting our way was so obviously friendly, that I didn't worry long.

He stood straight up, in his bearlike fashion, arms extended. The kids shot a concerned glance my way and took a step back, so I walked over to Vince and hugged him. Deirdre was next, then Luya stepped up. Kai, the shyest of all of us, flashed a nervous grin when Vince wrapped his arms around him.

"Nice to meet you," Vince said.

"Nice meet you!" Kai parroted.

"Nice to finally meet you in person," Deirdre said. "I've heard so much about you, you feel like a part of our family."

Vince brushed a tear away with a shaky hand, blinked a few times, and then his face crumpled in on itself. The kids looked on nervously, unable to tell if the man in front of them was smiling or grimacing in pain. I myself wasn't sure what to make of it. I couldn't get a read on what he was feeling—joy, sorrow, or some combination.

And then I realized: Vince had been in prison for almost ten years. He hadn't hugged a child since 2004, his last patient at Cane Creek.

Incarcerated people often talk about loneliness and isolation, but they also suffer from a lack of human touch. Often, the only physical contact they experience is violent, or connected with the logistics of their imprisonment: the brush of a hand as cuffs are applied, the brace of a forearm against the back of the neck as a hold is performed.

Affectionate touch is more rare. The children's hugs were short-lived, a greeting, the kind of hug that kids give all the time. But they had deeply moved Vince. He patted Kai on the head, then gently pushed his shoulder toward us.

"You have to stay on that side of the table now, kiddo," he said.

We played Uno that day, sliding cards across the table like we'd been doing it for years. Kai won the first game, Deirdre the second. Vince had a run of bad luck with "Wild Draw Four" cards, and ended both games with a fat stack of cards.

"How have you been feeling?" I asked him after the second game, as Deirdre and Kai got up to go to the vending machines.

"I'm . . . okay, let me . . . let me . . . I'm doing ridiculously better on the SSRI. I can think better. My mood is better. What's the word for it? I'm less anxious."

Vince did look better. He'd put on a little weight since the last time I'd visited, in August. He'd recently gotten a haircut, a clean buzz that I wondered if he'd asked for in advance of our visit. And although the dark circles under his eyes were present as always, they seemed less pronounced than usual.

"Dr. Angliker told me he could tell your medication was really helping," I said. "With your mood, with your tremors, with all of it."

"That's the holy truth," Vince said. "I'm actually starting to feel like my old self again. But I'm hot all the time. The summer was hell. I slept on the bare concrete floor because it was cooler. There is no air-conditioning here and I just sweat like a pig."

"What do you mean there's no air-conditioning here?" Luya asked.

"It's strange, Lu," I explained, "but they never installed it here."

Now Kai was coming back from the vending machines with Deirdre, the day's appetizers in his arms. It looked like about twenty dollars' worth of sugary junk.

"We've got Mountain Dew, Snickers, pork rinds," he said, dumping it all on the table, "cheese crackers, chips, and *peanut* M&M's for Dr. Vince."

"Yay!" Luya said, clambering into my lap.

Then all three of them—Vince, Luya, and Kai—ripped into the assorted candy, their eyes carefree and ecstatic. Vince looked so different to me then, so much more like the overgrown kid everyone at Cane Creek had described. Watching him laugh with my children on Thanksgiving, I finally felt—deep down, in my gut—what Gloria had been telling me for weeks:

We were all Gilmers. Vince, Deirdre, Kai, Luya, Gloria, and me.

We were family.

We stayed in the prison for two hours that day—long enough for the sugar high to crest, dissipate, then ultimately crash. When it did, Luya went to sleep on Deirdre's lap, and Kai practiced shuffling with the Uno deck. Both of them were remarkably well behaved as I took Vince through the paces of our clemency strategy.

"I want a fair trial," he said. "That's all I ever wanted."

"I want that for you, too," I told him. "But more than that, I want you to get the care you need."

It was awkward to bring up the fact that he didn't have many years left to live. But looking to see that Luya was still asleep, and Kai was engrossed in the cards, I lowered my voice and did just that.

"Your Huntington's is going to get worse, Vince," I told him. "I don't want to spend years getting you a new day in court, only to have you . . ."

"Dead."

"I was going to say incapacitated," I said. "But yes. I want you to experience the outdoors again, and be treated, not in a jail cell. Clemency is our best option for that. The new governor's going to be a Democrat and will probably be receptive. We have people working on the case—"

But Vince interrupted me.

"I want people to know what happens in here," Vince said, suddenly heated. "I want people to know that I have been tortured."

"You mean generally?" Deirdre said. "With solitary confinement? Stuff like that?"

Vince nodded, eyes gazing at the floor.

"They beat us. They pepper spray us. They take away our food," he began, before trailing off. "That was more at Wallens Ridge, but it happens here, too. They threw me into isolation for over a week because the CO thought that I cussed at him after he woke me up and went through my stuff. I don't think I cussed at him, but I don't respond well under stress. I went on a drinking strike for five days until Dr. Angliker came back from vacation and got me out. I don't know what I'd do without that man."

This was quite a monologue for Vince. It took him a while to get through it, and when he did, Deirdre and I didn't know what to say in response. There was an awkward pause.

Then Vince filled it.

"There are a lot of people like me here," he said.

"People with Huntington's?" I asked, alarmed.

Vince shook his head. There was a slight hitch in the motion, like his head could only move so far to the left.

"Mental illness," he said. "People whose brains don't work right."

That made sense. Marion is a correctional treatment facility, which meant that almost everyone Vince encountered there needed psychiatric attention of some kind. Whether or not they were actually receiving it was a different issue. Vince told me that in his clinical opinion, a majority of the other inmates he'd encountered had severe mental illnesses. They were clinically depressed, bipolar, schizophrenic. They suffered from anxiety, compulsive behavior, PTSD.

"Do you think they came in that way, or got sick in prison?" I asked.

"Both," Vince said firmly. "If something's wrong before you get here, it only gets worse inside."

"But you're finally getting care," I said, referring to Dr. Angliker's SSRI prescription and his visits with Michelle, the prison social worker.

"That's true, it's better now that Michelle and Dr. Angliker keep an eye on me," Vince said. "But I don't know how much longer I can survive here."

At five P.M., we said goodbye, promising to return soon. Since it was a weekend, and any legal business must be conducted during weekday hours, the prison would not allow Vince to sign the waivers and give them to me directly. But we were allowed to pose for a family portrait: all the Gilmers, together, framed by three vending machines and three toothless smiles. Kai and Luya flanked Vince, smiling radiantly with him. The CO took a Polaroid, which Vince proudly handed to us. I later found out that Vince had to pay for the photo, that it cost him a snack or a phone call to his mother. It has remained on our fridge ever since.

A year and a half before, I had been terrified that this man would find out where I lived. And now I was visiting him in prison, sharing a Thanksgiving meal, letting my children give him hugs. Posing for a Gilmer family Thanksgiving photo.

What would the next year and a half bring? How many more times would I have to make the trip up to this prison, before he finally saw justice? And what about the other men in there with him, all of the mentally ill who *didn't* have anyone fighting for them?

The Bureau of Justice Statistics estimates that 37 percent of people in prisons suffer from severe mental illness. My conversation with Vince that day made me ask myself, and not for the first time, why? If mental illness was one of the reasons they were in prison, then crime was not just a legal problem, but a medical one—not just for courts, but for us care providers, as well. Clearly, we could be doing a better job.

As we walked to our car, the cold air seemed to perk the children up. So did the wide-open space in front of the prison entrance, a field of incongruous green grass alongside the entry road. It looked desperately cheerful in front of such a dreary place.

Watched by the guards in their towers, my children ran across it, jumping and yelling, spinning in circles—happy to be in the open air, to have room to run, to be totally and unconditionally free.

As we drove away, we were all quiet for a moment, and then Kai's voice pierced the silence.

"Daddy, if Doctor Vince is so sick, why is he in prison? Shouldn't he go to your hospital?"

"He should, son," I said. "He should."

14.

CRUEL AND UNUSUAL

Three months later, I was sitting on the patio of a southern bistro in Abingdon, Virginia, surrounded by lawyers, spotlit by the early spring sun. I was already sweating in my twenty-year-old sport coat—but that wasn't so much because of the heat. It was because Dawn and I were about to make the most important pitch of our legal team's short life.

After eight months of working together, we'd lost a few members, and we were looking for reinforcements. Although she remained a mentor and guide, Deirdre Enright had mostly returned to her work at the Innocence Project, and Jenny realized she needed to step aside because of work commitments in Texas. But before she did, she reiterated one of her earliest pieces of advice: "Find a white-shoe law firm to partner with," she said. "Big, powerful, well respected. Even a little conservative. That matters, especially in Virginia." Certain firms' letterheads, she said, might get our petition to the top of the governor's stack.

We tried. We played to lawyers' sense of justice, their sense of fairness—and, sometimes, their pride. We flattered, we cajoled. But it didn't work. We were turned down by nearly everyone.

By July, we were starting to get desperate. We had one last shot on our A-list: Hunton and Williams. It was one of the oldest and most prestigious firms in the state, counting among its alumni Lewis F. Powell, Jr., who served on the Supreme Court. Most notably, though, it was the first law firm in the country to establish an office solely for pro bono casework.

And they were interested—interested enough to ask us to meet near Marion, so they could visit Vince afterward and make sure he wanted to work with them. But first, over a lunch of overpriced sandwiches, sitting outside at a restaurant called the Wooden Pickle, Dawn and I had to make our case.

And I was nervous. It was a do-or-die moment. If we wanted any chance of getting Vince out, we needed Hunton and Williams's power, their expertise, and their legal muscle.

Things were awkward at first. At the table were a bow-tied senior partner, a junior attorney who seemed eager to make his mark, and a younger woman who was so quiet that I assumed she was an intern of some kind. While the men made their introductions and confidently ordered lunch, she arranged a notepad and her pens. When her colleagues ordered a beer, she stuck to iced tea.

"I can lay out the legal case in a minute," Dawn said as we waited for our food. "But I figured I'd let Benjamin tell you the story from the beginning. Benjamin?"

In previous meetings, I'd tried to keep things straightforward and professional. I had the idea that lawyers wanted to hear just the facts, that the injustice of Vince's continued incarceration was so obvious that all I needed to do was convey it in a neutral tone. I was wary of overselling the story; I didn't want anyone to think I was straining for dramatic effect.

But something was different that day. Maybe it was the first sip of my watered-down lager. Maybe it was the knowledge that this felt like our best chance. Maybe it was the expression on Vince's face the last time I'd visited him, when he'd asked me if he had a chance of getting out, and I had to tell him I didn't know.

Whatever it was, I felt a huge upsurge of emotion, sitting at that table, and I went for it.

"Vince Gilmer's story is an absolute tragedy," I said. "Medically, legally, morally—he has been failed at every turn, by every system meant to help people like him."

I tried to read the lawyers' faces for a reaction. Nothing. The men just calmly sipped their beers. The younger woman took notes without looking up. They were probably used to tragedies, I thought. They probably saw them every day.

"Look," I said. "As a doctor, I've taken an oath to do no harm. Harm is being done to Vince right now. The question I come back to, again and again, is simple: How can we treat people with severe mental illness, the people who need us the most, like this?"

Over the next thirty minutes, I told the story from the beginning. I didn't skip over anything—not my fear, not my fury, not even the creeping sense of failure I felt now, years in, at having not done more to help Vince. Angry, embarrassed tears sprung to my eyes, and when I wiped them away with my cloth napkin I saw that something had changed—the lawyers were nodding along.

"That's so wrong," the woman, Geri, said when I described the way Vince had been kept in solitary confinement for weeks at Wallens Ridge, despite his desperate pleas to see a psychiatrist; punished because he could not eat fast enough due to his worsening tremor and missing teeth; disciplined because he could not remember the prison rules or even find his cell, his mind mired in Huntington's-inspired dementia.

"You don't know the half of it," I told her.

A week after our meeting, Hunton and Williams officially signed on, throwing the weight of their pro bono division behind us, with Geri taking the lead.

Geri Greenspan was not, as I first assumed, an intern or a law student. She was in fact a rising star at Hunton and Williams. She had all the qualifications that typically accompany employment at such a powerful firm—Yale Law, a Fulbright grant—but she also clearly had a passion for humanitarian concerns. A veteran of the Peace Corps in Mauritania, she was particularly interested in humanitarian immigration cases. Humble with a folksy laugh, she was the perfect mixture of empathetic advocate and steely tactician.

The first time we spoke, Geri laid forth a comprehensive plan for clemency. We were in the car on the way up to Marion with Dawn.

"What we really need," she told Dawn and me, "is a compelling argument."

Geri knew that I had memorized the ins and outs of Vince's story and his trial and appeals process, and that Dawn had started putting together a spreadsheet of every evaluation, medical appointment, and prescription Vince had had since 2004.

"Now we just need to braid the whole thing into a coherent story," Geri said. "Fill in all the gaps."

One gap in particular troubled me: Vince's phantom psychological evaluation. I had seen an excerpt of Dr. Feix's official state evaluation during my reading of Vince's trial transcripts. But what about the other consultation, performed earlier, while Vince was still in Asheville? We knew that Vince's first lawyer, Steve Lindsay, had arranged for him to be examined by Dr. Tony Sciara before Vince was extradited, but I had never seen the results. Both Dawn and Geri thought that seeing them could offer us a clue to Vince's mental state closer to the time of the event.

So I called Steve Lindsay, who was more than happy to reminisce about his work on the unusual case.

"I knew something wasn't right with Vince Gilmer," Steve told me. "I knew from the moment I talked to him that there was something wrong with him, and it wasn't that he was a cold-blooded killer. I knew he'd done it, of course, and I knew that he'd be going away for a long time. His case was like an airplane on fire. But I thought that I could crash-land it into a mental hospital, not a prison."

I explained to Steve what we were hoping to accomplish with our clemency petition, then asked what he thought should happen with Vince.

"The abuse that he's put up with and the lack of appropriate care for his condition really offends me as a lawyer and as a person," Steve said. "I think whatever price a person has to pay for what Vince went through has been paid a long time ago."

"Seems fundamentally wrong to me to punish people because of their mental illness," I said. "I don't know the details of the Eighth Amendment, but his punishment sure seems both cruel and unusual."

"Courts usually get around that by saying that the punishment isn't cruel, or isn't unusual," Steve said. "For it to violate the Eighth Amendment it has to be both. But you're right, of course. A mental illness diagnosis changes everything. That's why I had Dr. Sciara evaluate Vince in Asheville."

"Why did this never come up in his trial?"

"Because I wasn't his lawyer anymore," Steve said.

It seemed completely bizarre that no one would have accessed these records before committing a man to life in prison. It was the only snapshot of Vince's mental health from the time immediately after Dalton's death. Maybe Nicole Price hadn't wanted to know what that looked like.

But when we attempted to contact Dr. Sciara, we got nowhere. He avoided us, stonewalling for weeks when Dawn asked for the evaluation. And when I drove to his office to confront him in person, I never got past his receptionist.

What was in those files? And why couldn't I see them? Like so much else in Vince's story, the details didn't quite add up. Something was missing. If only I knew what it was.

Every clemency petition is different, but ours would be made up of a detailed memorandum laying out the argument for a pardon and the assorted evidence supporting it: Vince's medical records, his court records, and affidavits from expert witnesses, prison officials, and other people who knew Vince before the night everything changed.

Dawn and Geri's job was not only to formulate a legal argument but also to persuade a politician that a conditional pardon was the right thing to do—and that granting it wouldn't hurt him, politically. In brief, they would argue that Vince was suffering from severe symptoms of Huntington's disease when he killed his father, that he thus lacked the ability to control his impulses, and that because he was never properly diagnosed with Huntington's, his trial was premised on incomplete information. Vince should have been found not guilty by reason of insanity—and even if found guilty, he should have been convicted only of voluntary manslaughter, not first-degree murder. Murder in the first degree required evidence of malice or premeditation.

Under Virginia law, voluntary manslaughter charges carry a maximum prison sentence of ten years. Vince had already been incarcerated for that long, and so his continued incarceration was disproportionate to his offense—especially since he required medical care that he could not receive in prison, and his disease would accelerate there.

Geri combed through case law, searching for legal precedents for Vince's case. This was difficult, because Huntington's patients are rarely violent. And when they are, often they are too incapacitated by the disease to enact lasting harm on others. Still, Geri found several comparable cases. The first was Glenda Sue Caldwell, a woman with Huntington's who had shot and killed her son and wounded her daughter in Georgia in 1985. Unlike Vince, Caldwell suspected she had inherited Huntington's, and her attorneys made it a key part of her case. Unfortunately, she was tried years before genetic testing, so doctors could not conclusively diagnose her, and she was sentenced to life in prison. When, nine years later, DNA testing became available, she was conclusively diagnosed and granted a new trial. The judge found her not guilty by reason of insanity.

Another case was that of Gerald J. Wood, who in 2001 was put on trial for fatally injuring a fellow resident at the nursing home where he was receiving treatment for Huntington's. He was deemed incompetent to stand trial.

There was also Tonya McKee, a woman who in 2012 was charged with murder after drowning her baby in the toilet of the homeless shelter where she was living. McKee knew that Huntington's ran in her family, and a court-ordered evaluation and DNA test confirmed a positive diagnosis. Suffering psychiatric symptoms from the disease, she was deemed unfit to stand trial.

These stories were horrible tales of violence and suffering. But they showed that Vince would—and should—have been treated differently by the justice system, had his diagnosis been known at the time. At the very least, he should have been able to win a not guilty by reason of insanity verdict, Steve Lindsay's original plan for him. And McKee's and Wood's cases showed that he perhaps should not have been deemed fit to stand trial in the first place—much less represent himself.

"It is absolutely crazy that anyone thought this man could represent himself," Geri told me one day on the phone, after hours of reviewing Vince's medical history and the trial transcripts. "He was so obviously out of his mind."

"They didn't know that at the time," I said. "They didn't believe him."

"They will now," Geri said.

That was my job: to recruit experts in Huntington's disease to our cause, and make it clear to the governor how serious and progressively debilitating a condition Huntington's was. We'd have to convince the governor that, with Vince's diagnosis, his continued imprisonment was unjust and unnecessary—that he needed more care for his Huntington's disease than the prison system could provide, and the only humane place for him was a medical facility. And that once there, he would not be a danger to himself or to others.

My recruitment efforts introduced me to a number of brilliant minds. After I gave a keynote speech about Vince's story at the Huntington Study Group's annual meeting, a group of experts—who would become invaluable parts of the clemency efforts—invited Dr. Angliker and me out for dinner. I recognized immediately that these scientists and clinicians were special, united by the challenge to cure this disease. Many of them had family members with Huntington's.

While some approached the disease with a classical neurologic perspective, others came from a social work background, and others saw the disease as more psychiatric in nature. Vince's was a medical story that was no mystery to them. Their presentations were about the hard work: helping people to survive the day-to-day of this disease, supporting care providers, and exploring novel therapies. They were both doctors and foot soldiers, while Dr. Angliker and I were the newbies, stepping into a battle these people had been fighting for decades.

Much of our conversation that night centered on a scientific question important to treating Huntington's: How do you steer a nerve cell away from dying when it is fighting for survival?

At first, I thought we were talking only about biology: how to manipulate fragile nerve cells to inspire them to live rather than die. But the more we spoke, the more I realized that treating Huntington's could also be a metaphor for the way we treat the incarcerated. What scientists hoped to do was figure out a way to redirect nerve cells toward survival: to rehabilitate them.

Wasn't that what we should aim to do with the people in our prisons, as well?

And maybe it was bigger than that, even.

Because in the end, all of us are a reflection of our own cells: vulnerable, and consumed by the will to live. All living beings, even single cells, share this struggle in common.

Reverence came from taking note of it.

Once I began connecting with people in the Huntington's community, it quickly became clear how much passion they had for learning about this disease. I could only imagine that there were communities like this for nearly any condition you could think of—thousands of people devoted to helping others live better lives. After the conference, Dr. Francis Walker, who had invited me to speak, was eager to introduce me to yet another resource: Lauren Holder, the president of the North Carolina chapter of the Huntington's Disease Society of America. Her father had Huntington's, and like all children of HD parents, she had struggled for years to decide whether or not to be tested. She knew the path her life would take if she had the genetic defect, after witnessing her father's precipitous decline. She understood that a positive result might prevent her from having children, and would take her life early.

For Lauren, the certainty of knowing was important, and so, at age twenty she was tested—and confirmed to have Huntington's. Her diagnosis helped her plan the rest of her life—and it inspired her to pursue advocacy for others like her and her father.

"I feel for Vince," Lauren said, when we met at a café in Winston-Salem one afternoon that spring. "What happened to him could happen to me."

Sitting at our rickety outside table that day, I couldn't help but scan Lauren for symptoms of the disease. Aside from a slight hitch in her gait, there were none—she spoke without any visible effort, her cognition was entirely normal, and she showed no signs of chorea as she lifted her soup spoon to her mouth.

But there was a sadness in her eyes. Huntington's had already had an enormous impact on her. The unknown had haunted her since she was a little girl. And more recently, she'd been fired from her job after her diagnosis was revealed. In 2015, she'd had to stop work in order to take care of her father. Now every day she faced her own future living with the disease.

"How do you feel about knowing you have Huntington's?" I asked.

"Like a normal person," she said, "who knows her life will be cut short. It has a way of sharpening your focus."

Lauren had used that focus in service of activism, and she became an invaluable resource to me as we drafted Vince's clemency petition. Her advocacy work taught me something powerful: Vince wasn't alone. There were thousands of people living with Huntington's, and people like Lauren and Dr. Walker were advocating to make the world a better place for them. Lauren's organization had drafted a program to help educate law enforcement in North Carolina about Huntington's and its symptoms, since people with Huntington's far too frequently are homeless and misunderstood by police officers. The training could de-escalate situations so that, faced with a person like Vince, police officers would be able to recognize symptoms and direct them to services providing assistance—not jail.

Lauren's diagnosis made me imagine an alternate path for Vince. She was a heartbreaking reminder of how things could have been different for him, had he been diagnosed earlier—had he or his father been tested, had he known he would decline neurologically. It made me sad to think that his life, and Dalton's, would have been so different.

But I also found Lauren's work incredibly powerful. Faced with a catastrophic diagnosis, she'd found the strength to make positive changes for her family and for others. Meeting Lauren inspired me to keep advocating for Vince that year.

So did the reaction of my patients. I had worried, at first, that members of the community might not appreciate the spotlight trained on them by *This American Life*, but in the end, almost all of them were supportive of our mission to get justice—and healing—for Vince. After an article on our work appeared on the front page of the Asheville *Citizen Times*, many patients of mine told me they kept a clipping on their refrigerator.

It was clear that the community still supported their doctor, that they wanted, as I did, for him to receive the care he needed. Once they knew I was involved in legal efforts on his behalf, the equation of the previous years flipped; rather than ask them for information about their old doctor, they asked me for updates about his current condition.

And I told them. I told them about his good days, his bad days, his moments of levity, and his dark nights of the soul. I told them about his symptoms and about our efforts to treat them, the various successes we had with the limited medication available to him.

"What a shame," Donna Burton, still Vince's most passionate patient advocate, would say when she heard all of this, shaking her head full of gray curls. "I wish I could still travel to go out there with you."

Mrs. Burton instead brought me letters for Vince at nearly every visit, written in her flowery cursive. She would give updates about the community, her creative pursuits as a poet, and even her own health—as though he were still her doctor, and she were still his patient.

"He may be in prison," she said, "but he is not a bad person. And what is happening to him is—I'm sorry, just wrong. So wrong."

"Maybe you should write another letter," I said. "To the governor."

"Well what's his address, honey?" she said, her eyes flashing. "I'll bring you one next time I come up here."

I laughed, but I was also moved. Moved and impressed: If this eighty-year-old rabble-rouser was ready to write a letter to the governor, then why couldn't I?

In order to win a conditional pardon for Vince, we needed to recommend a secure medical facility to take him in. I found myself in the odd position of advocating for Broughton Hospital: the same facility where Vince had picked up his father that fateful night in his truck, the same facility where I'd started my career. Broughton was secure, it had a dedicated geriatric unit to care for patients like Vince, and it was a place I knew well. By the summer, I was meeting with officials there and at the Black Mountain Neuro-Medical Treatment Center to make preliminary arrangements. Both facilities were within driving distance of Asheville.

That was increasingly important, because it was clear to us that if Vince were granted clemency, someone would need to be appointed as his legal guardian. We had to demonstrate to the governor that someone would be responsible for him once he was released. Gloria was too far away in Alabama, and she was now in her midseventies. By this point, I was the most constant physical presence in Vince's life.

"Do you think you could make that commitment?" Dawn asked over the phone. "I know it's a lot to ask."

I didn't have to think about it.

"Of course I can," I said.

Vince was a part of our family now, a kind of uncle figure to our kids. Kai and Luya were at the age when they were coming to their own understanding of right and wrong, and even they could see how obviously wrong Vince's situation was. It brought tears to my eyes, sometimes, overhearing my children struggle to reconcile what they knew to be right with the wrong that they saw so clearly every time we visited the prison.

But Vince's presence in our family also occasioned strain. Being close to him took enormous emotional labor, and it was taxing—for me, for Deirdre, for the kids. It is difficult to be fully present with your family and also, in the back of your mind, think of the concrete floor, the metal bed, the un-air-conditioned cell. I felt guilty, no matter where I turned my attention: Watching a movie with Deirdre, I would sometimes imagine Vince staring at a wall. Visiting Vince, I'd think of all the Saturday afternoons I was missing, teaching Luya to ride a bike or kicking the soccer ball around our lawn with Kai or taking a walk with Deirdre.

There was no solution, of course. But getting Vince out—getting this other Gilmer into a hospital close by—would make our complex family dynamic more normal for all of us.

As we drafted the clemency petition that year and the next, I tried to remain present in Vince's life. I couldn't get to Marion every week, but I visited him every other month. I brought him updates about our progress, asked for his input, and checked on his medications and health. Most important, though, I checked in on him as a friend. That's what we were now.

Every visit to Marion, I began our meetings with a few baseline tests: I asked Vince to stick out his tongue as long as he could; I asked him to extend his arms in front of him, keeping his palms facing up; I asked him to rapidly tap his index finger to his thumb. Huntington's patients have trouble doing all of these actions. By comparing his performance visit to visit, I could get a rough idea about how he was progressing.

There was no question: Vince was declining. He was increasingly having issues with swallowing, and his speech was growing more halting. When he walked toward me, he was like C-3PO from *Star Wars*, unstable and ready to tip over at any moment. His memory continued to deteriorate, and finding simple words was often a struggle. He still had to keep his cell number scribbled on the back of his hand so he could remember how to find his way back.

But overall, Vince seemed to be adapting somewhat to prison. Or maybe the prison was adapting to him. More often than not that year, the guards seemed to be leaving him alone. They even seemed to be looking out for him.

I wondered if this was partly because of my frequent visits. Many people in the prison now knew who I was. Some thought I was mounting a secret lawsuit against the DOC, some thought I was Vince's personal doctor, and others assumed I was Vince's skinny little brother.

"What did you say he has?" asked the CO in the visiting room one day, as Vince walked to the vending machine for snacks.

"Huntington's," I said. "Think Parkinson's, plus Alzheimer's, plus Lou Gehrig's disease."

This CO had led me into the visiting room multiple times. He was young, fifty pounds overweight, with a pencil-thin goatee and kind eyes.

"We all thought it was fake for a while," he said. "But since you've been coming, some of us have changed our minds. We know he's not faking. He acts out sometimes, and gives us weird looks, but we know he can't always help it."

I explained to the CO how Vince's brain worked—or, more accurately, how it didn't. How his diminished brain function meant that he had trouble understanding others' emotional expressions, and regulating his own—following rules, complying with complicated social norms. How Huntington's symptoms could wax and wane, sometimes making him grandiose and arrogant, while at other times inducing anxiety and depression.

"I'm keeping an eye on him," the CO said as Vince shuffled toward us.

And after that, he and several of the others did just that. When

Vince had outbursts, some of the COs responded with more compassion, or at least more understanding. They knew better how to defuse situations before they escalated with other inmates. They knew when physical pressure would have the opposite of the desired effect, agitating rather than subduing Vince. They knew when to leave him alone.

I held fast to these moments of humanity. Because as we drafted our clemency petition, it had become all too obvious to me that there were tens of thousands of people inside Virginia's prison system who needed psychiatric help. A 2014 report by the state inspector general found that the number of mentally ill people in jail and prison in Virginia had risen 30 percent since 2008, and also that the state's jails held three times as many mentally ill people as its hospitals. Virginia's situation more than mirrored the nation's—it was worse.

Things got even more dire after Dr. Angliker was fired in October 2014. The official reason was for sending an inappropriate email from his work computer—but I knew that was just a pretext. Colin himself had been fully aware that he had been on the chopping block since the moment the *This American Life* episode aired. In fact, he told me that the day after the broadcast, early on a Monday morning, a group of officials from the Virginia Department of Corrections had shown up at Marion, asking Warden Larry Jarvis to discipline him in some way. The pressure came straight from the head of the DOC, who had reportedly been contacted by none other than a furious Judge Randall C. Lowe.

"I'm not a company man," Dr. Angliker had told me over the phone. "I said what I said on your radio show because I believe it is true: We have failed Vince, and we have been failing people like him for a long time."

"What about your job?"

"To hell with it," he said. "I spoke the truth. If that means the ship goes down, so be it."

Warden Jarvis had refused to fire him on principle. But since then, the state had been biding its time. And after Dr. Angliker was fired, the Virginia Department of Corrections didn't replace him—at least, not full-time. They brought in someone two and a half days a week, then switched entirely to telemedicine. To make matters worse, several of the clinical staff left Marion in protest, further reducing inmates' access to mental health treatment.

Marion had been one of the few prison facilities in the state with a psychiatrist on staff to treat patients with mental illnesses. That was the entire reason Vince had been transferred there from Wallens Ridge. And now he was on his own again.

"They aren't even pretending to rehabilitate people anymore," I vented one night to Deirdre in our kitchen. "These are people who are known to have severe psychiatric problems: schizophrenics, people with PTSD, sociopaths. People the state has already deemed seriously ill, to the point that they've moved them out of the general prison population and into a facility where they can receive treatment. And now there's no one there to treat them."

"Do they get any treatment at all?" Deirdre asked, frowning at a stack of Luya's finger paintings, deciding which would go on our crowded fridge.

"Telemedicine visits," I said. "Every few months. It's hard to receive effective therapy when you are locked up in solitary confinement."

"That's so wrong," Deirdre said.

She was right. But it was more than just wrong: It was a public health crisis. It exemplified everything that was broken about how Virginia treated its mentally ill inmates.

According to the Virginia Department of Corrections, the purpose of prison is to "help people to be better by safely providing effective incarceration, supervision and evidence-based reentry services."

But Vince's experience after a decade in Virginia institutions had not been safe, nor effective, and certainly not evidence-based in my mind. If people were sick behind bars, wasn't it both cruel and unusual to deny them appropriate treatment? According to Hippocrates, that spelled harm.

That got me thinking. If so many incarcerated people were mentally ill, it wasn't much of a stretch to believe that perhaps mental illness was one of the reasons—if not the primary one—for their incarceration. And if that was the case, justice needed to start before a person needed a lawyer or found himself behind bars.

Maybe it started in an exam room, in a psychiatrist's office, or on a guidance counselor's couch.

Drafting my affidavit for Vince's clemency petition, I found myself pondering these larger questions of justice. But when I visited him, I was hyper-attuned to the local, the specific, the day-to-day realities of a sick man trying to survive in prison. And I was increasingly grateful for the compassion from some of the guards. Hopeful, too. Because if a group of corrections officers could see the humanity in Vince, and learn to change their behaviors in ways that tangibly improved his life, I had faith that things could change.

Not just for Vince, but for everyone.

15.

WAITING

Getting a man out of prison takes a lot of time. It requires mountains of paperwork, months of research, and hours of interviews with experts—not to mention the sluggish machinations of politics. The legal team's efforts to put together Vince's clemency petition stretched through 2014, then 2015, then into 2016—long enough for Geri and Dawn to each get pregnant and give birth. Deirdre and I gave Dawn Luya's old orange jogging stroller. We cooed over baby pictures, recommended parenting books, and shared stories from the newborn trenches. All of it as we worked to free a terminally ill man from prison.

Dawn, Geri, and I were part of one another's lives now. Our mission had brought us together, and the more I got to know them, the more I admired their passion and dedication to providing a legal voice for those who couldn't speak. Either one of them could have entered far more lucrative areas of law. I once joked with Dawn that she was like the family medicine doctor of the legal profession: undervalued and underpaid, but doing the important work.

"Everyone told me to go into corporate law," she laughed, "but I just couldn't do it."

"Ditto," I said. "But cardiology!"

All those hours driving back and forth to Marion, talking on the telephone discussing strategy, and editing Vince's petition over Google Docs had fortified in us a sense of mutual trust. It was not lost on any of us that this trust was built on anger: righteous anger at the injustice being done to the mentally ill in our prisons and in our courtrooms. This fury was our fuel.

It also occasionally boiled over.

One Saturday in May 2016, I drove up to Marion to visit Vince. I didn't really have any updates for him, but I was trying, as usual, to keep tabs on his health and his mood. Marion had still not replaced Dr. Angliker, so I sometimes saw myself as his surrogate physician, in addition to his legal counsel and, of course, his friend.

But this confluence of roles did not sit well with the new warden of Marion prison. When I went to check in that day, I was told I wasn't allowed inside.

"Looks like your visitation rights have expired, Dr. Gilmer," the CO behind the counter said. I'd met her before—she'd been on duty several times when I visited, and we'd gotten to the point of light pleasantries during check-in. She'd said, one of the first times we spoke, that she'd known from the very beginning Vince had Huntington's. She had seen it before in other prisoners. Sometimes she gave me updates about how he was doing.

"He's been down lately, still walking slow, getting lost after chow," she would say. "But eventually, he finds his cell."

Today, though, she had a stern look on her face.

"There's a flag on your file," she told me. "I can't let you in. I'm afraid you're going to have to take this up with the warden."

Before grabbing my ten-dollar stack of change, I reminded her that I had just driven three hours for the visit. Was there any way she could make an exception for me?

She just laughed.

"Honey, we don't make exceptions in prison."

It was a long walk back to the car. I stood there in the parking lot looking through the razor wire, through the multiple fences and into the reinforced windows, imagining Vince sitting there alone, desperate to talk to someone. I was pissed, and on the long drive home, I got even angrier.

So I called the prison.

I was on hold for about fifteen minutes. But somewhere outside Johnson City, Tennessee, just as I was about to hang up, a voice came on the line.

She introduced herself as Dara Robichaux, the new warden at Marion.

"I understand you are confused about your visitor status," she began, in a clipped voice.

"I'm not confused at all," I said. "I just don't know why you've revoked my privileges. I'm the medical representative for his legal team, but I'm also Vince's friend. I've been visiting him for years."

I was trying to keep my voice down, but something was happening to me. I am by nature an even-keeled person and have always prided myself on being calm under pressure. But a huge swell of anger was rising in me, and I felt helpless to stem its tide.

"So you should know," Warden Robichaux continued, "legal visits are not allowed on weekends."

"But this wasn't a legal visit," I said. "I'm on the legal team for Vince Gilmer, but they visit him during the week, and I'm a practicing physician—"

"I'm not interested in your personal availability," Warden Robichaux continued drily. "I am interested in the continued security of my prison and the safety of the people incarcerated here."

The wave of fury crested.

"If you were interested in the safety of the people incarcerated in your prisons," I yelled, "you would have hired a staff psychiatrist after Colin Angliker was fired!"

"That is none of your concern," Warden Robichaux said.

"What are you talking about?" I scoffed. "It's all of our concern."

"What happens in my prison—" Warden Robichaux began.

But I cut her off.

"Vince is a very sick man," I said. "And he's not alone. There are hundreds of men—thousands—just like him in prisons all over this country. What are we doing to help them? What are you doing to help him?"

I was surprised at the strength of my anger—and the pleasure I felt expressing it. It was like a release valve had been turned and steam was coming out of my mouth.

Is this what justice would feel like? Or was this how Vince felt nearly every day, staring at the bars of his prison cell, trying to will the door to open with the sheer force of his hope and desperation?

When Warden Robichaux hung up on me, I was still fuming.

I reapplied for and was granted visiting privileges three months later—as a friend, not as a part of the legal team. But by then it didn't matter. In June 2016, we finally submitted Vince's clemency petition to Virginia governor Terry McAuliffe. It had taken about two and a half years to put everything together. In the end, the petition was more than a hundred pages long: thirty pages from Dawn and Geri outlining the argument for a conditional pardon, and seventy pages of supporting statements from doctors, lawyers, scientists, and people who knew Vince. Dr. Walker and others from the conference contributed. There were statements from Gloria, Tommy, and several of Vince's former patients.

There was one from me, too: a ten-page letter to the governor telling the entire story from my perspective. It ended with a direct and emotional appeal to his sense of fairness and justice:

> Vince has been and continues to be remorseful for kill-
> ing his father, and wants to do what he can to prevent
> other families from suffering the same devastation from
> Huntington's disease.

Whether you believe Vince Gilmer's trial was unfair or
not, he has now spent more than a decade in the Virginia
Department of Corrections, a prison system that is not
designed to treat terminal neurologic and psychiatric
illnesses. I can attest that this experience has been nothing short of emotional and physical torture. It is not long
before he will die in prison.

The fact that we continue to allow prisoners who pose
no threat to the public to die while incarcerated, without the presence of their families and loved ones, is a
question that goes beyond punishment—it is one of humanity and morality.

With all due respect, I ask you, sir, to make the humane
decision to grant a conditional release to Dr. Vince
Gilmer so that he may experience better treatment and
sunlight prior to the imminent dark days awaiting him
from Huntington's disease.

Soon after we submitted, I asked Dawn, "What do we do now?"

"We wait," she said with a laugh. "You're going to have to be patient."

This was hard for me to swallow. I thought I'd *been* patient. But
if I'd learned anything over the past two years, it was that the legal
world moved at a different pace than medicine. In medicine, I'd
grown accustomed to a kind of immediate gratification—a patient
presents with symptoms, you examine them, and then you take
steps immediately to address the problem. You don't wait until a
seemingly arbitrary time, after the midterms but before the end of
a governor's term, when a clemency petition is more likely to be
granted. If a patient needs surgery, you operate *now*.

But submitting a clemency petition was not like removing an

appendix. It was more like making a movie: It required the simultaneous, coordinated work of dozens of independent actors, most of whom were helping for free and also had other work. Geri was busy leading Hunton and Williams's pro bono partnership with the University of Virginia Law School, and Dawn was working all that year on the case of William Morva, a floridly mentally ill man who was on death row in Virginia—and whose case had unsettling resonances with Vince's.

William Morva had been incarcerated since 2005, when he and a friend had been arrested for attempted armed robbery. A year later, while awaiting his trial, Morva knocked out a sheriff's deputy, took his gun, and fatally shot a hospital security guard at Montgomery Regional Hospital, where he had been receiving treatment for a sprained ankle. After escaping from the hospital, he disappeared into the woods near the Virginia Tech campus, where a manhunt ensued. He was captured the next afternoon, clad in only boxers and a blanket—but not before fatally shooting a police officer.

Morva's case, like Vince's, at first seemed relatively straightforward. There was no question as to whether he'd committed the crimes. But also like Vince, Morva's mental health—or lack thereof—presented issues to the legal system. Before his trial, he was diagnosed as suffering from schizotypal personality disorder, which causes difficulties forming social attachments, odd behavior, and often eccentric views. Morva's conduct, even before his arrest, had alarmed his family and friends: Self-identifying as a survivalist, he consumed a raw diet, rarely wore shoes, and for long periods lived outdoors, in the woods near Virginia Tech.

Schizotypal personality disorder is not schizophrenia. It's a different type of cognitive fallibility. People with schizotypal personality disorder often fear social interactions and human relationships, but they typically can discern reality from delusion. As a result, the jury had not deemed Morva's personality disorder as important to his innocence or sentencing: Charged with two counts of capital murder, he was found guilty and sentenced to death by the Commonwealth of Virginia.

Dawn had first met Morva in 2009, early in her law career, about the same time I was starting at Cane Creek. In fact, he was her second client. Right away, she said, something seemed wrong.

"What I was seeing with William was so much worse than a personality disorder," she explained. "He was obviously psychotic and delusional. He believed that if we could just overturn his robbery conviction, everything else would fall into place. He referred to himself as 'Nemo.' He said that he'd attempted his initial escape because government forces were conspiring with the police to murder him in his cell—and he wasn't immortal yet."

So Dawn and a team of others did some digging. And she realized that the lawyers in the original trial had not delved very deeply into Morva's history of mental illness. They had never contacted many of the friends who had information about his mental state, and when they had, they hadn't asked for enough details about his slip into delusional thinking, his bouts of intermittent homelessness, his conviction that he was the target of a government conspiracy, or his litany of paranoid delusions.

In 2014, Morva's representation had him reexamined by a forensic psychiatrist, who diagnosed him with delusional disorder. Had this diagnosis been made before his trial, Morva would likely have been sentenced to life in prison without parole—not death. Dawn and a team of lawyers at the Virginia Capital Representation Resource Center had been mounting a habeas corpus case for more than seven years to ensure that an inmate suffering from severe mental illness would not be executed by the state.

To hear Dawn tell it, Morva had not exactly made things easy for them. He often refused—sometimes for years at a time—to meet with her or the other lawyers, who had slowly become part of his retinue of delusions. He believed that they had intentionally sabotaged his case, and at one point filed a complaint on his own behalf with the U.S. District Court accusing them of defamation. Affidavit by affidavit, he had disputed the claims made by those supporting his habeas case, the very people trying to help him.

By 2016, that team was nearing the point of no return. After a petition to the Supreme Court of the United States failed, they had only one option left: clemency.

The first time Dawn told me about William Morva, I immediately thought of Vince. There were major differences, of course. Morva was on death row, while Vince had gotten only life. Morva was hostile to his attorneys, while Vince was grateful for our help.

But both men had misdiagnosed mental illnesses, both were delusional at the time of their offenses, and both had been severely misunderstood at their trials. The jurors quickly declared both of them guilty. Both men had spent years deteriorating while incarcerated, so that they barely resembled the people they'd once been. And now both men had only one shot left to have their fates changed: the governor.

It was hard for me not to think that Morva's case was a kind of canary in the coal mine for Vince's. If Governor McAuliffe refused to grant the clemency application Dawn's team had spent months compiling—after years of state and federal habeas proceedings—Morva would be executed within the year. And if he sent an obviously mentally ill person to die by lethal injection, what hope was there for Vince?

We didn't expect to hear from the governor until the end of his term in late 2017, when many clemency petitions are decided. But as we waited, I resolved, as ever, to make sure Vince had visitors at Marion. I didn't always go alone, either. That first Thanksgiving visit with my family had gone so well that we repeated it in 2014, 2015, and 2016. Each time, my children grew more accustomed to the prison, more comfortable there. They grew to think of Vince as their friend, too. They played Uno with him and mailed him drawings. Their hugs grew longer and sincere. And at Christmas, when Vince sent us a ripped-out page from a coloring book, depicting Santa on his sleigh, they proudly posted it on the refrigerator.

It greeted me every morning—a pink and white Santa, shaded in with wax crayon, next to the greeting HE KNOWS WHEN YOU'VE BEEN GOOD OR BAD. The colors were off—Blitzen and Vixen were an odd shade of yellow—and the artist frequently strayed outside the lines, but I knew how much effort Vince had expended to keep his hands anything close to steady, or to write on the bottom of the page: *To the Gilmers. Love, Vince.*

I helped Kai and Luya write letters to him, in which they filled Vince in on their school lives and the exploits of our dog, Sammy. And Vince almost always wrote back. He cherished each contact, because he had so few of them.

"Those letters brighten the day a bit," he told me.

I wanted to do more for him. So one weekend, a couple of months after we submitted Vince's clemency petition, I sought out Tommy Ledbetter at his farmers market jam stand. We hadn't spoken since Sarah and I interviewed him. And although he'd asked to be removed from the *This American Life* story, he'd listened to it the night it aired.

"I thought you did a real good job," he said. "I'm glad y'all are telling his story."

I told Tommy that I was working with some lawyers to put together a clemency petition for Vince, and that I was going up to Marion to see him in a week.

"Think you could take a day off from the farmers market?" I asked. "I know he'd love to see you."

Tommy's face clouded over briefly.

"I don't know," he said. "It's been a long time."

"Think about it," I said.

A few days later I got a call at the clinic. He was in, he said.

So several weeks later, after Tommy got clearance from the prison, we drove up to Marion together. Tommy brought jam and toast for the ride, along with a thermos of coffee, which we shared. I was struck, as usual, by his easygoing charm and kindness—and also by the guilt he so clearly felt about not seeing his friend.

While driving to the prison, Tommy explained that he hadn't really known what to do when Vince was found guilty. In a way, Vince's imprisonment out of state took some of the pressure off him. It was clearly painful for Tommy to think about his friend, not being able to do anything for him after the trial.

"We all just had to pick up our lives and move on in order to survive," Tommy said.

I remembered Tommy saying that he didn't think Vince should be released unless he could be treated for his mental problems. I told him a little about his current situation—medicated, not violent, but without real care from a psychiatrist.

"You know," I said, "you were one of the only people to really get it. I didn't understand what you meant at first when you told me that he wasn't the same Vince, that he was a different person. But I do now."

"I couldn't make sense of it, either," Tommy flatly stated.

"Well, a lot of people believed that something was wrong," I said. "But you actually saw it. You knew that something had radically changed. And that what happened to him could happen to anyone."

Tommy looked at me, puzzled.

"You didn't think he'd become a psychopath," I said, trying to explain. "You didn't believe that he'd always been a sociopath, and had just been good at hiding it."

"No, of course not," Tommy said.

"You said something that really stuck with me," I told him. "*We're all just one step away.* That's true, you know. Huntington's is just a hereditary disease. It could happen to anyone."

"But it didn't," Tommy said. "It happened to my friend."

I was nervous about how the two men would react to seeing each other. I asked if Tommy wanted me to leave him alone to visit Vince by himself, but he said no—which was a relief, since the only place for me to go other than the visiting room was my car. As we signed in and made our way through the metal detectors, Tommy seemed nervous, but it was hard to tell if it was because of the prison's atmosphere or the prospect of meeting his friend for the first time after eleven years. Tommy, I knew, had a healthy fear of the law. And prisons are not the most congenial environments.

That day there were only two other people in the visiting room: two Black men in oversized T-shirts, one of them wearing a Charlotte Hornets hat with stickers still on its flat brim. They were visiting their brother, they told me when we sat down. He'd been inside for five years and suffered from bipolar disorder.

"It's good that you're here for him," I replied, pleasantly surprised to be having a conversation with other visitors. Usually, people didn't talk in the visiting room. A particular shyness seemed to arise there, a desire to hide the palpable shame from others. I had felt it, too, at first. But these two men were open and honest, laughing with each other, sharing stories about the old days. I found myself grateful to them.

"There're a lot of sick people in here," I told Tommy. "Vince is convinced that there's another guy with Huntington's in his unit."

"What do you think?"

"I don't know," I said. "The only incarcerated person I'm allowed to see is Vince."

When Vince walked in the room, he looked good to me—or at least, he didn't look any worse. But he didn't register at all with Tommy, who glanced at him once and then away. It took me a moment to realize it: Tommy didn't recognize him.

Vince didn't seem to recognize Tommy, either. So when he shuffled over to our table, I stood up and walked toward him, wrapping him in the bear hug we'd grown accustomed to giving each other. Then I stepped aside and took him by the shoulder.

"Hey, Vince," I said. "This is Tommy, remember? Your friend. He wanted to come visit you."

Vince's face didn't change at first. Or more accurately, it changed in only the normal ways, shifting in its usual involuntary progression of grimaces and tics. He looked confused, painfully searching his memory bank.

Tommy stood up, seemingly unsure of what to do. He smiled faintly, his hands shoved into his pockets.

"Hey, Vince," he said.

"Tommy," Vince said, finally placing him. He paused as his brain caught up with his eyes. Then he broke out into a huge smile, and his shoulders relaxed.

"Oh my god," he said. "Tommy."

We talked for an hour and a half. It was a bit awkward at first. I had to keep reminding myself that these two men hadn't seen each other in eleven years—and that during that time, their lives had gone in very different directions. Tommy's son, who as a young child had been Vince's patient, was now nearing middle school. The jam venture that Vince had helped fund now had jars of its wares all over Asheville's restaurants and co-ops. Tommy and his family had moved on. They were thriving.

The two friends caught up with each other, but it was clear early on that Tommy was keeping himself somewhat at a distance. He asked some questions about Vince's life, but Vince wasn't all that interested in talking about life in prison. He repeated some of his old standbys—the "unholy torture" at Wallens Ridge, the quest for calories—but mostly he wanted to talk about the old days.

"Remember Jack of the Wood?" he said. "Remember kayaking? Where was it, what's the word, what's the word . . ."

"The Nantahala," Tommy said. "How 'bout the time we spent just hanging out on the porch and playing some music? I miss those days."

I tried to give them some privacy by pretending to need things at the vending machine. I fake-deliberated over the fried pies, pondered the potato chips. And when I got back, Tommy and Vince were excitedly talking about their favorite singers.

"Was always more of a Willie Nelson guy, myself," Tommy was saying.

I dumped my bounty on the table, and Vince immediately pulled a Snickers and painfully opened a Mountain Dew before spilling it all over his shirt.

"I liked," he said, "I liked the guy. . . ."

He gummed the chocolate bar as best he could, then shakily washed it down with the remaining toxic-algae-colored soda. He paused, unable to remember the name.

"Glory days," he sang, in a reedy, off-tune, and hoarse tenor. "Glory days, glory days, glory day-ay-ays."

"Bruce Springsteen," I said, laughing.

Listening to Vince's out-of-tune warble, I realized something striking: It had been over ten years since he had heard music. He didn't have a radio or an MP3 player in the prison, and there were no performances or sound systems there. For over a decade, his requiem had been the clank of cell doors, the yells of other inmates, and the sound of his own thoughts, racing through his head. He had become accustomed to listening to the beating of his own heart, to the point that it was distracting.

Compared to the other indignities he suffered, a lack of music might seem relatively minor. But it was hard for me to imagine, because music had been one of my most important coping mechanisms throughout the entire time I'd known him. I had a Vince Gilmer liberation soundtrack that I turned to almost daily, filled with songs by Americana acts like the Avett Brothers and Johnny Irion. When I got discouraged, I often imagined Vince walking out of prison to Langhorne Slim's "Be Set Free."

Vince had no such remedy, although he had confessed to me that sometimes, he heard music. He knew that it wasn't real, that it was only his overwhelmed brain trying to carve out a space for peace. But it helped, he said.

Usually, at the hour mark of a visit, Vince would get fatigued, his mind slower, his posture drooping, unless he had an extra Mountain Dew. But today, he stayed sharp and alert to the end. I could see how much it meant to him. He hadn't seen a friend in about ten years. He hadn't seen anyone from the glory days, the days when he was a well-respected doctor, a normal guy who liked to boat on the weekends and play guitar with his friends. Being with Tommy let him become that person again—let him, for just those ninety minutes, transform back into the man he'd once been.

The two friends didn't touch over the course of the visit, and when it came to an end, I wondered how they would say goodbye. Would Tommy promise to come again? To write? Would they shake hands?

"It was so good to see you," he said. Then he stood up and walked to the other side of the table.

They hugged for what seemed like five minutes, then the CO came to lead Vince back to his cell. Vince slowly traversed the room, looking back at the door to the prison and giving a little wave. We waved back. And when we stepped into the air-locked space that would take us back to the outside world, Tommy turned away so I wouldn't see him use his sleeve to wipe the tears from his eyes.

"How do you feel?" I asked in the parking lot.

"Like I've just seen a ghost," Tommy answered.

That's what Vince was: the ghost of his former self. Not just neurologically, either. Back in Cane Creek, memories of Vince were vanishing, one person at a time. For Vince's loved ones and friends, this wasn't intentional. People's lives must march on, out of survival, or convenience. As I was learning, it was hard—both physically and emotionally—to maintain a relationship with someone in prison.

Getting him out would be even harder.

16.

COUNTDOWN

In November 2016, I got a call from a 347 area code. A man named Michael told me he worked for CNN and was producing a segment on medical mysteries.

"I loved your *This American Life* story," he said. "Would you be interested in partnering with us?"

My first instinct was: *Absolutely not.* But the longer I talked to Michael, the more I liked him. He said he was still a medical student at Stanford but was working at CNN to become a medical TV journalist. He referenced *Brain on Fire,* Susannah Cahalan's memoir about her bizarre experience with a rare form of encephalitis that left her delusional, violent, and confused.

"Your attempts to diagnose Vince remind me so much of that book," he said. "The strangeness of his behavior, the post-incarceration mystery diagnosis, the way no one believed him—it's such a sad but important story to tell."

"Hopefully, it'll have a happy ending," I told him, before filling him in on the clemency petition.

I was trepidatious at first. But a national spotlight on Vince's case might pressure the people in charge to make the right decision. So a few days later, I flew to New York, met Michael and the other producers at the CNN studios, and spent the afternoon taping interview segments.

It was a bit surreal. I felt, sometimes, like I was playing myself on television: looking straight into the camera, take after take, putting forth the image of a doctor who was impartial and who believed that Vince's plight was just plain wrong. I didn't want Vince's story to become merely another piece of dramatic entertainment. I didn't want anyone to think I was drawing attention to myself.

But it was difficult not to question my own motives, after a free flight into JFK and a fancy lunch at Columbus Circle.

"Great, Benjamin," the lead producer, Monica, said from the darkness on the other side of the camera. "Let's try that again—just be yourself. What do you think of this crazy coincidence—you and a killer having the same name?"

It was nothing like Sarah's process. And it wasn't just the makeup, the camera, or the lights. It was what I *didn't* hear from Monica, the questions that *weren't* being asked. Questions like:

Why is this so important to you?

What do you hope to achieve through Vince's case?

How might Vince's case affect the trajectory of mass incarceration?

The makeup artists darted in front of me, touching up the shine on my forehead, tucking a wisp of gray hair behind my ear. I thought about what Deirdre would say if she saw me here.

This isn't just a medical mystery, is what I wanted to yell between takes. *This is about a sick man who is dying in prison. This is about mercy. This is about the core of our ideals. This is about our fundamental humanity.*

"Was that okay?" is what I actually said, after take four.

"You're doing great," said Monica.

After a full afternoon of shooting, I invited the CNN team to join me on a field trip to visit Dr. Tony Lechich, who ran one of the largest treatment centers in the world for terminal Huntington's patients. It was a short walk away along Fifth Avenue, bordering Central Park, and I was sure they'd find it interesting.

Everyone politely declined.

But I wasn't alone. A good friend of mine, Jamie, had come down from Maine to see me, and we met up outside the CNN headquarters. As we trudged against a chilling headwind, I explained how I had met Dr. Lechich at a Huntington's conference, was inspired by his gregarious and soulful commitment to terminal Huntington's patients, and had arranged for a tour of the residential facility—the oldest in the nation—where he cared for more than fifty Huntington's patients, around the clock.

Dr. Lechich's facility had wonderful views of the park, and from the street it looked more like a museum than an assisted living facility. But once Dr. Lechich welcomed us inside, it was clear we weren't going to be looking at art.

Patients were shuffling around, some using walkers, some in wheelchairs. Some were talking loudly while others sat quietly in bed, being fed pureed food. Some were ambulatory, and some seemed sedated. But each patient lit up as Dr. Lechich talked to them.

Dr. Lechich told us that the older gentleman pacing the halls, his mouth silently writhing, was a brilliant retired mathematician who was hanging on to his autonomy by still walking. A man twisting his hands and looking out the window, eyes vacant, had for years been a bookseller on the Upper West Side, and still occasionally quoted lines from *Henry V.* The woman in her fifties confined to a bed in room twenty-two was a former pediatrician. Her speech was hard for us to make out, but Dr. Lechich understood every word and caressed her head while bragging about her medical career.

Dr. Lechich's commitment to his patients was palpable, his love for them radiant. They adored him, and it was clear that he had made a special home for each of them, a place where they were understood and treated with dignity at the end of their lives.

But it was also an overwhelming environment: the chatter, the shuffling feet, the food being dropped all over the floor, the confused stares from the patients. To most people, walking through such a facility would be an unsettling experience.

It certainly was for Jamie.

"Is it always like this?" he asked.

"Every day is completely unpredictable," Dr. Lechich replied, smiling. "I never know what to expect around here."

After an hour, it was time to go, and I thanked Dr. Lechich for sharing his world with us. As he led us out, we passed a team of nurses checking in for their shifts, pulling on gloves and scribbling down notes. They would be up all night.

Outside it was dark, and the late fall air chilled me to the bone as the sun sank behind the skyscrapers. I zipped up my coat, put on my hat and scarf, and thrust my hands into my pockets. Jamie stood frozen, tears filling his eyes.

"What a cruel disease," he said. "I had no idea."

I nodded and started crying myself, maintaining the Gilmer tradition of weepy men. It was hard to stomach the intensity of so many tragic stories, housed under one roof. After spending years watching Vince's slow decline, it wasn't hard to imagine where his story would end. He would resemble so many of the patients we'd just met.

But as we walked through Central Park that night, through the East Green and into Sheep Meadow and back again, I also cried for the amazing healing that Dr. Lechich and his team provided. Dr. Lechich's approach was one of the greatest examples of doctoring I had ever seen. He had renounced a lucrative career in urban private practice to take care of one of the most vulnerable patient populations you could imagine.

How might things be different, I thought, if Vince had been confined to a place like Dr. Lechich's facility, instead of a Virginia prison? How might he have fared if he'd been diagnosed earlier, or resided in a private room under a compassionate physician's care, instead of sleeping on the concrete floor in his bare prison cell?

Maybe Broughton could be that place for Vince. I wasn't sure. But it wouldn't matter if we didn't get him out.

The CNN piece wouldn't air for several months. Until it did, for the rest of 2016 and most of 2017, Dawn, Geri, and I were in what we called a "cone of silence."

We knew that governors often waited until the end of their terms to grant clemency. Pardons—even conditional pardons—can be politically risky, especially when the crime was violent. According to Dawn and Geri, it was better not to publicly pressure the governor too early.

"Why not?" I asked, exasperated, sometime early in the year. "Vince is a ticking time bomb. Every day counts if you are a dying man."

"Unless there is evidence he's going to die in the next six months," Geri said, "a high-pressure campaign could backfire. We want the governor to be thoughtful about Vince's case. We want to provide space for him to come to the right decision on his own without fearing the PR consequences."

"What consequences?" I asked, my voice cracking. "Like McDonnell got?"

Just a few weeks after I'd stood outside the governor's mansion that night in Richmond in 2014, and just ten days after he'd left office, former Virginia governor Bob McDonnell had been indicted on federal corruption charges. He and his wife had accepted over $130,000 in gifts from a donor, including Rolex watches. McDonnell was convicted and sentenced to two years in federal prison, and I had fantasized that he and Vince would be cellmates.

But McDonnell never spent a day behind bars. The case ended up before the Supreme Court, and they overturned the conviction.

"I know this is frustrating, Benjamin," Dawn said.

"You're damn right it is," I said. "Vince has been behind bars for thirteen years. The governor was tried, convicted, and exonerated in two and a half."

"We just have to be patient," Geri said. "The state has to do its due diligence."

I knew that the secretary of the commonwealth said they were looking into Vince's case, and that the Virginia Parole Board also had to conduct its own investigation before the governor could make a decision. Doing due diligence took time.

But knowing the process and accepting it were two different things. I was already starting to worry:

Was it too late?

Waiting for a clemency decision quickly became intolerable for me. In a single moment, with barely more than a snap of his fingers, Governor McAuliffe could completely alter Vince's course and my life. That he hadn't already done so angered me. That we might still have weeks, months, nearly a year to wait—it kept me up at night. I spent hours trying to discern the governor's attitude toward illness, the death penalty, and incarceration.

Stress took its toll. I was distractible, impatient with the kids, and absent from Deirdre on our infrequent date nights in downtown Asheville.

"You need to take care of yourself before you burn out," Deirdre told me one night over tapas at Cúrate, where we'd retreated after a long week. "You've spent half of this dinner on your phone."

In between bites of *espinaca* and *pan con tomate,* I had been reading an interview with the governor, combing it for clues about how he would respond to our petition. I put my phone down now, made a show of turning it off.

But Deirdre wasn't buying it.

"I want my old Benjamin back," she said. "The one who paid attention to me. Now I don't even know where I am on your priority list. And I'm worried about you. You're running yourself ragged."

She was right. As a teacher, I was always counseling my students to guard against burnout, one of the most pressing problems affecting physicians' health—especially emergency medicine and primary care physicians. The constant stress of being responsible for patients' lives, the endless medication refills and patient questions, and the punishing call schedules could wreak havoc on a doctor's mental health. It could be hard for physicians to leave the clinic in the evenings and transition back to their normal lives as spouses and parents. Letting yourself think of something other than a spiraling patient, or the labs you didn't order, or the correct medication dose for someone who really needed it could make you feel heartless and selfish.

"I'm sorry," I said now to Deirdre. "I know I've been all over the place. I just feel so helpless."

"You're not," Deirdre said. "You're doing everything you can for him."

It didn't always feel like that, though. Sometimes it felt like the only thing I could do for him was visit on the weekends.

So I did it as often as I could.

Oddly, the months of waiting were happy ones for Vince. I might have been stressed, but he was relatively stable. Although he still had no direct access to a psychiatrist—outside of occasional telemedicine visits—he had twice been bused the three hundred miles to Richmond to see a neurologist there. No new Huntington's treatments had been considered, but he was receiving daily doses of an SSRI, and the knowledge that a team of lawyers and doctors was working on the outside for him gave him hope—hope that I encouraged at every visit. I challenged him to start imagining life after prison and tried to convince him that he had a message to share with others. I told him I would organize medical students to come to Broughton to visit him so he could teach them about Huntington's. I reminded him that once there, he could receive visitors anytime—not on the schedule of the warden.

I liked to help him dream about the day of his release, rehearsing how it would go: I would facilitate the medical transportation from Virginia to North Carolina, driving him in an ambulance through Asheville to eat at his favorite pizzeria, Mellow Mushroom. Then we would descend the mountain to Broughton, where he would be greeted by his new medical team, walking freely into his new home.

I was surprised that he, at times, seemed more resilient than I did. For many incarcerated people, prison life enforces a condition of learned helplessness, a sense of powerlessness stemming from trauma. Like victims of abusive relationships, prisoners often feel that their destiny is out of their hands and cope with this realization by relinquishing what little agency they have left, sinking into a deep, lethargic depression.

Not Vince, though. Despite all of the traumatic insults he had endured, he still maintained a will to live and to give to others. His instinct to keep fighting for his life inspired me each time I saw him. He had bouts of depression and even suicidal ideation, but each time they came, he beat them back, asking for help and reaching out: to prison authorities, to the prison social worker, to me. He told me that he wanted to live—that all he wanted to do was live long enough to help people again, in some way.

If anyone felt helpless during those months, it was me. But when I sat with Vince in prison, and he asked me how I was doing, it felt absurd to say that I was anything but fine. What, after all, was my anxiety about his situation compared to his? How serious could my marital or family stress be to him?

But Vince didn't see it that way. When I opened up to him, as I did increasingly often that year, he was empathetic. He told me to spend at least an hour a day outside with Luya and Kai—fresh air and the outdoors brought people closer, he said. That's why he'd taken the nontraditional approach with patients at Cane Creek, moving the clinic outside if he thought a patient needed a walk or even just a few minutes at his beloved koi pond. He told me that Deirdre needed to be affirmed, that what she needed wasn't grand gestures but daily care.

"Make her coffee and bring it to her," he said.

It was a little odd to be getting marital advice from a divorced man serving a life sentence. But I welcomed Vince's input. It helped me see again the doctor he had once been—the unconventional and caring man who was interested in the totality of his patients' lives.

It did both of us good to come full circle in this way: to let him, for a brief moment, take care of me, treat me, give me advice. And for me to become someone who needed his help.

I wasn't allowed to bring Vince gifts, but I could mail books to him, and once they'd made it through the prison censor, we could discuss them. That year, we sent him Bryan Stevenson's *Just Mercy,* Doris Kearns Goodwin's *Team of Rivals,* and Laura Hillenbrand's *Unbroken,* about Louis Zamperini's time in Japanese POW camps. Although Vince's ability to write was deteriorating, his fine motor skills atrophying, he could still read and retain information. My visits came to resemble a prison book club, with each of us expressing our reaction to what we'd just read.

After Deirdre sent along a book on yoga, Vince asked for a more spiritual book to read.

"I can't do the poses," he said, "but I liked all the . . . what's the word?"

He sat, openmouthed, moving his jaw as though to dislodge the word from behind his teeth.

"Philosophy," he concluded.

So when I got home, I sent him excerpts from *Reverence for Life,* Albert Schweitzer's 1933 treatise laying out his life's philosophy, with the most important parts highlighted. When I returned, Vince had read them, and we talked about what Schweitzer's revolutionary idea meant to us, as doctors.

"It means respect for every living thing," he said. "Animals. The sick. People like me."

"I think what Dr. Schweitzer is saying is that we all share in this struggle to survive, that we all have a will to live," I told him. "It's what makes us human: recognizing that we are all fallible, and that we share a common purpose—to live."

"That's why I became a doctor," Vince said.

"Right," I agreed. "It's our duty as doctors, to help those who are less fortunate."

Vince got tearful at this.

"It gave me so much pleasure to be able to help my patients at Cane Creek," he said. "It's all I ever wanted to do. If I could only do it again, I would ask them for nothing."

"They know," I assured him. "They know."

Vince's most important visitor during the summer of 2017 was Trudy, an investigator for the Virginia Parole Board who had been charged with examining him for the governor as part of the state's due diligence. She had visited him before, the previous fall, but this time was different: She was in the final stages of evaluating his current health status and had just spoken to Detective Martin, who was still arguing that he was faking his symptoms.

So before Trudy arrived, Vince mustered up all the strength he had to speak clearly and walk steadily. He wore his best Sunday suit, an orange jumper. He knew that it was probably the most important meeting of his life, since Trudy's job was to assess his current condition and answer the central question, in the governor's eyes: Was he sick enough to be granted clemency?

This seemed like an odd question for a man who struggled to walk, talk, swallow, and think, but, according to Vince, the interview went well. Geri, too, was getting encouraging feedback from the secretary of the commonwealth.

"We're on final approach," I told Vince during one visit that summer. "Everyone's confident and hopeful that the governor will do the right thing and get you out of here."

Vince thanked me. But I'd started to notice something: When it came to his legal case, there were rarely follow-up questions. He never asked about how he'd done with Trudy, or the governor, or what his life at Broughton would be like on a day-to-day basis—things I would have wanted to know if I were in his shoes. It was as though he could not project beyond the bars of his prison cell, into the outside world—into the future. He could live only in the present, looking back into the past.

Similarly, his letters to me were usually one paragraph in length, concerned with one simple idea. This indicated to me that it was becoming harder for him to process complex thoughts, a natural consequence of his illness.

Yet Vince always appreciated my enthusiasm. Sometimes I truly felt that enthusiasm, and sometimes I felt like I was overstating it to make his life more bearable. Or was it for my own sake that I was holding on to hope? To prove that all our work was not for nothing?

During our visits, I always sensed that I received more than I gave to Vince. The time we spent together arrested some of the guilt I perpetually carried for not doing enough for him. I had assumed the responsibility for getting him out of prison alive and now understood, perhaps for the first time in my life, what it meant to be truly powerless.

Driving home from the prison after our visits, I sometimes imagined the world in a split screen. On one side was my life: mornings holding my stethoscope to patients' chests; afternoons at MAHEC teaching medical students how to use a portable ultrasound; evenings kicking the soccer ball with Kai, reading Luya bedtime stories, and relaxing with Deirdre, sharing a glass of wine on our back porch.

On the other side, in parallel, was Vince's daily routine, as he'd described it to me: the cold gray light in his cell blinking on at six A.M.; the slow shuffle to the cafeteria for a lunch of tasteless processed food; the struggle to find his cell after eating; the hours on his back on the cool cement floor, listening to the cries of fellow prisoners and the metallic clang of cell doors being shut. And through it all, the daily awareness that he was getting sicker—the ever-slower steps, the longer pauses between words, the struggle to eat without teeth and to swallow effectively.

Vince had many compulsions. But I was learning that I had one, too: It was to liberate him and end the torture that he had endured for years. I knew that failure would haunt me for the rest of my life. No one could understand this—not Deirdre, not my family. Losing Vince would be even worse than losing a patient—it would mean losing a friend.

I could not bear to think of him slowly dying in prison, the film of his life unspooling to no purpose. I did not want to see, in my mind's eye, the purposeless suffering of his days—especially when my own were so idyllic in comparison.

So I kept working. I kept calling, I kept writing, I kept driving up to the prison for games of Uno and sugary snacks with Vince. When we were together, the split screen vanished, absorbed into one shot. We were just two Gilmers, onscreen together: both of us waiting, both of us hoping, both of us under our cone of silence.

On July 6, 2017, the state of Virginia executed William Morva. He died at 9:15 P.M. by lethal injection. When asked if he had any last words, all he said was "No."

A dozen protesters had picketed the Greensville Correctional Facility, where Morva was being held. The United Nations had called for a halt to the execution. In the weeks prior, twenty-four

Virginia state legislators had pleaded with Governor McAuliffe to grant clemency. Even the daughter of one of Morva's victims had asked for him to be spared.

And for a time, it had seemed as though that might happen. As recently as that summer, Governor McAuliffe had claimed he was losing sleep over it. But in the end, the execution went forward as planned.

"I personally oppose the death penalty," Governor McAuliffe wrote in a statement.

> However, I took an oath to uphold the laws of this commonwealth regardless of my personal views of those laws, as long as they are being fairly and justly applied. Thus, after extensive review and deliberation consistent with the process I have applied to previous requests for commutation, I have declined Mr. Morva's petition. I have and will continue to pray for the families of the victims of these terrible crimes and for all the people whose lives have been impacted.

Dawn was devastated.

"None of it mattered to him," she said. "All the calls, all the media attention, all the appeals to common decency and humanity. The governor doesn't even believe in capital punishment and he still let William die."

Dawn hadn't seen William Morva in four years. Convinced that she and other lawyers were plotting against him, he had refused to meet with the people who were trying to save his life. He remained delusional. But she had never given up on him, never given up hope that the governor would do what she saw as the right thing: grant mercy to a severely mentally ill man.

"I'm sorry for your loss," I told her, as if someone in her family had just died. Then I realized that was exactly what had happened.

She had committed so much time, so much selfless energy, fighting for William Morva's life. Her work was unconditional advocacy, the sort of dedication that we typically reserve for only those we love.

"It shouldn't be like this," she began, fighting back tears. "The state should not be in the business of killing its own citizens."

I agreed. As a doctor, I believe everyone deserves to die with dignity, of their own volition. And on the phone with Dawn that day, I found myself thinking about a similar situation I'd recently faced in my own practice.

I had diagnosed a patient with ALS—Lou Gehrig's disease—and only a few months later, he'd deteriorated to a critical point. Bedridden, unable to speak or breathe on his own, he had been admitted to Mission Hospital in Asheville with severe pneumonia. He didn't have long.

This patient was heartbreakingly young, in his late fifties. Soon after his initial diagnosis, he had told me that he wanted to die in his own bed, surrounded by his wife, his daughter, and his dog. And even though he was now hooked up to a ventilator in the sterile confines of the intensive care unit and could no longer speak, he indicated to me that he had not changed his mind.

It was my duty to give him the death he wanted. So two days before Christmas, despite resistance from the critical care doctor and lukewarm support from the hospital's ethics committee, my medical student Lauren and I procured an ambulance and a ventilator to transport him home. After a bumpy ride over a snow-covered, steep mountain road, we made it to his house, then carried him inside to his bed, managing not to trip over or disconnect the ventilator. He couldn't talk, but his eyes sparkled as his dog jumped into his lap and licked his face.

I will never forget the next six hours. It was the most intimate party I have ever attended. The room was filled with his favorite music, *The Best of the Moody Blues.* Friends and family drank wine and reminisced, celebrating his life and toasting him, laughing and crying. When a gun-toting Appalachian pastor in overalls swung by, everyone scrambled to hide their wineglasses and joined him in a heartfelt prayer.

And then, a few hours later, it was time. The party could end only one way, and we had rehearsed it: I would give my patient some medicine for anxiety and pain, then remove the tube that kept him alive. This was what he wanted: five beautiful minutes to smile unrestricted, to say his last goodbyes, and to kiss his wife. He was joyous during those last moments, surrounded by the people who loved him the most.

And yet, watching this beautiful scene, I hadn't been able to help comparing my patient to Vince, imagining what his experience would look like if we couldn't get him out in time. The horrible mental image of Vince prostrate on the prison floor, suffocating alone in his cell from his own secretions, crying out to the darkness without a response, without anyone telling him he was loved or re- minding him that his life had meaning—it haunted me.

Was that how it had been for William Morva?

My conversation with Dawn that day reminded me of the funda- mental difference between how medicine and law treat death. In medicine, we can exert some control over how someone lives or dies. Doctors can try one antibiotic and, if it fails, try another; we can give fluids and norepinephrine to maintain blood pressure; we can anticipate when someone is dying and comfort them in their last moments.

Dawn's and Geri's work as lawyers always kept them at a slight remove, dependent on a jury, a judge, or a governor. There was a limit to how directly they could change their clients' fates, because they didn't have anxiolytics or ventilators—all they had were words.

Words that might inspire.

Words that might fail.

Most clemency petitions are addressed in the final six months of a governor's term, and we were counting down the days. We knew, by that point in the summer, that Governor McAuliffe was considering a 2020 presidential run. We were on tenterhooks imagining how that would affect his decision. Would an impending presidential campaign incline him toward mercy, or would it force him in a more conservative direction?

We had been unsure all year. But now, with Morva's death, we had our first indication of how the governor was leaning.

And it didn't look good.

The CNN piece aired in late August 2017. In the end, it was exactly what I was afraid of: a dramatic medical mystery tale.

Instead of a nuanced exploration of what it meant to have Huntington's disease in prison, or a tragic narrative about the frailty of the human brain, the network leaned into the most sordid aspects of the killing. Instead of an evenhanded recounting of the tragic events of that night, the producers filmed elaborate reenactments and zoomed in on lurid crime scene Polaroids. The entire production had the look of a horror movie. It was sensationalistic, flashy, and empty.

Vince's Huntington's diagnosis didn't even come into the story until the last ten minutes. And although it showed Steve Buie, the legal team, and me patiently explaining how the disease helped illuminate what had happened the night of the killing, the episode ended with Detective Martin reiterating his belief that Vince was a malicious killer, a faker who should remain in prison. He got the last word.

I was angry. I felt betrayed. More important, I was furious for Vince. For years, we had known that Detective Martin was wrong—that they were all wrong, all the people who had portrayed him as a sociopathic murderer, deceiving everyone around him in order to cover his tracks. And now Detective Martin was on national television, repeating the charge, in an episode that focused less on our broken criminal justice system or Vince's broken brain than on what his hands had done on that fateful night.

I drafted a short, fiery email to CNN to express my regret about their telling of the story. The story did not move the needle toward justice, I wrote. Advocacy had not been the objective of their reporting. They hadn't focused on what really mattered.

They politely responded that they were not taking sides.

After that, it was an all-out sprint.

We had broken the cone of silence for the CNN piece, but it had backfired. So in the months remaining to us, the legal team decided to focus less on media attention and more on political pressure. If we wanted to influence the governor's decision, we would need to enlist other powerful political figures to the cause.

I'm a country doctor. I'm not well connected with lobbyists or politicians or legal influencers, certainly not in Virginia. But the week after our Gilmer Thanksgiving celebration at the prison with Vince, I spent an afternoon on Yellow Mountain with my friend Jay. He'd trained as a lawyer for over a decade before retiring to his cabin on the mountain to write a novel and devote his life to land and water conservation. He was the kind of guy who knew everybody. He had played pickup basketball with Michael Jordan; testified on Capitol Hill about federal land policy; dined with the governor of North Carolina—and, yes, helped edit my personal statement for medical school.

So when I mentioned that I was trying to find my way to North Carolina governor Roy Cooper's ear, I was hardly surprised to hear that the state's attorney general was a childhood friend of his.

"Good guy," Jay said. "Maybe he can help us."

Jay put me in touch with his friend, who passed me off to the governor's chief lawyer, William McKinney. My plan was to get him on the phone before Christmas and explain what we needed: a statement of support from Governor Cooper, welcoming Vince back as a North Carolinian while assuring Governor McAuliffe that we had found a secure medical facility for his continued care, Broughton Hospital.

Which is how I found myself in the kitchen in my bathrobe, a turkey baster in one hand and my cellphone in the other, trying to get the general counsel for the governor of North Carolina on the phone before Thanksgiving dinner. The kitchen was a mess, Deirdre's parents were coming over, and I'd forgotten to brine the turkey.

I'd also accidentally made decaf instead of regular, burned the pancakes, and completely failed in my attempts to get the kids to clean their rooms before their grandparents arrived.

So I had my hands full, literally and figuratively, when my phone began buzzing through the pocket of my bathrobe.

"Dr. Gilmer? This is William McKinney," a clipped voice on the other end of the line said.

Over the next twenty minutes, I outlined the legal team's proposal. I tried to keep it short and sweet. I also tried to keep the barking dog out of earshot and the oven from burning the sweet potato casserole.

"We'll have to do our own due diligence, of course, and I'll need to speak to Dr. Gilmer's counsel," McKinney said, when I'd wrapped things up. "But I think the governor may be open to listening."

He paused.

"How often do you see him?"

"Every few months," I said. "Actually, we were there just last week. My family goes up every November to celebrate Thanksgiving with Vince. It's become a tradition."

I thought back to the previous week: Kai beating Vince again in Uno, Luya shyly presenting Vince with a drawing she'd done of him, Deirdre holding Vince's hand before we left. We had all been in good spirits.

"Next year, when I'm out of here," he'd said, "we're all going to have a big turkey."

Now Deirdre rushed in, eyes rolling as she saw the messy state of affairs in the kitchen. Within seconds, she had put most of it in order: turning off the tap, sliding the turkey into the roasting pan, quelling the chaos that I had naturally inflicted.

"It may be the holiday season," McKinney said to me, "but I'll be in touch."

"Happy holidays," I said.

I said that a lot over the next few weeks. Not just to my kids and my family, Deirdre and her parents, but to anyone I could think of who might be able to help: current legislators, federal judges, college presidents.

It didn't matter that it was the holidays. It didn't matter that I was calling people at home. Desperation had made me shameless and fearless. Time was running out.

A week before Christmas, Mr. McKinney called to tell me that Governor Cooper needed more time before he could consider making an interstate announcement. I understood this was a reasonable, safe response on their part. He mused that since Governor McAuliffe had only a few weeks left in office, he might not rule either way on our petition but instead pass it along to the next governor, Dr. Ralph Northam, who was set to begin his term in the new year. He encouraged us to be patient and wait. Maybe he knew something we didn't?

A part of me understood, even hoped he was right. Dr. Northam was a neurologist, which could help our cause.

But emotionally, I was through waiting. I wanted to know. I held on to the hope that one day, out of the blue, I'd get the excited call from Dawn or Geri announcing the news we'd all worked for: that Vince was free, that his nightmare in prison was finally over, that we'd succeeded.

But Christmas arrived without any word from Governor McAuliffe.

17.

HEALING CRIME

We waited. Through Christmas, through New Year's Day. No news.

We exchanged gifts. I gave Deirdre a gift card for a massage, Luya a bicycle, and Kai a new soccer goal. I wasn't allowed to send gifts to Vince other than books, but I wrote him a long letter of encouragement—telling him to keep his spirits up, that an answer would come soon. On Christmas Eve he sent us his customary Christmas card, this one a painstakingly crayoned depiction of Santa Claus on a rooftop, his globular belly stuck inside a chimney. On the inside it said: *Love to the Gilmers, Vince.*

We went to parties. At the Cane Creek Christmas party, I had my usual two spicy margaritas as we exchanged our "dirty Santa" gifts. Everything was completely normal. How odd to think that just five years before, I'd been waiting on a letter from Vince, terrified and hopeful—and now I was waiting on one from the governor, feeling much the same way.

We rationalized: There was still time before Governor McAuliffe left office. Maybe he was taking a cautious approach to his decision, reading our petition in detail, consulting his own office's findings.

December stretched into January, the holiday season giving way to the long early days of the new year, cold and leafless, the bright sun trying to resuscitate the dead grass. We heard rumors again that Governor McAuliffe was seriously considering a 2020 presidential run. We heard he was savoring his last days in office, that he'd already welcomed staffers for his successor, Dr. Ralph Northam.

We thought: *This is a good sign.*

We thought: *This is a bad sign.*

We read that Governor McAuliffe was pardoning a man who was serving 123 years for armed robbery, then that he'd given freedom to a woman serving thirty years over eighty dollars of crack cocaine. We looked up the number of pardons he'd granted over his term: 227, more than any governor in history.

We white-knuckled it through the first week of January, then the second.

Waiting has a way of making you reflective. Trying to ward off my frustrations over not hearing from the governor, I found myself thinking back to the beginning. Not just of my friendship with Vince—but to the very beginning of the story we were still creating together.

June 28, 2004. On that day, Vince Gilmer killed his father. And I, Benjamin Gilmer, was working in Gabon. We were continents apart, but I saw a new point of connection between our lives.

According to my journal, on the day that Dalton Gilmer died, my team visited the village of Bifoun as part of our outreach to the surrounding communities of Lambaréné. After a long truck ride over weathered roads, we stopped at a small cluster of huts, chickens and dogs running between them. At its epicenter was one small house clad with rusted sheet metal and recycled wood that allowed the smoke from inside to leak out through its walls and ceiling. Seated in a wooden chair next to the house was a woman with a floral shirt and an apron, striking a pose, arms outstretched, head cocked, while a young woman coiffed her thick, black hair. Surrounding her was an entourage of children, and an older man sat at her side.

Everyone's eyes were fixed on her. It was clear who the boss was here.

We stepped out of the truck and Mama Sophie, our chief nurse, greeted the woman.

I smiled at her, too. She didn't smile back.

"Who is this?" I asked Mama Sophie. "Is this the chief's wife?"

She laughed.

"No, Benjamin," she said. "*Voilà, la chef du village:* the chief herself."

I paid my respects in my best French, dressed in scrubs, sweating and covered in dust from the ride. And the *chef du village* did the same, thanking us for the work we would be doing that day.

Then she did something surprising. She stood from her chair, stepped aside, and motioned for me to sit down.

"*Assiez-vous, docteur!*"

At first, I hesitated. I wasn't sure what the local custom dictated—would it be better to refuse this invitation, as a sign of deference and respect to her authority? Social customs in Gabon could be very complex.

But the look on the *chef du village*'s face was so open and encouraging that I decided to take her invitation at face value. I walked up to her and humbly sat down on her wooden throne.

She laughed, then I felt her touch my shoulder.

"*Aujourd'hui, le médecin americain sera le chef,*" she said.

Today, the American doctor will be in charge.

No matter that I was just a third-year medical student. I thought of what the *chef du village* said all that day, as Mama Sophie and I treated children with acute malaria, schistosomiasis, and malnutrition in a small shack. What an awesome responsibility the *chef du village* had reminded me I had—not only to heal the bodies of her people, but also to be a leader, an advocate, even if it was only temporary. She trusted me, because she understood that we had come as an act of service and compassion for her people.

After nearly fifteen years of school, no one had ever empowered me the way she did. She had looked me in the eyes and asked me, a stranger, to help her people as if they were my own.

Wasn't that why I wanted to be a family medicine doctor? To treat not just the individual, but their family, their village? To effect broader change by addressing the things that really matter— keeping families together and communities healthy?

Working that day in Bifoun, I came to a new understanding of what my fellowship's namesake, Albert Schweitzer, had meant by "reverence for life." Before then, I'd thought of the phrase as a kind of philosophical anachronism. I knew that it was Schweitzer's attempt to formulate a basic theory of ethics, that he'd come up with the idea while piloting a boat down the Ogooué River and running into a hippo that threatened his life. Here's how he put it in his autobiography:

> By playing an active role, man enters into a spiritual relationship with this world that is quite different: he does not see his existence in isolation. On the contrary, he is united with the lives that surround him; he experiences the destinies of others as his own. He helps as much as he can and realizes that there is no greater happiness than to participate in the development and the protection of life.

But I didn't really understand what Schweitzer meant until I was within a few miles of the Ogooué myself. What had always seemed basic and obvious revealed itself as intentional and radical. As an idea, it was so simple that a child could grasp it. But as an actual ethic, something you did every day, it had immense power. It sounded easy, but in actuality it was perhaps our greatest human challenge.

All these thoughts ran through my mind as I distractedly went about my days, waiting for an announcement from the governor's office at any moment. I thought of Albert Schweitzer, stepping over chickens and stray dogs to get to his patients. I thought of Vince Gilmer at Cane Creek, holding mice in his hands, then releasing them into the fields. I thought of my pastorly fathers, serving last rites to their dying patients and parishioners. I thought about removing the breathing tube from my patient's larynx, surrounded by his family.

I remembered all the men Vince had told me about, there in the prison with him. The boy in his twenties who heard voices at night. The middle-aged man who spoke about his imaginary friend like he was a real person. The gentleman in his sixties whose dementia was so bad he didn't even remember, day to day, that he was in prison.

What did "reverence for life" mean, for people like this? For Vince? What was left to revere?

Seemingly nothing. But that was precisely Schweitzer's point: that true reverence extended compassion to the hopeless, the destitute, the scorned. It included the sick and the healthy, the poor and the rich, the free and the imprisoned. It included addicts and thieves, murderers and the men they killed. The chickens and the stray dogs, the mice and the man who held them: Reverence for life was unconditional.

That's why it was so difficult, and so necessary.

Schweitzer had found reverence for life in equatorial Africa, Vince in Appalachia. I'd found it in both of those places, too, but also in the bare visiting rooms of Wallens Ridge and Marion. It was through healing others that we three doctors had found a path to reverence—and I knew that honoring my patients' journeys, walking with them, gave my life meaning.

I felt the dawning of an idea, one that had been building in me for months. Ever since the night in front of the governor's mansion, I'd been asking myself why justice and medicine were often so far apart, so siloed, in both our policies and our personal lives. It was undeniable that the two were as intertwined as the two snakes of the caduceus, that centuries-old symbol of medicine. And yet each was often isolated from the other, working independently.

Maybe the solution was, on its face, simple.

We didn't need to fix crime. We understand that, like cancer, it cannot be eliminated.

We needed to treat it.

Healing crime. It sounded simplistic, almost naïve. As though the world's doctors could just take to the streets with their stethoscopes, diagnosing and curing all of society's ills. It sounded like something Luya—who sometimes referred to Vince's prison life as "time-out"—would say.

But the more I thought about it during that holiday season, the more complex it seemed. Healing crime was both an idea and a set of actions. It would require widespread, sweeping change in the way we understand medicine, crime, and rehabilitation. It would demand of us to think very differently about the health of communities, and the importance of propping up those who are just surviving. It would ask us to reconsider the American concept that we all have equal opportunities—because we don't. It would mean thinking like a child again and examining our world with fresh, loving eyes.

Over the course of my time working with Vince, I'd come to realize that the way we treat the mentally ill in this country is fundamentally broken. The United States has one of the highest incarceration rates in the world. A full 25 percent of the world's incarcerated population is within our prison walls. And, according to the Bureau of Justice Statistics, over a third—37 percent—of that population has a history of mental illness.

The reasons for this could fill an entire book. In fact, they very soon would—my friend Dr. Christine Montross was at that very moment writing *Waiting for an Echo,* an in-depth study of mental illness in prisons. Christine is a psychiatrist, professor, and poet who has written extensively about the ways our brains betray us. So as I cast about for direction in early 2018, I reached out to her to better understand the systemic underpinnings of Vince's situation.

"Basically," she said when I called her late that January, "the system is a mess."

Christine told me that a high rate of incarceration, coupled with decades of attrition within the state's mental health infrastructure, meant that prisons had become the landing pad for the majority of the nation's mentally ill. Patients who once would have been treated and rehabilitated in clinical settings like Broughton or my stepfather's rural mental health center were now, more often than not, trapped in the criminal justice system, relegated to prisons designed to punish, not heal.

Then Christine told me one of the most shocking things I had ever heard: There are *ten times* more seriously mentally ill people in the nation's prisons than in its mental institutions.

"Of course, most mentally ill people do not commit crimes," she said. "But those who do have few opportunities for rehabilitation, because they are denied effective treatment once they are incarcerated. We have a reactive, not proactive, approach."

"It's an upstream-downstream problem," I said.

"Exactly."

In medicine, physicians attempt to head off medical issues upstream, before they float downstream to become major problems. Every day, we try to identify anxiety before it blooms into major depression, or treat high blood pressure before it becomes a stroke, or counsel lifestyle changes before obesity evolves into diabetes.

But as Christine explained to me, the disappearance of mental health infrastructure—institutions, community health centers, and, especially in rural areas, trained psychiatrists—has meant that many of our most vulnerable citizens never encounter any institutional help until they're well downstream, over the waterfall: after they've committed crimes or behaved in a way that has landed them behind bars.

And was that where we wanted to rehabilitate our most broken minds? As Vince's experience in Virginia taught me, most states lack comprehensive programs to treat their mentally ill incarcerated populations. Most prisons don't staff a full-time psychiatrist. There is no ongoing therapy to address the reasons why an inmate might be there in the first place. That means illnesses go undiagnosed and untreated, putting prisoners at risk for violence, worsening mental disease, and—once they are freed—a higher rate of recidivism.

Vince had once told me, "If you are mentally ill, it only gets worse in here. It's only a matter of time before the mental hell catches up with you."

The more I thought and read about it, the more the mental health crisis in our prisons seemed to lay bare a central question about the purpose of incarceration: Was it to rehabilitate, or simply to punish? Despite all its claims to the contrary, a prison system that disproportionately locked up the mentally ill, then threw away the key—providing few resources to treat what was often a root cause of their crimes—was not seeking to heal. Whether through lack of funding, a rapacious profit motive, or sheer apathy, the American prison-industrial complex had become one focused almost solely on isolation and punishment.

The scholars and activists whose books I was reading were actively trying to change a system that they knew to be broken. Reading their work convinced me that I had to do my part—that I had a moral duty as a physician to bring a clinical voice to the fight for justice on the part of the incarcerated and mentally ill.

But I realized that I was part of the problem, too. For forty years of my life, I didn't seriously question why we locked up so many mentally ill people in our country. I didn't consider the larger pattern of how medicine and the criminal justice system intersected. I also didn't recognize the extent of our brain's vulnerability: to stress, to trauma, to contemporary life. Yes, in my care of patients, I tried to see past mere symptoms—to understand the roots of why one's nervous system could be so out of balance, to move past the brain to its owner. But I hadn't ventured into the darkness of my own privileged brain until Vince showed me his.

To be sure, I had always viewed my work as a moral calling, one I undertook in response to depressing political and economic realities. I had witnessed firsthand how vulnerable rural populations of this country had been left behind by larger institutions, medical corporatization, and shrinking public health departments.

Around the time that we submitted our clemency petition, I had filled in for a doctor in a neighboring rural community, and there I participated in the delivery of one of the last babies born in Avery County. Weeks later, the hospital's labor and delivery unit was shut down. This was the hospital where four of my cousins had been born and where my uncle had died. And now women could no longer deliver their babies in their own community. Within two years, western North Carolina closed four more rural labor and delivery units, a consequence of for-profit medicine and the corporatization of healthcare systems.

I had seen, over and over as a young doctor, how the business of medicine interfered with the quality of care. But medicine and the criminal justice system? This was a concept that had evaded my attention. I had several formerly incarcerated patients, but it was all too easy to avoid the conversation, to not talk about their shame or trauma, when I had only fifteen minutes to spend with them. It was much more convenient to prescribe an antidepressant to treat depression than to consider the range of experiences—including prison time—that might have brought my patient to need the medication in the first place.

I had always known that I had a duty to protect the health of my community. But I didn't always see the full picture, and in the end, it took the bizarre coincidence of Vince's and my life colliding to teach me something simple: My community, for whom I shared responsibility as a physician and as a fellow human, was far larger than I thought. My community wasn't just Cane Creek, or Appalachia, or rural America. It was also the community of our incarcerated, the community of our mentally ill. It extended beyond the exam room, beyond even the bars of the Buncombe County jail.

As the *chef du village* had told me that day back in Gabon, I was responsible for her people, too. But if I hadn't applied for a job at Vince's old clinic, and my name wasn't Gilmer, I probably never would have seen the inside of Wallens Ridge State Prison or Marion Correctional Treatment Center. Hell, I wouldn't have even noticed the outside, despite years of driving right past Marion on I-81.

That's by design. Most prisons in this country are engineered to be invisible. Hidden in rural communities, they are places where humans are stowed away and forgotten. Widespread privatization has only hastened the trend toward invisibility. Who, after all, wants to be known for making their money off the backs of those behind bars?

When we don't see the places where people are incarcerated, it becomes easy not to see incarcerated people. It becomes easy not to think about the widespread disparities—of race, of class, of cognitive fallibility—that affect the way justice is decided in this country. It becomes easy to ignore the young man who was sentenced to ten years in prison for an addiction to opioids that ravaged his developing brain when he was a teenager, changing it forever. The woman who drowned her child while in the throes of severe post-partum depression and woke up in a jail cell. The insecure child who joined a gang for a sense of safety and belonging only to find himself on the wrong end of a homicide charge.

I'm not saying that every crime is the result of undiagnosed mental illness, the same way that I'm not saying Vince Gilmer killed his father solely because of Huntington's, or his sexual trauma. But the truth is, with more than a third of federal inmates having a history of mental illness when they arrive to prison, to deny that mental illness is one factor among many leading to increased incarceration rates in this country is absurd.

In our approach to the mentally ill, we are not looking hard enough for healing solutions. If we saw the world through a "reverence for life" lens, we would accept and honor our shared moments of cognitive fallibility. Many other countries are already doing this. As Dr. Montross reminded me, Norway and Sweden have made returning incarcerated people back to their communities a priority. Norway's Halden Prison, a facility designed to hold that country's most dangerous criminals, achieves a recidivism rate that is half of ours—20 percent, as opposed to our 40 percent—by focusing on cognitive therapy, mentorship, and keeping their inmates engaged with the community.

Prisons like this are designed to minimize suffering and limit—not expand—the scope of incarceration. Our system in the United States, by contrast, aims to fill the cells. Tied to bringing in more profit, obsessed with punishment and payback, it needs a constant new stream of bodies to justify its continued expansion. Our prison system is an extension of Jim Crow, and we have not yet committed ourselves to healing as our endgame, nor recognized that mass incarceration is a public health crisis.

We haven't even gotten close.

Healing crime wouldn't just mean radically reforming the

prison system. It would mean abolishing the prison system as we know it. We have an obligation to do better.

We have lost sight, as a culture, of the people in our nation's prisons and jails. As a result, we have lost sight of the values that our nation professes to hold dear: respect for the individual, responsibility for our fellow man, and a fundamental recognition of shared humanity.

We have lost our reverence for life.

To heal crime, we must first heal ourselves.

On January 13, 2018, Governor McAuliffe's last day in office, I turned to the internet, hoping to see some update. But all I saw was the news: The Charlotte Hornets had beaten the Utah Jazz. President Trump's lawyer allegedly paid an adult film star for silence in a 2006 affair. An early morning ballistic missile alert had been broadcast across Hawaii, prompting hours of panic.

Nothing about Vince. Nothing about the governor. His term was over.

Maybe the response to our petition had gotten lost in the chaos of transition. Maybe Governor McAuliffe was kicking the can down the road to the next person to hold his office.

I called Dawn and Geri. They were optimistic.

"No news might be good news, in this case," Dawn said. "Sometimes, these governors don't want to take the hit for pardoning someone, but they don't want to condemn them, either. So they'll just pass the buck on to the next governor."

"If Governor McAuliffe wanted to deny clemency," Geri said, "I think we would have heard by now. He would have already said no."

"So we're happy with just not getting an answer?" I asked.

"This could be a blessing in disguise," Dawn said. "Governor Northam is a neurologist."

We made calls, but the governor's office was in disarray, in the midst of transition.

We left increasingly anxious messages with the secretary of the commonwealth.

We resigned ourselves to waiting.

Then, during the third week in January, after interviewing medical students in Chapel Hill for a rural health scholarship, as I climbed into a car full of my colleagues, Geri called.

"Vince got a letter," she said.

I held my breath, my hand on the passenger-side door, one foot inside the car and the other still planted on the pavement. A flock of geese flew overhead in formation, squawking through the icy sky, and I followed them with my eyes until they disappeared over the trees.

"Denied," Geri said.

"Tell me what the letter said," I pleaded, two days later, sitting across from Vince at Marion.

As Vince described the letter, I stared at the state seal of Virginia on the wall behind him, that emblem I'd passed so many times on the way into Wallens Ridge. It was hard now not to imagine Vince as the body splayed on the ground, beneath the foot of Virtus, a spear stuck into the ground at his side.

Vince said the letter was a one-liner, simply declaring that his clemency had been denied. No apologies. No details. No hopeful words.

"When did you receive it?"

"A week ago," Vince said. "After breakfast. It was all I got that week."

This, Dawn and Geri had told me, was a stunningly cold way to deliver the news. Usually, legal representation also received communication from the state so that they could confer with their clients, prepare them for success or head off disappointment. That, after all, was the purpose of legal counsel: to interpret, to act as a buffer between the client and the justice system.

But the commonwealth had sent their denial of Vince's clemency directly to him, without warning us. We'd had no way of prepping Vince for this rejection—which I had promised would not come. We didn't know until after he did.

And ever since then, we'd been worried about his emotional state. That's why I'd bolted to Marion on this Saturday morning: to make sure he was okay, that he hadn't slipped into depression or something worse. In truth, all of us were worried about suicide.

But in the visiting room, Vince didn't seem especially downcast. Resigned, maybe defeated, but not despondent.

"How are you feeling?" I asked.

"I'm okay," he said sadly. "Governor McAuliffe denied me."

"This is wrong," I told him, my voice breaking. "It's cowardly, it's unethical, it's ..."

"It is what it is," Vince said.

I'd expected Vince to be devastated. But if anything, he seemed to be taking it better than I was. I looked at him across the visiting table and came to a sad realization: *He was expecting this.*

Because when you've been behind bars for as long as he had, you learn to tamp down hope the moment it springs up. You learn to accept helplessness, to expect the worst.

And when you live with a degenerative disease, you come to terms with each day being a little worse than the one previous.

"We're going to get you out," I told him. "We're going to try again. It's actually a blessing. Governor Northam is a neurologist. He knows what Huntington's is. He understands how our brains can betray us. He'll know what it means. ..."

There would be a new clemency petition, I said. This time, we'd enlist even more support from the global Huntington's community, other legal voices, and the Cane Creek community. We'd increase public awareness of Vince's plight, go on a scorched-earth PR blitz. We would try to pressure the governor directly this time, a less passive course. I would appeal to Dr. Northam as a physician, reminding him of our Hippocratic oath. I'd drive up to the governor's mansion myself if I had to.

I thought I was trying to cheer Vince up and give him hope. But the longer I spoke, the more I realized that really, I was speaking for my own benefit, hoping to raise my own spirits. The truth was, I was crushed. I felt like a failure, like I'd been spreading false hope to Vince all these years—like we all had.

I could feel myself dissociating, not wanting to experience the pain—his pain. Outwardly, I was trying to pull it together, to be a compassionate anchor for Vince, but on the inside I was spiraling, my mind asking the same question, again and again.

How many doctors and lawyers, how many thousands of dollars, can it possibly take to deliver mercy?

Vince should have been transferred to Broughton by now, making his new home in a therapeutic community, getting the medication and psychiatric support that he needed. I'd been so confident that the state would recognize the injustice of his plight and that our years of hard work would pay off.

But here I was, again, sitting across from Vince in the Marion visiting room. It was easy to think that nothing had changed over the past five years—nothing, that is, except the firing of the prison's staff psychiatrist. Dr. Angliker's shepherding presence was just a memory to his former patients, fading just as surely as the Hungry Mother mural on the wall behind me.

It was easy to imagine, but hard to fathom, the years ahead: two men at the same table, for two hours at a time. When visiting hours were up, I would walk out a free man. And Vince would always shuffle back through the thick metal door of the visitation room, looking back and waving until he was forced to move on to his cell.

It defied reason. It defied morality.

"We're going to get you out," I said again. This time, I was choked up out of disappointment, out of anger, but also because I wasn't so sure we would succeed.

"Please don't be sad," Vince comforted me. "It's okay. You came over that mountain. You believed in me. That was a gift I never thought I'd get. You helped me to understand myself, even though it wasn't what I hoped to find. Even if I never get out of here, I have a new friend, a brother. I know you, Dawn, and Geri did everything you could."

"Did we? I keep thinking . . ."

What if I'd made one more call? What if we'd broken our cone of silence earlier? What if I'd negotiated a one-on-one with the governor? What if I'd taken more control with the CNN producers?

The questions unspooled in my mind as we sat silent in the visiting room, the wounds from the state's letter still gaping and fresh.

"My mother," Vince said, out of nowhere.

He shook his head.

"She shouldn't . . ." he began. "She shouldn't have to keep driving up here."

"I can help her," I told Vince. "She loves you, Vince. She wants to keep coming out here. We all do."

"I'm just sorry," Vince said.

"For what?"

"For . . ." He looked past me, over my head, then back down. "Wasting your time."

That was the moment that broke me. I leaned over, resting my elbows shakily on my knees, and craned my neck to get as close to him as possible. But all I could see was a shadow. His face was lifeless, except for an uncontrollable twitch in his left cheek. His sadness took me to a distant, childlike memory, somewhere deep in my brain, that felt strangely familiar and paralyzing: sitting alone in my room, listening to AM radio from Chicago, where my dad lived, and longing to be closer to him.

When Vince broke the silence and stood up, wrapping his arms around me, I sobbed into his chest like a child. One of the COs shot a cautious gaze in my direction. They don't like scenes on their watch.

"That's enough," the CO said.

So I stepped back, and when I looked at Vince again, something had changed. The light was back on in his eyes. I saw the doctor his patients had known, the one who only wanted to heal. And right now, he was healing me.

"You have not failed me," he said. "I am so-o-o appreciative."

"I will not let you die in this place," I told him.

In the weeks and months after Vince's clemency petition was denied, I struggled. I was angry. I was lost. I felt a new responsibility to the plight of the mentally ill in prison and a compulsion to speak out, but I had no idea how to effect any change.

After a clemency rejection, there was a two-year waiting period before another petition could be made. What was our next move?

What was mine?

The legal team and I had a phone call shortly after the governor's decision. We were accustomed by then to doing our work on the phone or over email, after hours, in between soccer practices and breastfeeding sessions, dinner and daycare. But there was a new weight on us now, audible even through the phone line. Time had marked us—in Dawn's and Geri's voices I could hear their fatigue from parenthood, from the battle wounds of our fight. I could hear my own exhausted voice, too.

"How's Vince?" Dawn asked. "I feel so horrible. I haven't made it up to Marion to see him since everything."

"He's okay," I said. "Given the circumstances."

"It was a slap in the face," Geri said, her voice raised. "To just blindside him like that."

"So what happens next?" I asked.

"We try again," Dawn said. "We keep trying."

"I thought you two might want to jump ship," I said. "No offense. You've got lives, careers, families, and there is only so much generosity your firms can give."

"What are you talking about?" Geri interjected, her voice raised. She sounded furious—no longer the quiet new lawyer, but the seasoned courtroom veteran, mercilessly cross-examining a witness.

"This isn't over," Dawn said.

"This is the next chapter," Geri said.

I'd expected a grand finale, but the story continued. And that's what bothered me most: not that Vince's story didn't have a happy ending, but that it might never end. His symptoms would only get worse. He could easily die in prison or commit suicide at any moment—and we still had two years to wait, then likely another couple for Governor Northam to pick up the case.

For years, I'd thought of our lives as an evolving story: one that began with a mysterious coincidence, took off with the revelation of his diagnosis, and ultimately became a protracted battle for freedom. It was a *Twilight Zone* episode that morphed into an episode of *House, M.D.;* a *This American Life* episode that became my actual American life. In Act I, Vince and I discovered each other. In Act II, we discovered what was wrong with him. And in Act III, in all my imaginings, we were supposed to get him out.

But now Vince was stuck inside the plot. I had a clear ending for him, but with time, it grew harder and harder for him to imagine anything other than a jail cell, a decaying mind, and an undignified death.

He deserved a better ending.

And we remained—we remain—resolved to give it to him.

Since I met Vince Gilmer, I have often asked myself one simple question: *Why?*

Why did this coincidence happen?

Why did I end up in the mountains of North Carolina, working in a country clinic?

Why did this story choose me?

I am not, like Vince's mother, Gloria, a big believer in divine intervention. But I do believe that the universe can conspire in one's favor if you humbly follow the signs and pay attention. I believe that life has a way of putting us in situations that demand of us our utmost courage, composure, and grace—and that it is our duty to respond in ways that show reverence for the life we all as humans share.

These are not original ideas, I know. I have been taught by so many people to appreciate and love the life I have been given, and that means doing so even when we are most vulnerable. It is only by confronting life, in all of its valences, that we can learn to live with ourselves, and to make life better for everyone. Creating a more just world requires that we look at it with clear eyes, open hearts, and a charitable spirit.

That has certainly been the case in my years working with Vince. Seeking "reverence for life" has required that I see past the rope and the gardening shears, the courtroom outbursts, and the terrifying rumors. It has meant seeing past a diagnosis, beyond my own internal biases, to what made the person behind it. For those of us who have only captured glimpses of losing conscious control, whose brains have been bathed in safety and security throughout life, it is hard to understand the fallibility of our minds.

My blindness, I see now, is emblematic of a larger cultural blindness. Waylaid by trauma—emotional, psychological, and neurological—the vast majority of us cannot see the struggle all of us as humans share. We have become myopic, even in our best moments. Our sense of community has atrophied.

Mired in brokenness, we can't see that brokenness is what we share.

"Reverence for life" means recognizing Vince Gilmer's fight to survive as my own. Because Schweitzer was asking us—all of us, not just physicians—to act: To celebrate and aid people in their will to live. To lead when called upon.

Vince's story chose me not only because it needed me, but because I needed it.

In the end, understanding the other Dr. Gilmer, getting to know him beyond my initial preconceptions, has forced me to look inside, to the other Dr. Gilmer—myself.

What kind of man am I?

What kind of doctor do I want to be?

What can I learn from this man the state says is a murderer, this man with my name?

AFTERWORD

Getting Vince the ending he deserved meant a new clemency petition, of course. But it also meant continued work to free him—in the press, in public, in the ear of anyone who would listen.

"You could write that book," Deirdre said one day, hiking with the kids. Kai and Luya were sprinting ahead down the dirt path, chasing our new puppy, Prince Peanut Butter.

I had thought of writing about my experiences with Vince often, throughout the years I'd known him. I'd even put pen to paper a few times, on the weekends, late at night. But I'd never gotten past a few pages. The idea of a book seemed daunting.

"I'm no writer," I said. "I'm a doctor."

"Who cares?" answered Deirdre. "This is a story that must be told."

"It needs an ending."

"Maybe you'll have to write one," Deirdre said.

I thought about it for a few weeks. And the more I thought about it, the more inspired I became.

If I could write Vince's story, it could be a persuasive tool. Instead of an overly dramatized CNN true-crime special, I could hand Governor Northam a copy of the true story, the real story, the one that actually captured Vince's mind and his redemption, his disease and his health, his suffering and his hopes—all of our hopes—for healing.

The real story didn't fit into an hour-long radio episode, or a twenty-minute television special. The real story was a medical mystery, a legal thriller, and a heartbreaking saga of intergenerational abuse and how a disease ravaged a family. It was about more than just Vince or Dalton or what happened that night. It was about more than me, too.

It was about the truth, and justice, and the systems that were tasked with upholding both. It was about crime and punishment. It was about all of us recognizing that our brains are fallible, as fallible as any other organ, and that humans make mistakes. It was about life and death, sickness and health, and our shared responsibility to heal each other. It was about two men with the same name, who somehow—through exam rooms and prison cells, radio interviews and trial transcripts—found each other.

It was a huge story, and I wasn't sure I could write it. But I knew that I had to. And if I did, I'd need Vince's help. It was, after all, his story, too.

So a month later, I was back at Marion, armed with more questions and some releases for him to sign.

"So good to see you," he muttered as we sat down at the table like usual.

"This one's for Wayne Austin," I said, pointing to the line. "There's Dr. Sciara and your first lawyer, Steve Lindsay, too. That will let us get more information about your earliest psych evaluations."

We still hadn't seen Dr. Sciara's evaluation, but he had shown a willingness to cooperate, if Vince gave the okay.

Vince sighed. He looked a little worse for wear. Not horrible, but definitely tired and run-down.

"How are you doing with all of this?"

It would be understandable, I thought, for Vince to be

inconsolable—for him to have lost all hope. To have his appeal for mercy so unceremoniously rejected, after years of effort, had depressed *me* beyond measure. I couldn't imagine what it felt like for him.

"I'm all right," he said. "What's the word . . . I'm . . ."

Indeed, what was the word? How could anyone describe the hope of freedom, followed by the despair of the cell door, clanging shut?

"Gutted," Vince concluded, with a spasmodic flourish of his hands.

I detailed to Vince the plans I'd already started making with Dawn and Geri. In the two years before we could submit our new petition, we could do a lot. We would interview more Huntington's experts, I told him. We would enlist the help of more neurologists, in the hopes of appealing to Governor Northam's history as a pediatric neurologist. I would consult with Bryan Stevenson, the author of *Just Mercy* and founder of the Equal Justice Initiative, who had inspired me and was leading this fight on a national level. We would tell Vince's story again, and again, in any way we could.

This brought me to my big ask.

"One other thing, Vince," I said. "I want to write your story into a book."

Vince had been distracted, looking down at his hands. But now he looked up at me.

"A book?"

I nodded.

"This story is so complex," I told him. "It's hard to do it justice on a screen or in a legal document. I want people to know you—to hear you, to understand you and learn what you've been through."

"Do I get to help . . . write?" he asked.

"Of course you do," I said. "It's your story."

This pleased him, I could tell.

"When do we start?" he asked.

"Right now," I said.

"When do we finish?" he asked.

"When we have an ending," I told him.

We are still looking for that ending. But in the process of writing this story, Vince and I are hoping to find it. Together, I think we will.

Before I left the prison that day in 2018, I asked Vince to tell me the most important things he wanted this book to say.

This is what he said:

Prison is torture.

Sexual abuse changes you forever.

We are all at the mercy of our brains.

Listening is healing.

Vince bear-hugged me as he always did. He told me he was grateful that I listened to him. I reminded him again that he would one day be free.

As my advocacy for Vince expanded, I kept wondering about the people who had helped the state put him behind bars: the jurors, the lawyers, the police. I wondered if any of them had ever had a change of heart, or had found themselves questioning their bedrock assumptions about justice and mental health. Dr. Jeffrey Feix, the forensic psychologist who had evaluated Vince and testified that he was malingering, was especially on my mind. He was now the chief of forensics in Tennessee, charged with implementing systemic change to protect the mentally ill. His phone number was easy to find. So I decided to reach out.

To my surprise, Dr. Feix agreed to meet me at a Nashville coffee shop. A slender, casually dressed man with sharp features, he greeted me with a handshake and a guarded smile.

"Nice to finally meet you," I said.

We ordered drinks and breakfast and found a quiet table. It was awkward at first. He fidgeted. He paused. I sat up in my chair.

"What do you think about Vince's trial now?" I asked.

"Had we known he had Huntington's and had I understood it better," he told me, "both a psychiatrist and a neurologist would have evaluated him, rather than just me. He probably still would have been deemed competent—but he would not have been branded a malingerer. I think the outcome would have been different—but I'm not a judge, nor a jury."

I realized, as we spoke, that I had been angry at Dr. Feix for years. I had always seen him as someone who couldn't see beyond his own biases—after all, he had published extensively on malingering. But now, as the two of us sat face-to-face, I could see that I was wrong, that my own biases had tainted my seven-year perception of him.

Because Dr. Feix *did* see Vince differently. He still believed that Vince had been manipulative and not entirely truthful at his trial. He believed that he had played up some of his symptoms. And although I could not blame him for missing the signs of Huntington's—he was not a medical doctor, and it is a rare diagnosis—Dr. Feix seemed genuinely bothered by the fact that he had missed *something*.

After a few minutes, I asked him point-blank, "Should Vince Gilmer be in prison?"

There was no hesitation.

"No," Dr. Feix said. "The mentally ill should not be locked up. He should be in a treatment facility. If I had known then that he had Huntington's, that's where he'd be."

I smiled. I wished, more than anything, that Vince could be there to hear Dr. Feix's words. I allowed myself a brief daydream, while Jeff Tweedy played in the background over the café's speakers: Vince drinking a latte with us, remembering the fiasco of his trial, maybe even forgiving the man whose failure to see his mental illness had helped consign him to Wallens Ridge.

But I knew I had to let it go. Dr. Feix was genuinely remorseful for what had happened to Vince, and had spent years trying to make things in the prison system better for people just like him. For one, he introduced me to the Sequential Intercept Model, an approach designed to identify crimes tied to mental illness. The model had been very successful in helping to divert people with mental illness who had committed crimes to community-based intervention rather than incarceration.

I told him about my slowly cohering ideas about healing crime.

"What would that really mean, though?" he asked.

"Let's figure it out," I said, ordering a second round of cappuccinos. And for the next two hours, instead of just rehashing the past, we brainstormed ways to reform the system for the future.

Healing crime would mean a higher degree of integration among law enforcement, the criminal justice system, and clinical practitioners: a vision of justice that incorporates healthcare providers and social workers with police officers, lawyers, and judges.

It would mean a recognition in the judicial system that we *must* treat mentally ill people differently.

It would mean replacing the antiquated system of psychiatric evaluation—one evaluation, performed by one clinician, at one moment in time—with a more collaborative, team-based approach. The question of whether or not a person accused of a crime is mentally ill would not be left to one isolated encounter, as it was for Vince, but would instead incorporate the input of a group of psychiatrists, psychologists, and medical doctors. Before any major medical decision for the treatment of a complex cancer, a dedicated interprofessional *team* often meets to discuss the case. If we could do that for a brain cancer patient facing chemotherapy and surgery, shouldn't we be doing it for the accused who were facing life behind bars or the death penalty, at a cost of potentially millions of dollars to the state?

These were big ideas. And before I met Vince Gilmer, I would have thought they were out of my reach—that they were best left to the politicians, to the strategists, to the governor. But so many other societal issues—voting rights for minorities, equal pay for women, basic protections for LBGTQ+ people—had also been left to these same people, and it had taken decades to achieve lasting change. How many more generations did we need to wait for them to recognize the injustice of locking up people with mental illness?

I finally looked up from my notebook, wired and jittery from too much coffee. It was getting close to lunchtime. Dr. Feix had a job to return to, and I was facing the long drive back home to Asheville.

"Thanks for meeting with me," I said. "I appreciate your open-mindedness. This was a healing conversation for me."

He smiled.

"Me, too," he said.

Over the course of writing this book, I returned to several of the other principal actors in the story, to ask them how their perception of Vince's case had changed in the intervening years. Judge Lowe, who oversaw Vince's trial, refused to speak to me. The prosecutor, Nicole Price, still believes Vince had a fair day in court.

But Dr. Feix restored my faith that there are people within the system who are trying to make it better. And although Detective Martin still believes that Vince was manipulatively faking his symptoms, he did admit to me at the end of our meeting that we had found common ground moving forward: Law enforcement cannot solve this problem alone, and neither can doctors.

"We need each other," Detective Martin told me.

To me, these men's changing attitudes signal that the old ways of doing things are finally evolving, and that the outmoded preconceptions that each man brought to Vince's case are in the process of revision. It cannot come too soon—for Vince, and for so many like him.

Vince hasn't read this book yet. Due to prison rules, he will not be able to do so until it is published. But he is still alive.

He has still never been able to listen to the *This American Life* episode Sarah and I made, so he has never seen his life reflected back, or heard his story told by someone else. Writing this book, I've wrestled with my responsibility to him, wanting to make sure I treated him with honor and respect while staying true to what happened, recognizing how extreme intergenerational trauma shaped him. I see his story as an example of hope and survival, not death and darkness, and my only hope now is that by the time this book is published, Vince will be able to read it sitting outside in a chair, shrouded by the North Carolina mountains, secure in a facility equipped to care for him, listening to the spring songs of the wood thrushes in the surrounding oaks.

But everything depends, yet again, on the mercy of our elected leaders.

In April 2019, Dawn, Geri, and I submitted our second petition for clemency to Governor Northam's office.

We waited.

We built political relationships.

We started making a feature film.

I wrote this book.

Through it all, I had high hopes that Governor Northam, a physician himself, would understand Vince's plight, in both clinical and legal terms. I was confident that he would listen to Vince's story and arrive at the same conclusion I had: that dying in prison from Huntington's was cruel and unusual. After all, he was a neurologist, someone who had intimately experienced the vulnerability of the human brain throughout his professional career. Surely he would understand the justice of transferring a terminally ill, incarcerated patient who had already spent seventeen years behind bars to a hospital so that he could receive appropriate care before dying.

I worked overtime to connect with Governor Northam. With the help of Virginia state senator Creigh Deeds, I wrote him a letter outlining the case, which Senator Deeds personally delivered. I spoke with the governor's secretary of equity, diversity, and inclusion (EDI), Dr. Janice Underwood, about using Vince's case as an opportunity for the governor—as a physician—to bring a powerful political voice to mass incarceration. Through Dr. Underwood, I set a plan in motion for a personal meeting with Governor Northam to discuss the case. I was confident he would understand that prison is no place to take care of a patient with Huntington's.

I was wrong.

On a Friday afternoon, one week before I submitted the final draft of this book, Kelly Thomasson, the secretary of the Commonwealth of Virginia, called us. After considering the nature of the crime, the length of Vince's incarceration, and the level of care he was receiving at Marion, Governor Northam had rejected our clemency petition for Vince's release.

It is difficult not to react to this latest setback with anger and disillusionment. It is difficult not to see Governor Northam's decision as a death sentence for Vince. I will admit that as I write these words, I am filled with fury and sadness—for Vince, for his family, for all of the mentally ill people in prison just like him.

We all mourn this latest decision. But even now, some ember of hope still burns in me and in the rest of the legal team. We have already started planning for the next clemency petition, for the next governor. But the truth is that there is no new argument to make, no new twist to this plot. Vince is not out of options, but he is running out of time. There are fresh minds like Dr. Underwood and Senator Deeds who are hungry for change and recognize that Vince's story isn't only about clemency for one man. It isn't only about ending one man's suffering. It's about all the mentally ill people in our prisons. We're fighting for them, too.

We hope that this book will be a tool to begin a fresh conversation.

In this spirit, we continue to follow the example of Dr. Colin Angliker, who died in August 2018, at the age of eighty. I will always remember Dr. Angliker's courage, his humor and—most important—his clear-eyed vision of justice for the mentally ill. His widow, Sarah, recently gave me a trove of letters and articles he wrote in the late sixties and seventies, detailing his work building a diagnostic and treatment center within the Clinton Correctional Facility in Dannemora, New York. The policies he and his mentor, Bruno Cormier, implemented—"maximum freedom" of movement within the prison, daily therapy sessions, mentors who followed inmates even after their release—were ahead of their culture's time.

I can only hope that they are not too far ahead of ours.

Dawn, Geri, and I will not stop advocating for the other Dr. Gilmer until he is out of prison and getting the treatment he deserves in a hospital.

And even then, the fight won't be over. Neither will this story. I am a doctor, and have taken an oath to do no harm. More importantly, I am a human, and I believe that we must be responsible for one another—our fellow humans. Even if we do not free Vince, I will continue to honor him as someone who, despite the violence that landed him in prison, healed thousands of others during his career as a doctor. His life should not be defined by one moment of profound mental illness. He is a human who deserves dignity.

So do thousands of other people in our nation's prisons and jails. That's why I will continue to advocate for everyone like Vince, and for a clinical shift in our approach to mental health, public health, and mass incarceration. I believe that one day we will recognize our own cruelty, and will use medicine for its highest purpose—to heal those who need it most. If we continue to lock away our most vulnerable humans, our humanity—our very civilization—is at risk.

There are so many other Dr. Gilmers out there in the world.

They all need our compassion. Our righteous anger. Our reverence.

But most of all, they need our help.

Vince, for his part, sees his neurologist through a video screen once or twice a year, and continues to take an SSRI. The Covid-19 pandemic essentially put him and the other inmates at Marion into solitary confinement, so I have been unable to visit him in person since January 2020. But it is clear from our phone conversations that his Huntington's symptoms continue to worsen. His speech is getting harder and harder to understand, and his cognition continues to slow down. Every day, he becomes more unsteady on his feet, less able to swallow his food, and more likely to choke or fall. Like many incarcerated people, he battles clinical depression and despair on a daily basis.

But he hasn't given up. Neither has Gloria, who still believes that she will see her son again as a free man. I truly believe that Gloria's faith is justified, that justice is in reach for Vince. I believe that he can be healed, but not in prison.

In one of the letters Dr. Angliker's wife gave me, written three months before I was born in 1970, Colin put it well:

> To treat the convict as a human being is but one of our
> aims and it is an approach we as citizens should take.

The world of the 1970s wasn't yet ready to hear words like these. But there are more people now who are willing to listen. Leaders in the state of Virginia—people like state senator Creigh Deeds—have recognized the importance of treating mental illness and putting laws in place to address inequality and lack of access to care. On February 22, 2021, Virginia's senate voted and passed a historic bill to abolish its death penalty, joining twenty-two other states. Describing capital punishment as "ineffective, inequitable, and inhumane," Governor Northam signed the bill into law—which means that Dawn's client William Morva will be memorialized as the last person to be killed by the Commonwealth of Virginia.

The wheels of justice are turning more slowly than we would like, but things are changing. We are all learning and evolving. When I started working at Cane Creek, I was a fledgling doctor trying to find my way in the wake of a very strange story that spoke to me—perhaps because of my name, or maybe because I finally decided to listen.

Vince's story has changed me.

And I hope it changes you, too.

POSTSCRIPT

November 2022

The day before this book was to go to press, in early January of 2022, our legal team received word from Virginia's secretary of the commonwealth that Governor Ralph Northam was reconsidering his original rejection of Vince's clemency. I was on a Zoom meeting when I saw a call from Geri that I couldn't pick up. Then a text came through.

"Take a break! Northam may reverse his decision. We have work to do! Need you to reach out to Broughton, have to talk about guardianship!"

I spent the rest of the day in ecstatic tears, calling everyone I knew who was close to Vince, starting with my wife, Deirdre, then the rest of my family and Vince's mother, Gloria.

I ran down the halls of Cane Creek, screaming to anyone who would listen, "Vince is getting out!"

As I spread the news, I wondered what had happened to change the governor's mind. Before Christmas, I had shared early versions of this book with Governor Northam and others in his cabinet. We made calls. We talked to anyone who would listen: parole board members; Dr. Janice Underwood, the secretary of the Office of Diversity, Equity and Inclusion; and Senator Creigh Deeds. But our hopes had not been high. As Governor Northam's days left in office dwindled to hours, we all knew that reversing a clemency ruling would be nothing less than miraculous.

But that's exactly what happened. Something had clearly changed.

What was the final trigger to shift the governor's heart? All I could imagine was that finally, the right people had heard Vince's story. Not only had they decided to listen; they had changed their minds.

They had chosen compassion.

I was tearful as I spoke to Dawn and Geri over the phone. We had worked so hard together for nearly ten years. We had become dear friends and seasoned parents. We had imagined this victory for Vince a thousand times but always remained fearful it would never arrive.

And when it did, it was hard to believe at first. In a way, getting this news reminded me of the moment when Dr. Angliker told me: "Vince has Huntington's." I felt a sense of shock and disbelief—but also, this time, a deep sense of relief. I could feel my shoulders relaxing and sense the tone of my voice softening for the first time as the news sunk in.

After confirming the details with the legal team, I sat in silence, peering through my office window—past the small lawn, the fenced-in koi pond, and the cornfields, to where the silhouette of the mountains melted into the horizon.

There was only one more person to tell, and he was understandably ecstatic to hear the news.

"Vince," I said when I reached him by phone in prison, "we did it! You are going to be released finally to a hospital!"

Words came slowly as his mind sluggishly processed news he doubted he would ever hear. Then the silence was broken by an eruption of joyous, childlike laughter.

"Thank you, thank you, thank you! And thank you to Deirdre, and thank you to Kai, and thank you to Luya!"

I was surprised that he was still capable of laughing like that. The last rejection of his clemency appeal had almost extinguished what life force remained. But now it was coming back. The laughter continued until he teared up. Vince was like a newborn, waiting to take a breath and cry for the first time.

Once he was freed, I would be Vince's legal guardian. It would be my responsibility to find him a clinical home that could take care of his complex needs: to begin therapy, to initiate medications, and to begin processing a lifetime of trauma. There were no words to describe my emotions as I imagined Vince shuffling through the prison doors for the last time. I had fantasized about this moment for years. We would pick him up in our van and, per his request, drive to Asheville to eat Mellow Mushroom pizza while blaring some Bruce Springsteen. I had already received numerous gift cards from people who graciously contributed to his first night out.

But unfortunately, that is not exactly how things went.

People ask me often about Vince's case. How is he doing? How is his health? Has he been set free?

In the weeks after the governor's announcement, my answer was joyous: He had been granted clemency! He would finally receive appropriate medical care! He would find a new home in a hospital and be seen as a patient for the first time in nearly two decades, no longer a prisoner!

But as time went on, my answer had to change.

Weeks, then months passed by while the Commonwealth of Virginia slow-walked the process of granting Vince his freedom. In our clemency petition, we made one request to the governors of Virginia: to transfer Vince to a hospital where he would receive care and remain for the rest of his life. But the Commonwealth of Virginia refused to collaborate on transferring him from Marion to one of their state mental hospitals—which was only a few hundred feet away, sharing a parking lot with the prison. The official explanation was that it was our responsibility to land him in a hospital. And that was easier said than done.

As one of the psychiatrists at the mental hospital told me, "I can't just let him in." They needed the collaboration and accord of the Department of Mental Health and, of course, the Department of Corrections. "An inmate can't just walk over here; it takes extensive coordination."

I wondered if the Commonwealth just didn't want him on their hands, a reminder of the miscarriage of justice that had led to a seriously ill man rotting in prison for years instead of receiving care. I imagined that they were tired of the press and didn't want to pay to house him for the rest of his life.

They wanted him to be someone else's problem. They didn't care about getting him treatment or righting a wrong. And, strangely, they didn't care that it cost more to house Vince in prison than in a hospital.

I began to feel something akin to embarrassment, or guilt, at having to explain to people that even though Vince had been granted clemency, he was still awaiting transfer. It sounded ludicrous. I told people that Vince must be one of the only clemency-granted incarcerated persons in the whole country. Even though he was a free man, Vince was still sitting in a cell, still being punished in solitary confinement—or, in prison parlance, "administrative segregation."

To Vince, it was "the hole," and it was still torture.

Again, we sprang into action. We petitioned every public mental hospital in the state of Virginia to take Vince on as a patient. Without help from the Virginia Department of Mental Health or support from the attorney general's office, everyone refused.

I asked the appropriate public mental hospitals in North Carolina, but they required that Vince first be in a Virginia hospital for a state-to-state transfer. Vince was stuck in a bizarre no-man's-land.

"It would only take picking up the phone, one call from someone in the governor's office or Mental Health, to get him across the damn street!" I fumed to Deirdre one afternoon after a particularly fruitless attempt to convince another government official to act.

We quickly came to the conclusion that our only options were private hospitals. After transferring Vince to a private hospital in any state, he would be eligible to transfer into a public hospital in North Carolina like Broughton. But those places also had long waiting lists. I learned that the neurobehavioral center in Black Mountain, a public mental health hospital that had a history of taking Huntington's patients, had a waiting list of up to three years. It could take months for a geriatric bed to open up at Broughton. With closure after closure of our state mental hospitals, few options remained for people experiencing chronic, severe mental illness.

Getting Vince out would cost money—a lot of it. Simply transferring him from Virginia to North Carolina could cost $5,000 for an ambulance ride. One month at Mission Hospital in Asheville could cost a minimum of $45,000, and we might need three months.

So in August of 2022, we started a fundraising campaign for Vince's case. I directed anyone who asked about Vince, anyone who cared about medicine and justice, to donate to a fund that would pay for private care for Vince so that we could extricate him from Virginia.

The response was extraordinary.

As of this writing, we have raised more than $100,000 for Vince. People gave a little—$5 here, $10 there—and people gave a lot. What touched me was that close to 1,500 people chose to act. These individual actions also made a statement to Virginia: The continued incarceration of a now sixty-year-old terminally ill man who could no longer walk—and who was legally a *free man*—was unacceptable, the very definition of cruel and unusual punishment.

———

Just as the funds started to add up, my father fell seriously ill. It was soon apparent that he did not have long to live.

One afternoon, sitting next to his bed, I asked him, "Dad, what will it take to achieve justice for Vince?"

My father barely had the strength to do more than breathe. But lifting his head, he opened his eyes and grasped my hand.

"Love," he said. "It requires love. Vince deserves to die with the same love and support I am receiving. Don't we all? He deserves dignity. He deserves forgiveness. This is justice."

My father's words were unequivocal: Vince deserved the same compassionate care he was receiving. He told me that he'd always wanted to meet Vince, that Vince felt strangely like family. He said he was proud of my commitment and perseverance. "This is the work that priests should be doing, too," he said.

A few days later my father, Lyonel Wayman Gilmer, died, surrounded by his loving family, a compassionate palliative care team, and an empathetic young priest from his church who aspired to be the humanistic leader that my father was. Together we cared for him until his last breath.

In the days after he left us, my father's words echoed in my brain. *Love. It requires love.*

In those dark days, I felt lost. I felt guilty. But my father's words, and his example, spurred me to continue the fight for Vince. He taught me that it is our duty to help those who are less fortunate. As I mourned his death, I was once again inspired by his example, his love for service. My father believed in the power of compassion. He understood that every human life was worth saving—that everyone deserved mercy.

Ten years ago, when my father had his cardiac bypass surgery, Sarah Koenig and I were sprinting to finish our *This American Life* piece. And in the wake of my father's death, I once again went on a full-court press, calling everyone I knew to find a landing spot for Vince in a hospital.

I had learned over the course of my decade-long advocacy journey that people inherently want to do what's right, but that means battling one's entrenched internal biases, overcoming fear, and working to shatter the inertia of complacency. It means making the harder decision. It means sometimes sacrificing yourself.

I had also learned the power of stories to change people's minds. Many readers of this book had told me that Vince's story inspired them to start their own advocacy journeys. Perhaps, I thought, the same change of heart that Governor Northam experienced would occur with the hospital leaders I had been hounding on the telephone.

And that is exactly what happened.

In the fall of 2022, I approached the lead psychiatrist at Mission Hospital in Asheville, who asked me about Vince. She had just read this book, she said, and had been moved by it.

"What can I do to help?" she asked.

Over the ensuing months, we had numerous meetings: with lawyers, public relations teams, the CEO and COO, the psychiatry team, the Virginia attorney general, state public health officials, and other hospitals.

And then, the week before Thanksgiving, Mission Hospital officially decided to take Vince as a transitional step to long-term care. Eleven months after Northam's clemency reversal, after nearly nineteen years of incarceration, Vince would begin his healing journey, and it would be in his own community hospital.

He was getting out.

I got the news as I was preparing to fly to Virginia to give a rural health talk about Vince. Just before boarding, I spoke to him.

"Vince!" I yelled. "We found a bed for you!"

There was silence on the other end of the line. It went on for so long that I thought maybe we had been disconnected. Or maybe Vince didn't believe me. After so many years and so many setbacks, he was cautious about any good news.

But then I heard something that surfaced rarely: laughter. Child-like, joyful, unrestrained laughter.

There were no words after that. We didn't need to say a thing to each other.

Vince laughed. I listened.

I wanted to shout it out loud to everyone around me in the Asheville airport so that they could understand my endless smile and tearful eyes.

This Thanksgiving, Vince was coming home.

ACKNOWLEDGMENTS

I would like to first acknowledge Dr. Vince Gilmer for his commitment to serving others throughout his life and as a physician before this terrible tragedy. His remarkable tenacity to hold on to life while his body and mind deteriorate as an incarcerated person with a terminal condition continues to inspire me.

My deepest thanks to my wife, Deirdre, who has been my anchor throughout this journey. Embracing every challenge with strength and humor, you made innumerable sacrifices to support me and our family over the last eight years. You challenged me, wept with me, and inspired me to keep fighting so that the world could know Vince's story. This book would not exist without you.

To Kai and Luya, our beautiful children: Your keen insights and ability to so clearly see the injustice of Vince's plight give me hope that one day another generation will find a better way to punish and rehabilitate.

Thank you to my parents, Day Kennon and Lyonel Gilmer, and my stepparents, Mary Jo Gilmer and Larry Kennon, for teaching me the importance of service and seeing the world with compassionate eyes. You gave me the incredible gift of growing up in a safe, life-affirming world. Without your patience and endless support, the seed to pursue medicine and this story would not have been planted.

I would like to recognize Gloria, Vince's mother, who has endured a life filled with trauma. Despite losing a husband and both of her children, she still fights to mother Vince from afar. Her unconditional love is an example to us all. It is important to also recognize the many tragedies that Vince's father and his forefathers suffered as a result of undiagnosed Huntington's. Through the generations, this lurking disease ravaged the Gilmer family. It pains me to think of how different this story might have been had they known its name.

I cannot thank enough the legal partners who have fought over the past seven years to achieve justice for Vince. Thank you to Jennifer Brevorka for sparking our liftoff, to Deirdre Enright for her guidance during the early phase of our legal journey, and to Hunton Andrews Kurth for its generosity in supporting Vince's case. Infinite gratitude is due to Dawn Davison and Geri Greenspan, who have spearheaded this legal battle and given so much of their time pro bono to advocate on Vince's behalf. Their tireless commitment to justice has been a constant source of inspiration. The friendship we have developed over the years reminds me that there is always some light embedded within tragic tales.

I have had the opportunity to work with many superheroes over the past eight years but none as inspiring as the late Dr. Colin Angliker. Thank you for listening with open ears and seeing with childlike eyes while tirelessly serving incarcerated populations for over forty years. The compassion you shared for your patients never wavered from your first patient to your last: Vince. Your example of truth-telling has changed me forever.

There are many people across the country who are advocating for justice and prison reform who have committed their professional lives to this cause. Thank you for your tireless work that so often goes unnoticed. In particular, two people have informed me deeply: Bryan Stevenson, a crusader for social justice and prison reform at the Equal Justice Initiative; and Dr. Christine Montross, a brilliant writer, physician, and advocate at Brown University, who gave me insightful support, encouragement, and guidance while writing this book. I would also like to recognize Dr. Jeffrey Feix for opening his eyes to Vince's case years later and owning that a grave mistake had been made. I admire your professional efforts to enhance mental health services.

I cannot thank Sarah Koenig enough for seeing the value of Vince's story. Her brilliant storytelling and dogged pursuit of truth remind all of us of the important role that the media has to play in our democracy. My sincere thanks to Ira Glass for his support and giving us the space to develop this story for *This American Life*.

I appreciate the hundreds—if not thousands—of people who have reached out in support of Vince's case. I would like to particularly recognize Emily Sottile, whose letter about her father I quote in this book. I am also deeply grateful to Vince's friends and patients, and his clinical crew at Cane Creek—especially Terri Worley, whose belief in Vince inspired me to keep asking why.

I recognize that reading this story has opened deep wounds for many, but especially for Vince's previous wife. I sincerely hope that it helps your process of healing.

I am thankful for the many others who have supported me and this project along the way: Jamie Nicholson for his friendship and the many hours processing with me the unfolding of Vince's story; Jay Leutze for his brotherly support and coaching; my cousins Jonathon Milner and Cary Clifford for their honest feedback and steadfast encouragement; and Dr. Patricia White for all her mentoring and reverence for life over the years. Dr. Tom Irons, thank you for being such an inspiring teacher and crusader for the poor. Enormous gratitude is due to Dr. Steve Buie for helping me see what needed to be seen and the many psychiatry lessons. Thanks to all my Cane Creek partners—Dr. Mike Coladonato, Dr. Amy Santin,

J. T. LaBruyere, Angella Zarella, Laura Lira, Robin Whiteside, and Terri Ippolito—who provide amazing care for our community. A special note of gratitude to my MAHEC mentors, Dr. Jeff Heck and Dr. Steve Hulkower, who have both supported this advocacy mission and who remind me that it is our duty as physicians to speak out.

I am extremely appreciative of the Huntington's community and its many clinical leaders: Dr. Francis Walker, Dr. Mary Edmondson, Dr. Daniel Claassen, and the many others who have taught me about this disease and supported our legal efforts. I have never experienced a group of clinicians and advocates so committed to healing a disease. Lauren Holder, you have been an amazing source of information about living and working with HD. Your choice to advocate for others with this disease inspires all of us to rise up when confronted with life's cruel blows.

I would like to recognize a special group of people who have been advocating for Vince through a parallel film project. My deepest thanks to Zak Kilberg and Iz Web (Social Construct Films), Jenny Halper and Celine Rattray (Maven Screen Media), and Jonathan King (Concordia Films). Witnessing your process of creative advocacy through film continues to inspire me and has taught me that media plays an important role in making social change.

My deepest gratitude to Jennifer Fox, who has been the creative lead for this film project while I have written this book. Your compassionate storytelling and indomitable spirit to advocate for Vince have informed me profoundly. Thank you for being such a great friend, mentor, and creative partner throughout this journey.

Special thanks to Johnny Irion, who has supported this story from day one. Thank you for your inspiring music.

One of the great joys of writing this book has been learning from the professionals whose job it is to tell stories. I feel so fortunate to have had so many incredible teachers, especially my editor at Ballantine, Emily Hartley, whose discerning feedback, sensitivity, and bottomless enthusiasm shaped these pages. I appreciate so much Mark Essig for being my first writing coach and for his tremendous and always honest feedback as I put pen to page for the first time.

Finally, this book would not have come to fruition without the brilliant minds and personal mentorship of Lara Love and Doug Abrams, my agents extraordinaire and partners at Idea Architects. I am indebted that you believed in me and grateful for your clear-eyed mission to support stories that seek to change the world. I cannot thank all of you enough—especially Jordan Jacks, who has been the most amazing writing partner, coach, and friend during this process.

Without all of you this book would not have been possible.

NOTES

CHAPTER 5: SEROTONIN

58 **one in six Americans:** Thomas J. Moore and Donald R. Mattison, "Adult Utilization of Psychiatric Drugs and Differences by Sex, Age, and Race," *JAMA Internal Medicine* 177, no. 2 (2017): 274–75, doi.org/10.1001/jamainternmed.2016.7507.

59 **SSRIs were not originally designed:** R. W. Sommi, M. L. Crismon, and C. L. Bowden, "Fluoxetine: A Serotonin-Specific, Second-Generation Antidepressant," *Pharmacotherapy* 7, no. 1 (January–February 1987): 1–15, doi.org/10.1002/j.1875-9114.1987.tb03496.x.

59 **From another article about his trial:** Matthew Lakin, "Strange Twist," *Bristol Herald Courier,* March 23, 2005.

CHAPTER 6: THE LETTER

63 **Shoulder to Shoulder:** Shoulder to Shoulder is an NGO in rural Honduras started in the early nineties by my mentor Dr. Jeff Heck. It is an organization that serves the medical and educational needs of one of the country's most rural and impoverished regions. Readers who would like to learn more about the vital work Shoulder to Shoulder does can visit its website: www.shouldertoshoulder.org.

CHAPTER 8: WHAT HAPPENED

103 **"Basically, the District Attorney wants to lose":** All quoted material in this chapter related to the trial is drawn directly from the trial transcripts of the Commonwealth of Virginia v. Vince Donald Gilmer, case no. CR-05-62.

CHAPTER 9: REVELATION

128 **a psychopathy checklist:** Robert Hare, *The Psychopathy Checklist—Revised,* 2nd ed. (Toronto: Multi-System Press, 2003).

129 **ACE (Adverse Childhood Experiences) score questionnaire:** Vincent J. Felitti et al., "Relationship of Childhood Abuse and Household Dysfunction to Many of the Leading Causes of Death in Adults: The Adverse Childhood Experiences (ACE) Study," *American Journal of Preventative Medicine* 14, no. 4 (May 1998): 245–58, doi.org/10.1016/S0749-3797(98)00017-8.

135 **he'd been thrown in the hole:** On any given day, some eighty thousand incarcerated people are held in solitary confinement in America. The data is indisputable that this causes emotional and mental harm. For further reading, see Mimosa Luigi et al., "Shedding Light on 'the Hole': A Systematic Review and Meta-analysis on Adverse Psychological Effects and Mortality Following Solitary Confinement in Correctional Settings," *Front Psychiatry* 11, no. 840 (August 2020), doi.org/10.3389/fpsyt.2020.00840.

CHAPTER 10: SICK

141 **Huntington's is difficult to diagnose:** The academic literature on Huntington's is intense and ever changing. For an accessible summary, see the National Institute of Health's overview of the disease: www.ninds.nih.gov/Disorders/Patient-Caregiver-Education/Hope-Through-Research/Huntingtons-Disease-Hope-Through.

149 **inmate population in excess of one thousand:** As of this writing, the Virginia Department of Corrections lists the Wallens Ridge prison population as 1,029: vadoc.virginia.gov/media/1627/vadoc-monthly-offender-population-report-2020-10.pdf.

CHAPTER 13: FAMILY THANKSGIVING

186 **Reverence for Life:** Albert Schweitzer, *Out of My Life and Thought* (Baltimore: Johns Hopkins University Press, 1998), 235–36.

187 **"It's not enough to merely exist":** I first encountered this quotation on the wall of the inpatient ward of Hôpital Schweitzer in Lambaréné, Gabon. Although it is widely attributed to Albert Schweitzer, I have never been able to find its source in his written work, so I have always assumed it was something he said that was later transcribed.

201 **The Bureau of Justice Statistics:** Jennifer Bronson and Marcus Berzofsky, "Indicators of Mental Health Problems Reported by Prisoners and Jail Inmates, 2011–2012" (U.S. Department of Justice, Office of Justice Programs, Bureau of Justice Statistics, June 2017), 1, bjs.ojp.gov/content/pub/pdf/imhprpji1112.pdf.

CHAPTER 14: CRUEL AND UNUSUAL

202 **Hunton and Williams:** In 2018 Hunton and Williams changed its name to Hunton Andrews Kurth LLP.

216 **A 2014 report:** Michael F. A. Morehart, "A Review of Mental Health Services in Local and Regional Jails (Office of the Virginia State Inspector General, 2014), 1, www.osig.virginia.gov/media/governorvirginiagov/office-of-the-state-inspector-general/pdf/2014bhds004jailstudy.pdf.

CHAPTER 16: COUNTDOWN

237 **former Virginia governor Bob McDonnell:** For a good overview of the case, see Alan Blinder, "U.S. Ends Corruption Case Against Former Virginia Governor," *New York Times,* September 8, 2016, www.nytimes.com/2016/09/09/us/us-ends-corruption-case-against-former-virginia-governor.html.

245 **"I personally oppose the death penalty":** Governor Terry McAuliffe, "Statement on the Execution of William Morva," July 6, 2017.

CHAPTER 17: HEALING CRIME

253 **a man who was serving 123 years:** Sandy Hausman, "McAuliffe Pardoned Record Numbers of Prisoners, but Many Are Still Waiting," Radio IQ, Roanoke, Virginia, WVTF, January 23, 2018.

257 **25 percent of the world's incarcerated population:** This statistic has been widely repeated by a number of politicians, policy makers, and human rights organizations. For an overview of the statistic, see Michelle Hee Yee, "Does the United States Really Have Five Percent of the World's Population and One Quarter of the World's Prisoners?," *Washington Post,* April 30, 2015, www.washingtonpost.com/news/fact-checker/wp/2015/04/30/does-the-united-states-really-have-five-percent-of-worlds-population-and-one-quarter-of-the-worlds-prisoners/.

258 *Waiting for an Echo:* Christine Montross, *Waiting for an Echo* (New York: Penguin, 2020).

259 **scholars and activists whose books:** To name a few: Bryan Stevenson, *Just Mercy: A Story of Justice and Redemption* (New York: One World, 2014); Michelle Alexander, *The New Jim Crow: Mass Incarceration in the Age of Colorblindness* (New York: New Press, 2010); Shane Bauer, *American Prison: A Reporter's Undercover Journey into the Business of Punishment* (New York: Penguin Press, 2018).

AFTERWORD

273 willingness to cooperate: In 2021, I had the opportunity to meet with Dr. Sciara virtually, and he expressed a willingness to review the studies, but still couldn't find them.

281 diagnostic and treatment center within the Clinton Correctional Facility: Jack Kapica, "How Are Things in Dannemora?," *McGill News*, September 1970, 5–8.

282 people like state senator Creigh Deeds: Senator Deeds's story is a tragic one with an uplifting coda. For an overview of how he became one of the country's foremost advocates for mental health care, see Stephanie McCrummen, "A Father's Scars: For Creigh Deeds, Tragedy Brings Unending Questions," *Washington Post*, November 1, 2014, www.washingtonpost.com/national/a-fathers -scars-for-deeds-every-day-brings-questions/2014/11/01/2217a604-593c-11e4 -8264-deed989ae9a2_story.html.

Dr. BENJAMIN GILMER, M.D., is a family medicine physician in Fletcher, North Carolina. He is an Albert Schweitzer Fellow for Life and associate professor in the department of family medicine at the University of North Carolina School of Medicine at Chapel Hill and at the Mountain Area Health Education Center. A former neurobiologist turned rural family doctor, Dr. Gilmer has lectured widely about medical ethics, rural health, and the intersection of medicine and criminal justice reform. He lives with his wife, Deirdre; their two children, Kai and Luya; and their dog, Prince Peanut Butter, in Asheville, North Carolina.

benjamingilmer.com

ABOUT THE TYPE

This book was set in Chronicle, a typeface created in 2002 by Hoefler&Co. It derives from the Scotch Roman typeface family originated by Alexander Wilson and William Miller. Historically, the Scotch Roman style worked harmoniously with book printing, yet faced limitations when paired with fast-paced printers, such as those used for newspapers. Chronicle was developed as a typeface that would translate well into different styles of media usage.